WHO KNEW?

*Roadside Revelations
in Western Massachusetts*

Big Indian on Rt. 2 (Mohawk Trail)

Front cover image: The Tin Man at Goshen's Three Sisters Sanctuary

WHO KNEW?

Roadside Revelations in Western Massachusetts

Text and Photos by

Robert E. Weir

Levellers Press

AMHERST • MASSACHUSETTS

Copyright © 2021 Robert E. Weir

All rights reserved, including the right of
reproduction in whole or in part in any form.

Levellers Press, Amherst, Massachusetts
Printed in the United States of America

ISBN 978-1-951928-38-4

Dedication

For Abigail, Carita, Cristina, and Jeanette

For 39 years I had the greatest job imaginable: I was an educator. I taught high school, at a community college, in several private women's colleges, and at the University of Massachusetts Amherst. I have no idea how many students I've instructed — probably over four thousand. I was tempted to dedicate this book to every student I've ever taught, but I have a confession to make. Educators aren't supposed to have favorites, but over the years, four young women stand out as extra special. I dedicate this book to them.

Inside Nash Dino Track Site

Table of Contents

Introduction ... 1

Section I: Western Mass BC
Introduction ... 7
Chapter 1: When Monsters Roamed ... 8
Chapter 2: Heath: Burnt Hill ... 15

Section II: Hard to Overlook
Introduction ... 21
Chapter 3: Mohawk Trail: Big Indian ... 23
Chapter 4: Whately's Colossus of Roads ... 29
Chapter 5: Northampton's Misunderstood Monument ... 35
Chapter 6: Great Barrington's Newsboy Statue ... 43
Chapter 7: Conway: Small Town, Fancy Library ... 50
Chapter 8: Three Men Lost on Florence Road ... 57
Chapter 9: Mt. Greylock: A Whale of a Mountain ... 64
Chapter 10: I Can See for Miles and Miles ... 71

Section III: Famous Long Ago
Introduction ... 81
Chapter 11: Chicopee: Where Utopia Began ... 84
Chapter 12: Northfield: Dwight L. Moody ... 92
Chapter 13: Spingfield: Erastus Salisbury Field ... 100
Chapter 14: North Adams and Its Chinese Drama ... 108
Chapter 15: Hadley: It's Not Easy Being a Green ... 116
Chapter 16: You Don't Have to Go to Vermont to See Covered Bridges ... 124

Section IV: Follies, Choices, and Causes

Introduction	133
Chapter 17: Tyringham: Santarella	136
Chapter 18: Montague Castle: A Wizard's Vision	143
Chapter 19: Goshen's Three Sisters Sanctuary	150
Chapter 20: Lee: Pouring Cold Water Over Alcoholism	156
Chapter 21: Orange: The Peace Memorial	164

Section V: Sports

Introduction	171
Chapter 22: Not Entirely Red Sox Nation	174
Chapter 23: Wahconah Park: Pittsfield's Field of Dreams	180
Chapter 24: Right Up Your Alley in Shelburne Falls	185
Chapter 25: The Revenge of the Broom Makers: Curling in Petersham	190

Section VI: (Not Your Ordinary) Museums

Introduction	197
Chapter 26: Pelham: Small Tokens of Large Disputes	200
Chapter 27: Indian Orchard's *Titanic* Museum	207
Chapter 28: Dalton: Give a Damn About Greenback Dollars	213
Chapter 29: The Story Behind *The Cummington Story*	220
Chapter 30: Gardner and Greenfield: When Factories Founder	228
Chapter 31: Great Barrington: The Guthrie Center	236
Chapter 32: South Hadley: The Skinner Museum	244
Bibliographic Essay	253

Who Knew?
Roadside Revelations in Western Massachusetts

Introduction

Who knew that an elaborate fountain in Lee, Massachusetts, was part of a plot to wean citizens from the allure of demon rum? Why does a 20-foot concrete milk bottle sit on the front lawn of an elementary school in Whately? Did you know that one of the most influential visionaries in Western history lived most of his life in Chicopee Falls? Whose crazy idea was it to build a sprawling fairy-tale house in the Berkshires hamlet of Tryingham? Who decided to associate Mohawk Indians with metal teepees with wooden doors?

Who Knew? Roadside Revelations in Western Massachusetts tells the stories behind follies, oddities, and curiosities that folks stumble upon when they journey through the region. Many are things that even local residents no longer "see," and probably never knew much about in the first place. Commonplace things have a habit of sliding into the blurry background of our everyday routines. When Northampton friends ask me for an example of this book's content, I often mention the monument on West Street. Invariably they ask, "What monument?" Once you "see" it, it's pretty hard to miss. (See chapter 5.)

As a professional historian, I've written my share of meaty tomes for specialists. This is a book for ordinary folks. The tone is sometimes puckish, but informative. It has taken me longer to write than I originally planned, for the selfish reason that I was enjoying myself too much to hurry. Now it's time to share.

I will make only passing reference to things you'll find in any tourist brochure. I intend no slight to gems such as the Basketball Hall of Fame, the Emily Dickinson House, the Clark Art Institute, Mass MoCA, the Norman Rockwell Museum, Tanglewood, the Bridge of Flowers, or other well-known sites and attractions. Instead, I focus upon what archaeologist/historian James Deetz called "small things forgotten"—objects, structures, and ways of life that often puzzle modern viewers. I opted for a *CSI* approach to things neglected and ignored, with the hope of enriching appreciation, imagination, and historical understanding.

I'm pretty sure this teepee is historically inaccurate!

Why Western Mass?

Who Knew? focuses on Berkshire, Franklin, Hampden, and Hampshire counties, with an occasional foray into the western edge of Worcester County. Locals call the region "Western Mass," and that term is more contentious than you might imagine.

I was tempted to call this section "Will the Nightmare Never End?" after a 2017 incident. The Economic Development Council of Western Massachusetts (EDCWM) decided it was time to rebrand the section of the region known as the "Pioneer Valley." That wasn't a terrible idea per se. That head-scratching label was itself an invention, and nobody seems to know where the Pioneer Valley starts and ends.

What followed was like a lame *Saturday Night Live* sketch. The EDCWM sent $80,000 to an Oklahoma ad agency to develop a new tag line and logo. It came up with "West Mass" and a design that looked like it was lifted from a bank that went under in the 1970s. If you count a space between words, it works out to $26,666 and change per character to transform "Western Mass" into "West Mass." This, mind you, came from an agency in the middle of the country, a slap in the face to a region that has as many designers as Oklahoma has oil wells. Locals hoisted their metaphorical pitchforks and torches to storm the airwaves, op-ed pages, and social-media sites.

The EDCWM came in for such ridicule that its brainchild disappeared faster than a plate of brownies at a church supper. Pioneer Valley signs remain in place, even though most of us still can't find its borders on a map and have no idea why it's called that. For the record, tourism boosters developed that label in the 1940s to promote the region's innovative and independent spirit, and the region is mostly, but not entirely, confined to the Connecticut River Valley. No wonder most people prefer to reference everything from the Quabbin Reservoir to the Berkshires as "Western Mass."

At least the emphasis on independent thinking was on the money. There's not much that peeves folks more than being dissed by outsiders. When I first hatched this project, I approached several intrigued publishers who told me they'd offer a contract if I expanded my reach to include Boston. They were less than amused to learn that their offers were just about the most insulting thing they could say to someone who has made Western Mass his home for nearly 35 years!

Western Mass is renowned for its scenic beauty, its institutions of higher learning, its literary output, its cultural richness, and its live-and-let-live attitude. It is also an underappreciated, understudied afterthought even within the Commonwealth of Massachusetts. Political power isn't just concentrated in the Greater Boston area east of Route 95/128, it's waterlogged. Too often, Western Mass—the 150 miles of Massachusetts Turnpike west of I-95—gets short shrift.

If we want to get geographical about it, there are (at least) three distinct physical regions of Massachusetts. Greater Boston hugs the low-lying eastern seaboard. Moving west, the singular features and climate corridor of the Greater Worcester area from the New Hampshire border to Rhode Island is often called "Central Massachusetts."

Worcester is close enough to Route 128 that Bostonians at least occasionally *think* about it. I obtained my Ph.D. from the University of Massachusetts Amherst. It's in American history, but I could have majored in Boston insults. I'll mention this again later, but in 1994, U.S. Senate candidate Mitt Romney pledged to canvas "the entire state—from Boston to Worcester." Ouch!

For most of the time I've lived in Western Mass, the commonwealth's flagship university in Amherst has lacked a single local representative on its governance board—one that sits in Boston, by the way, though only one of its five campuses is located there, and 42 percent of all UMass students are found in Amherst. A former *Boston Globe* sportswriter liked to refer to the Amherst campus as "UMass Hooterville." If you have a thick skin, that's amusing. It's also emblematic of how little Greater Boston residents actually think about Western Mass. To some, it's even mysterious.

In the pages to follow, I'll discuss the distinct character of Western Mass. That's tricky stuff, but for now let's observe that patterns of non-Native-American settlement in Western Mass differed from those along the seaboard, and that its economic patterns also followed a different trajectory.

Western Mass topography also plays a part. The region is more rugged, more heavily forested, and less populated than the rest of the commonwealth. Much of the area is in a different U.S. Department of Agriculture growing zone than Eastern and Central Mass. Agriculture is, perhaps, more challenging in Western Mass, but its persistence probably contributed to the strong streaks of independent thought that permeate the region.

Western Mass was an epicenter of back-to-the-land communalism in the 1960s and 1970s, was an early enclave of support for LGBTQ rights in the late 20th century, and remains considerably more liberal than most of the United States, including other parts of New England. It has long been so; 19th-century Western Mass. had strong abolitionist movements, various utopian experiments, diet reformers, water-cure centers, and social redeemers. Their spirit lives on in the region's alternative lifestyles, political activism, and vibrant arts and cultural output.

The bottom line is that Western Mass. eccentricities, quirks, and social history make it unique. So, yeah, it raises hackles when someone tells you to "include Boston" in a book about Western Mass. I bring a touch of irreverence into this look at Massachusetts west of Worcester. Mostly, though, my goals are to help readers appreciate the perplexing things in plain view, and to see the history lurking behind them. Even the wacky stuff!

Dinosaur-foot fossil, Beneski Museum, Amherst

Section I

Western Mass BC

There's nothing like starting with the stuff you know the least. Remember, I'm a historian, so give me credit for moxie! These two chapters look at things that may have happened before recorded history. So some material is speculative by nature.

The first is on dinosaurs, and is constructed from available scientific evidence. It led me into fields such as botany, evolutionary theory, geology, paleontology, and a few other "ologies" about which I am a rank amateur. I did some double-checking to make sure I got things mostly right, but if any factual errors slipped by, I am entirely to blame. My goal is to point you in the direction of cool things. Dinosaurs, for example, are pretty awesome and we're learning more about them every day.

Burnt Hill is a site that might be archaeologically important, but it could also be a complete fabrication, even a gigantic goof. In my mind, the fact that it's so mysterious makes it worth contemplating. Of all the things in this book, though, it's the one for which it's most acceptable to plead ignorance. If someone asks you what Burnt Hill is, you can say proudly, "I don't know. Nobody knows. And that's the point of it."

I
When Monsters Roamed: Dinosaurs in Western Massachusetts

Wally, a full-sized stegosaurus replicated in fiberglass, greets visitors to the Berkshire Museum in Pittsfield. Those entering the Springfield Museum of Science shiver at the skeletal feet of a 20-foot model of a carnivorous Tyrannosaurus rex. Just moments from the antique-stuffed historic homes of Old Deerfield, children frolic among an assortment of faux ancient reptiles at the Rock, Fossil, and Dinosaur Shop. What gives? Does Western Mass think it's Montana East?

When it comes to dinosaurs, Western Mass doesn't have to resort to pretense: the Connecticut River Valley is rich in reminders that once upon a time, monsters roamed, including *herds* of long-necked herbivores, lumbering duckbills, and carnivores of all sizes. Pliny Moody, a South Hadley farm boy, discovered the first fossil in 1802,

One of hundreds of dinosaur prints at Smith's Ferry

and new finds take place regularly. It's not hard to find shops selling fossils, museums displaying them, and weighty college courses interpreting them.

Wally, though, is a poseur. He came to Pittsfield by way of Cleveland, Ohio, where he stood for 30 years before making the trek to Western Mass in 1997. He's just a teaser for the Berkshire Museum's Gallery of Dinosaurs, which is informative, though the Berkshires didn't have many dinosaurs—for reasons I'll get to in a moment. Not to slight the equally fine Springfield Museum of Science, but the three go-to sites for a Western Mass dinosaur experience are Amherst College's Beneski Museum, the Smith's Ferry dinosaur tracks on the outskirts of Holyoke, and Nash Dinosaur Land in Granby. The Beneski is filled with fossils and learned interpretations of them. Kids can walk in dino-track casts and gawk at the skeletons of giant mammals and a 27-foot-long Gryposaurus, but most folks go there to polish their intellectual apples. Overall, though, it's more fun to walk where the dinosaurs walked, or indulge in the eccentricities of Nash's Dinosaur Land. First, though, a tiny bit of geology and prehistory.

How Dinosaurs Came to Holyoke

If you believe the Earth was created just 6,000 years ago, stop reading this chapter. Scientific evidence suggests the planet is around 4.5 billion years old and that it took billions more years for landmasses to assume their current shapes and positions. If you wonder how cold-blooded dinosaurs could survive in chilly New England, it's mostly because New England was once part of the supercontinent Pangaea, which had a subtropical climate and was situated near the present-day equator. Our particular part of Pangaea (Laurentia) was formed through various geologic events during the Mesozoic Era (252 to 66 ma[1])—including volcanic eruptions, earthquakes, colliding supercontinents, and tectonic shifts.

We can subdivide the Mesozoic Era into three periods that correspond with the age of the dinosaurs: the Triassic (252–201 ma), the Jurassic (200–145 ma), and the Cretaceous (145–66 ma). Think of them as the early, mature, and late dinosaur ages. It's highly unlikely that anything like Wally roamed the greater Pittsfield region. Nearby Mount Greylock's 3,491-foot summit makes it the highest peak in Massachusetts today. That's impressive, but in the early Mesozoic Era, Berkshire peaks were as high as the Himalaya are today, pretty rough terrain for a 15,000-pound plated reptile!

When Laurentia began to split from Pangaea about 175 ma, a north/south fault line developed. The Berkshires were the eastern edge of the North American Craton, a continental shield. But the same forces that thrust the mountains upward depressed the thin strip that makes up much of today's eastern seaboard. The 410-mile-long Connecticut River Valley—then marked by shallow, warm water and abundant vegetation—was ideal for dinosaurs, especially during the Jurassic Period. Their tracks— impressions left in mud and cooling lava—can be found in many places along the Connecticut River. The best site is along Route 5 about a mile and a half north of the center of Holyoke at a place known as Smith's Ferry, so called for the ferryboats that used to carry passengers and goods between Holyoke and South Hadley. It contains dinosaur tracks from at least 130 separate beasts. Be glad no humans appeared in the Connecticut River Valley until some 5,000 years ago, or your ancestors might have been lunch; most of the dinosaurs that sauntered through the greater Holyoke region were meat-eating theropods.

Thero who? We have a lot more knowledge about dinosaur diversity these days. We now know that Amherst Professor Edward Hitchcock was right when, as early as the 1830s, he insisted—though some thought him crazy—that evolutionary ancestors of birds made some of the unusual fossils over which he puzzled in his laboratory. The term "dinosaur" wasn't coined until 1841, and research remained, shall we say, primitive into the 20th century. Only since the 1970s has a critical mass of scientists accepted the idea that some dinos had feathers and evolved into birds, or that many prehistoric reptiles were brightly colored and some might have been warm-blooded. To date, over a thousand dinosaur species have been discovered in North America. To make it a bit easier, though, most dinosaurs are grouped by hip types as either saurischia or ornithischia, the first meaning "lizard-hipped" and the latter "bird-hipped." But don't get too comfortable, the lizard-hipped saurischians are the ones from which birds evolved!

Want to feel small? Try to walk in the prints of the 15-foot-tall Eubrontes giganteous that once traipsed through Holyoke mud. Good luck with that if your stride is less than six feet. It wasn't even the biggest creature in the pond—four-legged sauropods akin to brontosauruses grew to over 100 feet in length. At least they were herbivores. At just three-to-six inches in height, the smallest known critter in the region was the three-toed Grallator cuneatus, but you wouldn't want to have encountered it because it was carnivorous.

Nash Dinosaur Land

A dose of nostalgia is often a good way to imagine an even more distant past. Nash Dinosaur Land is a relic in its own right, a reminder of days when "motoring" was its own reward and tourist attractions were less commercially slick. It lies in a section of Granby hard by the South Hadley line accessed via Route 116, and is a strong-armed fossil's throw from where Pliny Moody unearthed the Bay State's first dinosaur tracks in 1802. No one knew exactly what they were, and locals dubbed them "the tracks of Noah's raven," a Biblical reference to the bird whose non-return to the ark signaled receding flood waters. But the story of Nash Dinosaur Land has less to do with the Old Testament than with the fact that George Harlan Nash lived nearby. During his time at Amherst College (class of 1896), he developed a lifelong interest in geology and often took his son, Carlton Snell Nash, to peruse Amherst College's fossil collections.

Carlton had the misfortune of graduating from high school in 1932, one of the harshest years of the Great Depression, and had to work various jobs to make ends meet. Luckily, by 1939 he amassed enough capital to buy a two-acre piece of land near the Nash homestead, where he had secretly found dinosaur fossils six years earlier. In addition to his main job with the Holyoke Water Power Company, Nash made extra money from selling geodes and fossils he chiseled from the quarry on that land. In 1950, he shocked his wife by quitting his job with the power company to operate a rock and fossil shop.

Nash was good at self-promotion, but was he a huckster, an eccentric, or a visionary? It depends who you asked, but a good guess is that he was a bit of all three. One could buy a variety of things at Dinosaur Land: trilobite fossils, dinosaur tracks, gemstones, gizzard stones that helped herbaceous sauropods digest plants, sharks' teeth, unusual rocks, and petrified plants. Dinosaur tracks were and remain the big-ticket best sellers for a simple reason: the quarry lies on private property and is immune from most restrictions that curtail trade in paleontological finds. Nash's clients included various museums, cowboy star Gene Autry, positive-thinking advocate Dale Carnegie, comedian Stan Laurel, General George Patton, and TV personalities Dave Garroway and John Cameron Swayze.

Nash dinosaur-track site today

Carlton Nash invited controversy, but not for his retail or wholesale practices. In the increasingly rigorous world of academic paleontology, Nash was accused of being a P. T. Barnum-like con man. He covered his shop with fossils and declared it "the world's oldest building," aggressively hawked the goods housed therein, and reveled in the post-World War II thirst for celebrity. He was interviewed on the radio and spotlighted in numerous urban newspapers, on the pages of mass-market magazines, and on the device that came to dominate American households: television. He made appearances on both *The Today Show* and *Good Morning America*.

Back in Granby, a retro "dinosaur delivery wagon" served as a mobile advertisement, and a sign along Route 116 touted Nash's claim to have discovered a cure for leukemia. The fact that the cure involved chickens and a "secret formula" encouraged the suspicion that he was a cranky eccentric, as did his loud complaints that the scientific community was marginalizing him. It might also have had something to do with the corny papier-mâché dinosaur models and in-shop signs warning that unattended children would be fed to dinosaurs.

But Carlton Nash was also civic-minded, welcomed school groups, and approached his work with the scholarly zeal of a well-informed amateur. When he died in 1997, his son Kornell took over the shop, rechristened it Nash Dinosaur Track Site and Rock Shop, and jettisoned a lot of the provocative flamboyance. Nonetheless, it remains a quirky delight. Approaching it is akin to time travel. The current shop—the third on the site—is a one-story stone block building built in 1960 and looks its age; the fake dino on its left side has weathered even less well. You can peruse the shop for free and tour the quarry for a small fee. Inside, illustrations and displays are dusty, fading throwbacks to the pre-digital, do-it-yourself age. For all of that, it's still a serious place to do business. Kornell adroitly helped my wife locate a particular type of moss agate for which she was searching and dispensed advice on how to how to set it for a necklace. And, yes, you can still buy dinosaur tracks.

Ironic postscript: Carlton Nash might have been weak on specifics—including whether it was he or his wife who was cured by his secret anti-cancer formula—but he wasn't nuts to think chickens were the key. Since 1937, hundreds of studies have looked into chicken/cancer connections and as recently as 2017, interferon injected into chicken cells, extracted from eggs, and used on humans has shown promise in treating kidney cancer, some melanomas, and a few varieties of leukemia!

1 ma = millions of years ago. It is one of several measurements used by geologists and paleontologists to measure prehistoric time. After all, they study events whose exact dating is flexible by millennia. Although I have had history students seeking such leeway, you only get away with it before dates are recorded.

2
Those Who Walked Before Us?
Burnt Hill in Heath

The weathered hills of Western Massachusetts and the Berkshires show their geological age. The cultivated valleys, altered stream beds, abandoned structures, and museums clogged with archaeological finds alert us that human beings have been here for a long time as well. How long, though, is hotly contested. That's one reason Burnt Hill remains a mystery. At least 21 hefty rocks rise atop a hillock near the center of Heath. It's dubbed Burnt Hill because the exposed bedrock upon which the standing stones sit seems charred by centuries of exposure to the elements.

Native Americans populated Massachusetts well before Anglos or African Americans, but were they here first? Did ancient Celts or Egyptians or Iberians venture into New England before or at roughly the same time as Indians?[1] Mysterious sites across Western Massachusetts invite us to imagine ancient peoples and ponder what they

might have had in mind when they relocated wicked heavy rocks to the top of a remote hill. We do not know the actual "who" or "why." Barring some spectacular and incontrovertible discovery, what Burnt Hill means depends on whom you ask.

The town of Heath lies near Route 2, more than 400 feet above the valley carved by the Deerfield River. Europeans settled Heath in 1765, but even today it has a population just a shade over 700—and that's a generous counting inflated by its 25-square-mile boundaries. Those who live there praise its solitude and independent spirit; non-residents wonder why anyone chooses to be so isolated. I pass no judgment, but Heath's relative remoteness makes Burnt Hill all the more puzzling.

The center of Heath lies at 1,680 feet above sea level. To catch a glimpse of Burnt Hill, you must travel a few miles beyond the center, meander back a few gravel roads, and climb another 170 feet. Burnt Hill lies on private land, so you can't walk among the stones, but you can see enough from Flagg Hill Road to pique your curiosity. Some call the site a "stone circle," but that's inaccurate. Burnt Hill looks at once planned and haphazard. Three larger stones form a rough triangle and the remainder frame the complex, but neither in a straight line nor in a perfect circle. A field littered with stones is the punch line to many a New England joke, but I have explored enough standing-stone sites across Europe to suspect that those of Burnt Hill were not randomly placed. If fact, if they were a bit more orderly, Burnt Hill would evoke a smaller version of Callanish on Scotland's Isle of Lewis.

Who Built Burnt Hill?

There are plenty of theories about who built Burnt Hill, but most are akin to speculation about the Loch Ness monster—more wishful thinking than hard science. Is it an ancient religious center? A gathering point for scattered peoples? An astronomical sun wheel? A 2001 field report from the New England Antiquities Research Association dowsed the sun wheel idea by noting that the possible sighting stones are too short. The same report speculates that blueberry pickers may have enhanced the site through the decades by placing other stones near the main cluster. Who knows? Maybe the entire thing is a 19th-century farmer's practical joke, though he must have had a serious perverse streak to lug 21 boulders weighing 300–500 pounds each to the top of a rocky outcrop just for a laugh. But that's not the weirdest theory. Some have imagined Burnt Hill as the outline of a whale; others see a dragon. One observer slapped a purple filter on his camera and claimed to have witnessed an ethereal glow. Aside from the fact that ancient peoples would have lacked such a filter, it's no secret that camera filters alter our perceptions of reality.

Once we get beyond the fanciful, the top three "rational" theories are that Burnt Hill is evidence of Neolithic peoples, was a Native American site, or was erected by medieval Europeans. Neolithic means "new stone age" and is used to label the period of Western civilization from roughly 12,500 BCE to around 3,000 BCE.[2] It was marked by the domestication of plants and animals, which meant that food came to people rather than vice versa. Humans could build permanent settlements instead of wandering in search of sustenance, which was a big deal if you wanted to build something like England's Stonehenge. During the Neolithic period, stone circles cropped up across Europe. Whenever we see standing stones in places like Burnt Hill, it's tempting to make analogies, as I did to Callanish. Ancient Celts, Iberians, and Phoenicians are frequent suspects, though there's not enough evidence to convict any of them.

Neolithic analogies suffer from what I call Mystery Hill Syndrome. Salem, New Hampshire, is home to a conundrum that has been called "America's Stonehenge." It's an impressive 30-acre complex allegedly discovered in 1826 by a farmer named Jonathan Pattee. It is either proof that Neolithic Europeans came here, or that William Goodwin made up the whole thing when he bought the land in 1937 and dubbed it "Mystery Hill." There are loads of stone chambers, suggestive scratches, and rock foundations that invite both scientific and romantic speculation. Is a giant grooved slab a "sacrificial stone," or just creative drainage? Are striations really ancient runes, or chisel marks? If they are runes, who carved them, when, and for what purpose? Pottery and charcoal samples dating to 2000 BCE prove nothing more than the fact that people camped there a long time ago.

In fact, a huge problem with all presumed Neolithic sites is that no one seems to have died there or left much garbage. Every now and then a well-preserved body—like one found in New Bedford—invites Egyptian mummification comparisons, but the same body might be from the 16th century, and that leaves quite a lot of historical space in the middle. Why are Iberians or Phoenicians mentioned? Mostly because Burnt Hill's small, rounded stones are a bit like some sites in Portugal, and the Phoenicians are suspect because they were great sailors who *might* have made it across the Atlantic.

Burnt Hill is seldom associated with Native Americans because they are not known to have made such stone structures. Key word: *known*. Recent research suggests that ancestors called Paleo-Indians made their way to North America around 30,000 years ago. That's a hint about how much we've learned; we used to think they arrived only about 15,000 years ago. Insofar as we can tell, those classified as Eastern Woodlands peoples show up in Western Massachusetts around 7500 BCE, but we still don't know much about those earliest arrivals. We do know, however, that Indians throughout Central and South America built impressive things out of stone a little bit later. Given that the New England landscape is lousy with stone, why dismiss the possibility that Indians once erected a ceremonial center? After all, the Deerfield River Valley was a highway for native peoples long before Route 2 was built.

European Origins, Or Not

The most suggestive evidence, though, is that medieval Europeans could have had a hand in shaping Western Massachusetts. A 15-foot-deep subterranean chamber in Goshen was fashioned without mortar. This is known as dry stone construction and dates to Neolithic times. It has been a staple of wall and chamber building since the Middle Ages. There is an enigmatic stone chamber in nearby Leverett that bears a striking resemblance to the building techniques of 8th-century Irish monks, as is the case with some 105 similar sites elsewhere in Massachusetts. Unusual stone walls and chambers in Pelham, Petersham, New Salem, Shutesbury, and Wendell also evoke medieval European structures. In legend, the Irish monk Brendan voyaged across the Atlantic with 16 followers in the 6th century. Many doubt this tale, but we do know that Norsemen ("Vikings") made it across by 1000 CE and built the L'Anse aux Meadows site in Newfoundland and probably a few more outposts.

All of this proves next to nothing. The elaborate cave in Goshen could be nothing more than the well-built retreat of an unknown recluse. We know for certain that an immigrant Scottish eccentric named John Smith lived such an existence in the Millers River town of Erving from 1867 to 1900, a site now whimsically dubbed "Erving Castle." Doubters insist that unusual structures are little more than root cellars, ice houses, and foundations made from available materials by those using whatever skills their builders possessed. Their skepticism is fueled by other overzealous assertions, including tendencies to declare any unorthodox space not dubbed ancient as either a smuggler's den or a stop on the Underground Railroad.

As a historian, I remind students not to confuse correlation with causation. There's simply not enough evidence to unravel the mystery of Burnt Hill. In 1997, astronomy professor Judith Young spearheaded a project that gave rise to construction of a stone sun wheel on the campus of the University of Massachusetts Amherst to help study sites such as Callanish or Burnt Hill. Imagine that a future cataclysm destroyed UMass. What would future archaeologists make of those carefully placed stones? In the absence of hard evidence, is it okay for us to dream about what happened at Burnt Hill? Why not?

1 Some view the term Indian as disrespectful, though most Native Americans embrace the term. Although "Indian" is associated with Christopher Columbus' false conclusion that he had found a westward route from Europe to India, the term is also linked linguistically to the word indigenous and is liberally applied to various pre-Columbian peoples.

2 BCE = Before Current Era. This is often used because much of the world does not date time via the Christian convention of BC (Before Christ) and AD, anno Domini, Latin for "the year of the Lord," or 1 AD. The use of BCE is a generally agreed upon compromise.

Section II

Hard to Overlook

America is such a big country that it's only natural that we have a fondness for eye-catching things. One way to attract attention is to go *really* big, a phenomenon Karal Ann Marling recognized in her delightful tribute to gargantuan drive-by distractions, *The Colossus of Roads: Myth and Symbol along the American Highway*. The subject can be anything from ice cream cones to Paul Bunyan. You name it and someone has supersized it in plastic, concrete, tin, wood, fiberglass, stone, or some unorthodox material such as corn, as in the famed Corn Palace in Mitchell, South Dakota.

As you will read in this section, Western Massachusetts is no stranger to such colossi. How do we classify these things? Are they

"Hail to the Sunrise" statue

folk art, kitsch, amusing diversions, or marketing gone mad? I enjoy things that disrupt my normal routines, though I admit that every now and then I'm perplexed. There is, for example, a storage unit complex between Becket and Lee that sports a worse-for-wear giant beaver that blurs the line between beavers, sumo wrestlers, and hamsters on steroids. Other large statues are throwbacks to another age, a few of which might offend delicate sensibilities. Mostly, though, these things are just weird and fun.

Size isn't the only way to attract attention. There are monuments and features across the region that jar the senses because they are unexpected and, unless someone tells you about them, inexplicable. Why is there a giant rock perched atop a hillock on Route 66 west of Northampton? Why is there a newsboy statue in a Great Barrington residential neighborhood, a fancy library in Conway, or an enormous milk bottle in Whately?

Finally, there are things we need to contemplate to appreciate. Western Mass is known for its scenic splendor, but you have to take the time to look. This section also spotlights what Herman Melville imagined when he looked at Mount Greylock, and offers some lesser-known places where you might want to look around and engage your own imagination.

3
Big Indian and Big Hype: The Mohawk Trail

You'd have to be seriously distracted to miss "Big Indian" when traveling west from Greenfield toward Shelburne Falls. He stands erect upon a platform and looms nearly 20 feet above Route 2. Although the original Big Indian Shop has changed owners and names several times since the statue appeared in 1974, Big Indian, with his right hand raised and adorned in a colorful attire and feather headdress, continues to entice tourists to check out the souvenir shop behind him. Whether he's amusing or problematic depends on your politics, but for certain Big Indian is a load of hooey! So too are many other representations you'll encounter along the sections of Routes 2 and 2A known as the Mohawk Trail.

If Indians aren't the most represented figures in American sculpture, they are surely the most *misrepresented.* You'll find them on everything from ship figureheads and weather vanes to cigar store come-ons and circus wagons. There are numerous parallels to Big Indian across the country. I used to get a chuckle whenever I drove to Freeport, Maine, where a very tall Indian statue on Route 1 once bore a sign for a store named Levinsky's, which suggested that one of the lost tribes of Israel got seriously rerouted. The figure is still there but, alas, Levinsky's is not.

It's obvious that the purpose of such statues is

commercial, not historical. That's also true of most of the things purporting to be "Native American" along the Mohawk Trail: metal and concrete tepees, faux totem poles, trading posts, and ferocious concrete black bears that make grizzlies look like kittens. The trading posts also provide amusement. You'll find some goods actually made by Native Americans—though it's highly unlikely they're from local crafters—but mostly it's foreign-made kitsch, decades-old musical recordings, and stereotypical mass-produced items. I can assure you that the only thing you can "trade" for these items are the pictures of American presidents adorning U.S. currency.

The best way to learn actual history along the Mohawk Trail is to accept that—aside from the occasional summertime powwow—little of what you encounter has much to do with Massachusetts Native Americans. Take Big Indian. His bonnet and clothing are those of Great Plains natives, not the Algonquians of Western Massachusetts or the Mohawks who wandered over from today's New York state. Ditto those teepees. There are totem poles along the Mohawk Trail as well, but most are pale imitations of those from the Pacific Northwest. Don't get me started on shop offerings such as plastic tomahawks, plastic-soled moccasins, or toy tom-toms.

When Native Americans Actually Roamed the Mohawk Trail

Today's Mohawk Trail is a 60-mile-plus ribbon of asphalt. Its exact eastern starting point depends on which brochure you read,[1] but it terminates at the New York line near Williamstown. Much of it follows the Deerfield River, but it also meanders along or crosses the Millers, Connecticut, Green, and Hoosic rivers. These waterways were important to various native peoples, but when Route 2 was rebuilt in 1914, it was christened the Mohawk Trail as part of an early auto-tourism marketing campaign. It parallels what was an east-west byway long before Europeans set foot in the region.

Among Native Americans, the section west of the Connecticut River was contested turf between Algonquian peoples along the Connecticut and Deerfield rivers, and Iroquoians north of New York's Mohawk River.[2] There were as many as 125,000 Algonquians in pre-contact New England, though Western Massachusetts was more sparsely populated, with peoples scattered among small villages, such as Agawam (Springfield), Norwottuck (Hadley), and Woronoco (Russell). Each group had a leader (*sachem*) and lived semi-nomadic lives in which hunting, fishing, and gathering supplemented foods grown near the villages—often the "three sisters" crops of beans, squash, and maize. Regional Algonquians shared language similarities, but sometimes warred against one another.

Many of the Algonquians along the Deerfield River were called Pocumtucs, and they had the dubious distinction of being on a trail traversed by Mohawks, who spoke an Iroquoian dialect. Iroquois peoples such as the Mohawk, Oneida, Seneca, and Onondaga mostly lived in arc extending north, west, and south of the Algonquians. But the Deerfield River was rich in salmon, bass, trout, and shad, which were favored by Mohawks. Untold thousands lived to the immediate west and north of the Pocumtuc Algonquians.

At the risk of grossly oversimplifying, let's say that the borders between the Algonquians and Mohawks were a delicate dance of cooperation, hostility, renegotiation, and nervous coexistence. The coming of Europeans complicated matters further. The Mohawks lived in areas under the control of the Dutch; the Pocumtucs dwelt among English settlers. Each native group saw its numbers dwindle precipitously because of disease, warfare with each other, and blood shed in conflicts with or led by Europeans. The Pocumtucs were on the losing end of most 17th-century turning points, including England's alliance with the Mohawks, a smallpox epidemic (1633–34), the Pequot War (1636–38), a war against the Mohawks (1644), and King Philip's War (1675–76). During the last, also known as Metacom's War, the

Mohawks took full advantage to assert control along the Deerfield River. It's no wonder the route is today called the Mohawk Trail; by the time those Iroquois allied with France raided Deerfield in 1704, the 300 or so remaining Pocumtucs also took part; most came down from Canada, as nearly all of their kin in the Connecticut Valley had been obliterated.

The future, though, belonged to the English, and later to their heirs who led the American Revolution. The Mohawk Trail, like the Bay Path once used by natives traveling from Massachusetts Bay to the Connecticut River for the shad run, became trade and travel routes used by Euro-Americans. By 1914, automobiles, tourism, commerce, and romanticism laid claim to the Mohawk Trail.

Dressing in Feathers

In 1932, 42 years before Big Indian appeared on the scene, another fanciful native took his perch along Route 2: the "Hail to the Sunrise—In Memory of the Mohawk Indian" monument just west of Charlemont. (See photo, Section II Introduction.) A scantily clad native stands atop a boulder, his arms spread skyward—presumably in praise of the Great Spirit. At his feet are 100 carved stones from various so-called tribes honoring the five Mohawk "nations" that once roamed the region. The only thing truly native about any of this is that the central figure is wearing more appropriate headgear than Big Indian.

The aforementioned tribes are local chapters of the Improved Order of Red Men, a fraternal organization. Each "tribe" is headed by a "sachem" and assisted by "sagamores" that officiate at the local "wigwam" and represent the tribe at state gatherings called the "Reservation." There is also a national Great Council of Red Men and a Board of Great Chiefs. Today there about 15,000 Red Men and the organization is largely a charitable organization, but members were originally for the well connected. Its most famous offspring is New York's Tammany Hall, a political machine.

Hail to the Sunrise Park

Here's the kicker: The Red Men were never about Native Americans. They evolved from groups inspired by whites disguised as Indians that took part in the 1773 Boston Tea Party. The statue at Charlemont is the work of Joseph Pollia (1894–1954), a Sicilian-born, Boston School of the Museum of Fine Arts-trained sculptor best known for war memorials and monuments to public figures. In 1932, only "free white male(s) of good moral character" could join the Red Men. Its constitution is littered with fanciful (and embarrassing) Indian terms; Red Men practiced what anthropologist Elizabeth Bird dubbed "dressing in feathers."

Most of the Mohawk Trail is dressed in feathers—way too many of them, in Big Indian's case. You'd never know that the natives of the region made temporary domed wigwams from birch bark and wood, that they lived in permanent wooden long houses, that they burned fields to fertilize them, or that they seldom wore elaborate headdresses or cavorted about half naked. (This is New England, after all!) Nor

would you know that women held great power among the Mohawks, and you'd learn little about the rhythms and precariousness of everyday life for people wholly dependent upon abundant fish, game, and crop yields. Needless to say, you won't hear much about political intrigue or the destruction of native ways. The Mohawk Trail belongs to a time of movie and television cowboys and Indians in which the displacement of native peoples was viewed as the triumph of civilization over savagery.

We feel differently about these things now, among the reasons why many of the Mohawk Trail "attractions" have faded. You can still enjoy the Mohawk Trail, though. It is one of the most scenic drives in Massachusetts, and there's no harm in a giggle or two at the expense of Big Indian and other attempts at dressing the trail in feathers—as long as you also think about the history that's *not* displayed along Route 2.

Footnote: The only instance I know of in Western Massachusetts where dressing in feathers was (sort of) appropriate lies in a display case at the Forbes Library in Northampton. There you'll find a Great Plains war bonnet and a photograph of President Calvin Coolidge wearing it. Coolidge looks uncomfortable, but the event was laudatory. The headdress was given to the president in 1927 by Sioux Chief Henry Standing Bear to thank Coolidge for signing into law the 1924 Snyder Act, which belatedly recognized Native Americans as citizens.

1 Because its starting point is imprecise, the Mohawk Trail shows up in brochures as 63–69 miles in length.

2 The term "tribe" is a bit misleading when thinking of the region's native populations; "language groups" and "kinship villages" are more helpful labels.

4
What School Doesn't Need a Giant Milk Bottle? Whately's Colossus of Roads

You drive down the main drag (Center Street) of the Franklin County town of Whately and there it is. The town's iconic concrete milk bottle stands 16'2" high, weighs more than 6,800 pounds, and sits in front of a throwback two-story red-brick elementary school. But the bottle—emblazoned with the logo of Quonquont Dairy—wasn't always on that spot, and no students attend the old school, which now houses some items from the Whately Historical Society.

The Whately milk bottle is an advertising come-on from the early days of automobile travel—a "colossus of roads," to borrow a term from art historian Karal Ann Marling. Western Mass advertisers and marketers are no strangers to the bigger-is-better ethos. The Clarkdale Fruit Farm in Deerfield, for example, is probably known as much for its giant apple as for its cider.[6] Whately's tall milk bottle definitely attracts notice but, to invoke another slogan, there's more to it than meets the eye.

When Fred and Clara Wells began their dairy enterprise in 1923, they named it Quonquont —sometimes spelled Quon-Quont—the name of a 17th-century Native American *sachem* of the Nonotucks. Whether this was his actual name is open to interpretation. He was also known as Wampshaw, just as the Nonotucks—an Algonquin people—were also called the Nolwottogs and Norwottucks. It is possible that Quonquont may have been a mishearing of the native word eventually rendered as Connecticut: *Quenicticot*.

In the 1920s, Quonquont Dairy was one of three within the town of Whately. It and Fairview Dairy sold raw milk. Back then, Franklin County was a decidedly agricultural region sporting 3,130 farms among its 12,300 households (49,361 individuals). More than one-quarter of the county's labor force was involved in agriculture, which made dairy farming competitive as well as arduous. Enterprises such as Whately's Hillside Dairy, which sent milk out to be pasteurized, had to have it ready for the morning train; those storing raw milk needed to maintain ice ponds to keep it cool throughout the year—or at least long enough to send it to the local bottling works at Whately's Graves Corner.

The Wells family, however, saw how the automotive age was transforming local economics and opened the seasonal Quonquont Dairy Bar to diversify. They sold motorists ice cream, pie, and sandwiches. Tellingly, it was located on Route 5, some seven-tenths of a mile from the dairy. They chose it because Route 5 was (and is) a well-traveled road between Northampton and South Deerfield.

In 1925, Clara had the idea to build a giant milk bottle for the dairy bar. It was finished in time for the 1926 season, though it was a little bit different from what one sees today. Originally, it had a rubberized tarp covering its top to simulate the tin caps used on pre-1940s bottles. This eventually cracked, allowing water to seep into a structure fashioned from wood framing over which a coarse mix of plaster was slathered. The outside is finished with a fine concrete/plaster coating and whitewash. The structure's hollow interior is accessed by a door on the opposite side from the logo—convenient for making repairs such as replacing timbers and, eventually, the original lip and cap. The latter two are now made of stucco with painted details. The logo we see today uses the original script that adorned the embossed bottles of Quonquont milk sold to locals.

From 1926 until August of 1943, the giant bottle was part of the everyday landscape of Western Massachusetts. It had an interesting journey after Fred and Clara retired, but first let's take a small departure into advertising's past.

The Myth of an Illiterate Past

The Whately milk bottle is a product of the 20th century, but it also helps put to rest a hoary myth. Gigantic roadside novelty signs are the offspring of trade signs that date to the Colonial era. There's scarcely a local historical society that lacks old signs from its town's commercial past. Especially prized are those with carved trade symbols, such as tobacco-store wooden Indians, the baker's grain sheaf, the cobbler's boot, the wool merchant's ram, the dentist's tooth, and bigger-than-life tin men. Many are prized today as folk art, and the same historical societies (and quite a few art historians) regale audiences with tales of bygone days when these signs supposedly guided the illiterate masses to needed local services.

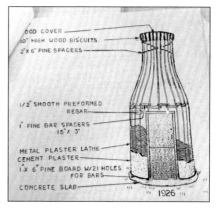

Nonsense! Those old trade signs were *exactly* analogous to the Whately milk bottle— they were advertisements; what today we'd label "branding." Many reflected merchants' pride in their wares or their aesthetic preferences, but symbols weren't needed to tell clueless locals where to shop. To think so is what historians call "presentism"; that is, viewing the past through contemporary eyes. Presentism often shows itself in assumptions of modern-day superiority. Since we know so much today—or so the logic goes—people long ago must have been poorly educated bumpkins. It's closer to the mark to assume that what we mean by "education" varies from generation to generation, but if illiterates populate your view of Colonial and Early American New England, you've fallen victim to a myth.

First of all, people traveled less often before the advent of trolleys, trains, and automobiles. No local needed a carved tooth to know where to have one extracted—it was common knowledge. More erroneous still is a belief in an unlettered past, especially in New England, which was founded by Protestants for whom Martin Luther's "priesthood of all believers" was a touchstone that required Bible reading. By 1650, an estimated 60 percent of Massachusetts residents of European ancestry were literate. Primers circulated after 1690, and Massachusetts laws required tax-supported schools for every community of more than 50 families. By 1776, as much as 90 percent of the population had at least rudimentary literacy skills.

Signs back then, in the 1920s, and now attract attention. You can go online and find lots of scientific studies that tell you how signs and symbols stimulate brain neurons, but it comes back to the same thing: stimulus and response. Have you ever seen a store sign and remembered that you needed milk? Has the sight of a familiar fast-food symbol brought on sudden pangs of hunger?

Saving the Milk Bottle

Still, some signs are cooler than others, and a giant milk bottle definitely qualifies as cool! Whately came perilously close to losing its iconic symbol. Quonquont Farm was sold to sisters Jeanne and Nathalie Kulesa in 1943, but they closed the dairy bar and, in 1946, sold the land to the Rice Oil Company. It had little need for a milk bottle, and planned to demolish it. Instead, the company gave it to Sabin Filipkowski, who hauled it to the other side of Route 5, where he operated the Pal-Mel Steakhouse. When the bottle deteriorated, he had it trucked to Malick's Garage, where it sat in storage. In 1963, Charles Selicious bought the Pal-Mel Steakhouse and renamed it the Lamplighter Inn. He sensibly realized that he wasn't in the dairy business either, so when the garage asked him to move the milk bottle, Selicious offered it to the town.

When Whately refused the gift, Selicious contemplated destroying the bottle, but instead moved it to the restaurant's parking lot, painted it gray, threw a tarp over the cracked cover, and ignored it.

In 1980, the Whately Historical Society began to discuss restoring the bottle, by then an eyesore. At the time, the society lacked both ownership of the bottle and the resources to repair it. The first problem was resolved in 1990, when Selicious retired and donated the structure to the town. It took five more years before the bottle was moved again—with the help of the Air National Guard in Westfield—to its current location at the junction of Center Street and Chestnut Plain Road. Under the supervision of retired engineer Henry Baldwin, restoration began in earnest in 1996. Quonquont Farms issued a commemorative one-pint bottle to help raise funds, an effort partly spearheaded by Stephen Bond, whose grandfather, Lincoln Bond, actually built the bottle.

Local community spirit continues to surround the bottle, which is now a focal point of an annual fair in May. Appropriately, free ice cream is served from the back of the structure. None of the milk comes from Whately, though; there are no active dairies in the town. Quonquont continues, but as an orchard, farm stand, and events center.

Marling notes that colossi of roads such as the Whately milk bottle were supposed to "sell the American Dream." They've certainly done that, but over time they've also become symbols of community memory and pride. And what could be more "American" than milk? By Stephen Bond's reckoning, there are more than 4,300 oversized milk bottles that still grace the countryside, including one in Granby at the site of the former Manny's Restaurant. These days, neither it nor the one in Whately has much to do with diary farming, but they sure do grab your attention.

1 'The Clarkdale apple is mostly red plastic stretched over a wooden frame and stuffed with straw, but it does the job for this 102-year-old, fourth-generation farm. The sign has even been in a few films.

5
Reinventing the Past: Northampton's Misunderstood Monument

Route 66 (West Street) is a well-traveled access into and out of Northampton. The crest of a rise near the bridge over the Mill River used to be called Hospital Hill, as it was once the site of the Northampton Lunatic Asylum, or the Northampton State Hospital, as it was later more sensitively renamed. Today, Hospital Hill is a favorite spot for winter sledding; in the spring, the field at the bottom is used by  Smith College for rugby and equestrian events. Few people pay much attention to a small hillock across the street at the intersection of West and Earle streets. Upon it sits a rough-hewn upright stone on a red sandstone base. It's not very attractive, which makes it all the more puzzling why it has been appropriated as a memorial to events that never happened there.

I know; I'm a victim of historical mythmaking. When I moved to Northampton in 1985, I was told that the stone crests what used to be Gallows Hill, where miscreants met their maker. It sits across the street from the Smith College stables, which made it an irresistible prop for telling students about the 1806 hanging of two unfortunate Irishmen–Dominic Daley and James Halligan— for a robbery and murder they probably did not commit. If any of my former students are reading this, please accept my red-faced apology. Daley and Halligan were indeed hanged and are memorialized on that hill, but their hangings took place elsewhere. In fact, nothing of note took place on the hill at all until the 1950s, though the West Street stone inadvertently informs us about how we recall history, how history's focus changes over time, and how professional historians untangle mysteries.

Northampton as a Protestant Anti-Irish Town

Daley and Halligan have much to teach us. We often hear of the vicious anti-Irish/anti-Catholic discrimination suffered by the ragged sons and daughters of Erin who came to the United States fleeing the Irish potato famine of 1845–52. Daley and Halligan alert us that prejudice had deeper historic roots. In many ways, the fate of Daley and Halligan was sealed 272 years earlier.

In 1534, King Henry VIII's Act of Supremacy dismantled the Catholic Church and established the Church of England with the monarch, not the pope, as its head. It also paved the way for English anti-Catholicism, which intensified after England's conquest of Ireland in 1691. The English Separatists and Puritans who settled Massachusetts in the 17th century viewed "papism" as superstition and blasphemy, which is why all but 20,000 of the estimated quarter-million Irish to immigrate to Colonial America were Protestants.

There were no Catholics in Western Massachusetts until the arrival of a "Celtic" indenture to Springfield in 1662.[1] By 1806, Northampton was overwhelmingly Congregationalist—the heirs of Puritanism—in keeping with the rest of Massachusetts, where tax dollars helped fund Congregationalism until 1834. For much of the 19th century, only Mormons (and later the Chinese) were as despised and feared as Catholics. Roman Catholicism had a small presence in Boston, but the faith was officially a "mission" church in New England, where there were reputedly just 1,200 Catholics in the entire region.

In brief, 34-year-old Dominic Daley (whose surname appears under various spellings) and 27-year-old James Halligan were accused of the robbery and murder of farmer Marcus Lyon near the town of Wilbraham. The evidence against the pair was slight and the prosecution's star witness was 13-year-old Laertas Fuller, whose eyewitness testimony was based mostly upon seeing two strange men in the area, one of whom he thought resembled Daley.

Nonetheless, the pair lingered in jail for five months, were appointed counsel just 48 hours before the trial, were found guilty, and sentenced to hang. Father Jean-Louis Lefebvre de Cheverus journeyed from Boston to administer last rites. He stayed with a local family, as no inn would admit him. Ironically, though, his was the first mass ever administered in Northampton. According to reports, 15,000 people witnessed the execution of Daley and Halligan, a veritable throng for a town whose population was around 2,500 at the time. If those numbers are even remotely accurate, the West Street hill could not have accommodated such a crowd.

It didn't need to; it was never Gallows Hill. And it was certainly not, as another tale holds, the burial spot of Daley and Halligan; their bodies were rendered at a South Street slaughterhouse and their bones discarded. For most of the Colonial period, Northampton hangings took place in the courtyard of the jail on Pleasant Street. Sometime around the American Revolution, executions moved to West Street, but to Pancake Plain, a site about seven-tenths of a mile west and south of the monument. Daley and Halligan died on a large open plain—near where there are now playing fields—a much more commodious space for a large crowd, though located in an area with an unsavory reputation.[2] Although the gallows were dismantled after the Irish duo's hanging, for several decades thereafter, local toughs used a nearby maple tree for morbid reenactments of the event.

The Silence of Changing Northampton

By today's standards of jurisprudence, the Daley-Halligan hangings were a great injustice. Irish-Americans eventually revered the victims as martyrs and used their deaths to highlight the indignities suffered by Northampton's Irish citizens. Today there is a memorial plaque to Daley and Halligan on the faux Gallows Hill, but that story embodies Northampton's longer demographic and religious transformation.

In 1838, the town got its first Roman Catholic priest, and in 1866, St. Mary of the Assumption became its first parish—catering to a predominantly Irish congregation. By the time St. John Cantius opened in 1904—just in time for the town's Quarter Millennial (250th) celebration—there were *five* parishes in town and 15,000 Catholics. Each parish was active in Quarter Millennial activities and, though the Daley and Halligan case was mentioned in the official Quarter Millennial booklet, noticeable by its absence is any reference to the West Street hillock. Neither was it listed in the "Historical Localities in Northampton" section of *The Meadow City's Quarter Millennial Book.* Nor will one find such an association in official documents relating to the city's 300th birthday bash in 1954. To reiterate, that's because Daley and Halligan met their end on Pancake Plain, not on the hill on West Street.

The stone holds another clue: "1878" is clearly chiseled into the stone, an indication that this was when it was erected. Although some say a group called the Sons of St. Patrick erected the stone that year, such a claim is problematic for several reasons. The year 1878 was of no particular significance in Northampton history, and no Irish-American group would have erected the stone in that year. It was when the Molly Maguire trials ended in Pennsylvania and when the final Irish-American was hanged for alleged acts of terrorist murder.

Across the nation, Irish-Americans scrambled to disassociate themselves from the Molly Maguires, whose very name became a synonym for terrorism. In other words, it was a good year for those of Irish descent to lie low.

Telling Tall Tales

Some local sleuths once thought the stone honored Joseph Maminash, though such a view is even more fanciful than the Daley and Halligan claims. Maminash was an assimilated Pocumtuc Indian who fought for the British at Louisbourg in 1745, and then against them during the American Revolution, serving in the same 4th Hampshire Regiment as future rebel Daniel Shays. Although probably born in Connecticut, Maminash lived upon Pancake Plain in Northampton and was buried there upon his death on August 31, 1778. In the 1860s, Maminash's grave marker was stolen. A folktale holds that his daughter Sally was the last Native American resident of Northampton and that the family with whom Sally was living raised the stone in Joseph's memory. Two small problems: Sally died in 1853—well before her father's marker disappeared—and she was not the last native in Northampton![3]

Two other, more prosaic, explanations also fail the sniff test. One tale claims that workmen grading West Street—a dirt road until the 20th century—hoisted the stone atop the hill because they liked how it looked. This is romantic nonsense; grading roads with draft animals and manual labor was far too arduous for working men to waste their time on such tomfoolery.

I initially thought the West Street monument was a road sign. Massachusetts had a law requiring that regularly spaced highway markers of durable material should line the roadsides. The law further stipulated (though it was often disobeyed) that these markers should be at least eight feet in height. The hilltop stone in question would fit these criteria.

Pliny Earle's Obsession

The truth is less romantic than anything thus far discussed. A clue lies in the hill's current configuration. If one gazes downward from the crest, a water containment pond that empties into a sewer marks its eastern base. This was the hill's 1878 purpose and the one it serves today. There *was* no hill on this spot until that year. Although Hospital Hill and Pancake Plain are part of a glacial drumlin that contains large boulders, the hill is a human-made feature, not the end of the drumlin.

The Northampton State Hospital opened its doors in 1858, and expanded greatly under its second superintendent Pliny Earle, who headed the institution from 1864 to 1885. Part of Earle's vision for treating the mentally ill involved work therapy, much of which involved farm work and manual labor. To that end, the hospital acquired land on both sides of West Street, including the land upon which both the real and faux Gallows Hill sit. There was a brick kiln across from where the monument now stands, convenient for Earle's many build-

ing projects. Earle was a fastidious man, and hospital's annual reports contained numerous mentions of grounds-beautification efforts—as well as complaints about the unsightly approach to the hospital, the tendency of rains to erode the hillsides, and disruptive Mill River floods. He ordered construction of numerous drainage ditches and sewers as part of his constant crusade against wet grounds.

The city of Northampton also struggled with flooding along the Mill River, a problem not entirely settled until 1940 when the stream was diverted away from the city's center. In 1878, however, the city took a stab at addressing the problem by rebuilding West Street. The part near Main Street was lowered several feet and some of the material was used to reconstruct Green Street. Further up the hill, West Street was cut back, graded, and partly rerouted. The October 29, 1878, *Daily Hampshire Gazette* contains this simple remark, "A sewer is being laid on the south side of Hospital Hill road, to carry off the water which has hitherto run into the gutter, and made constant work on the hill necessary. The grounds near the bottom of the hill are being graded and seeded down, and a huge stone monument has been set up."

That's it, folks! The hill was constructed from scratch and in such a way that water running down the hill would swirl around the cone-shaped hill and then into a sewer carrying it into the Mill River. As for the monument, Superintendent Earle ordered workmen to haul a boulder from the woods and place it on a pedestal; in his mind, it made the entrance to the NSH grounds look more imposing and beautiful.

Reclaiming the Hill through Accident and Intention

The stone signified nothing until the 1950s, when local Irish-Americans began to retell the long-forgotten Daley and Halligan saga and to gather on the hillside for St. Patrick's Day celebrations. In recounting the tragedy of 1806, either a local tale spinner stretched the truth or an inattentive *Springfield Republican* reporter misheard details. Thus, by 1956, sewer hill had become Gallows Hill.

But the monument was still not a memorial—not until St. Patrick's Day in 1984, when Governor Michael Dukakis awarded a posthumous pardon to Daley and Halligan. A bronze plaque appeared on the monument to commemorate the governor's proclamation. Today, it's a historical site marking something that never happened there. But with all the tales circulating around the hill, it would be inaccurate to say that the hill is without deeper historic and folkloric meaning. You could argue that everyone associated with the hill—Irish victims, forgotten Native Americans, Irish-American-pride groups, road crews, and the countless individuals who passed through the Northampton State Hospital—deserve to be memorialized. Alternatively, you could take the position that it's pretty cool to have a monument to a sewer!

1 We don't know much about the indentured servant, but the term "Celtic" usually denoted either an Irish or Scottish Catholic. Protestant Irish were generally called Ulstermen or Anglo-Irishmen, and Scottish Protestants were simply Scots or Scotch [sic]-Irish. Note: Scottish people seldom use the term "Scotch" to reference anything other than the fiery alcoholic beverage.

2 The neighborhood had a poor reputation for several reasons that are troubling in their own right. Pancake Plain was where Algonquian Indians once maintained a small village, and a few mixed-race residents resided there in the late 18th and early 19th centuries, a time in which antipathy toward Native people ran high. It was also occupied by the poor and others deemed outcasts by Northampton elites.

3 Northampton residents followed the example of many towns in creating legends of the "last Indian" in their town. These stories tell us more about the fading of Native American heritage in the East than about actual ethnic bloodlines. Beginning in 1860, the U.S. Census enumerated only "Indians" who paid taxes, which fueled the idea that Native Americans had died out in many places where they had not.

6
Extra! Extra!
Great Barrington's Newsboy Statue

Mention that you once had a newspaper route, and you'll probably get one of several reactions. If there are young folks in the room, they might not know what you mean. These days, most paper carriers are adults and their ranks are thinning given the precipitous decline in "hard copy" newspaper readership. Chances are good, though, that anyone born between 1946 and the mid 1970s either had a route or recalls kids on bikes flinging papers onto driveways and front lawns.

In popular memory, delivering newspapers was an activity straight out of *Leave It to Beaver,* a rite of passage that gave children their first brush with wage earning and responsibility. Such memories are largely those of white suburbanites, but this chapter isn't about them; it's about "newsies," kids from diverse backgrounds who hawked papers on urban streets from the Colonial era on.

Picturing Newsies

Their stories are more complex, as most of them worked out of necessity. We hold other images of these youngsters. Perhaps you have seen either the Broadway musical *Newsies* or the 1992 Disney film of that name. The spirited song-and-dance numbers notwithstanding, you can't get around the fact that you're looking at child labor, even if things do (sort of) work out okay in the end. Another view is darker, that of late-19th-century newsboy child laborers captured by the camera of Jacob Riis (1849–1914), or the even grittier early-20th-century photographs of Lewis Hine (1874–1940).

None of our mental pictures is accurate 100 percent of the time, but for now let us agree that newsies performed an important task and are worthy of a statue to honor them. Here's where it gets weird. You might expect Western Massachusetts to salute newsies in one of its larger cities: Springfield, Chicopee, Pittsfield, Westfield, Holyoke … Nope. It's in Great Barrington, a town that never had a daily paper of its own.[1] Even odder, the bronze news carrier on the statue is holding a copy of the (old) *New York Daily News*, a paper few in Great Barrington would have read.

Even if you've been to Great Barrington dozens of times, you may have missed its newsboy statue. That's understandable, given that it sits in a small triangle of land carved from Maple and Silver streets half a mile from Route 7, where routes 23 and 41 intersect. It fronts a quiet neighborhood and isn't easy to access when traveling west. I drove by it several times before it caught my eye.

Though he's cast in bronze, we see what we imagine to be towheaded lad of about 12. He's five feet high and stands atop a 10-foot granite base, a newsie cap pushed back toward the nape of his neck, his right arm thrusting a paper toward an unseen customer, and a portfolio of additional papers tucked under his left arm. As befits the 1895 date on the statue, this newsboy is dressed in a jacket, open-collared shirt, buttoned shoes, knickers, and over-the-knee socks, the latter two accoutrements making up what the British call "plus fours."

Colonel Brown and the Newspaper Wars

The statue's presence in Great Barrington is the easiest part of the story to tell. The Berkshires have long been where wealthy New Yorkers built retreats, summer houses, and retirement homes. The statue informs us that one of them, Colonel William Lee Brown (1840–1906), gave the monument to Great Barrington. Brown was born in Vermont, grew up in Ohio, briefly taught in Mississippi, returned the Ohio when Mississippi seceded, and served with the 88th and 125th Ohio Volunteers during the Civil War. After the war, Brown drifted to the Montana Territory for a few years, before returning to Ohio and immersing himself in Democratic Party politics and publishing a Youngstown newspaper. He gained the rank of colonel in 1874 for his service as an aide-de-camp (assistant) to Ohio Governor William Allen. Colonel Brown moved to New York City in 1880 to join Benjamin Wood and co-publish the *New York Daily News*. He also found Tammany Hall politics irresistible and served in the New York State Senate from 1890 to 1893.

It was, however, the newspaper world on which Brown left his biggest mark. Brown and Wood ran the *Daily News* in a world very different from our own. In 1890, the daily circulation of American newspapers stood at 69 million—a figure that exceeded the total U.S. population of 62.9 million! Each year some 4.6 billion papers were sold. New York, with its 50 dailies, was easily the journalism capital of the nation. Brooklyn had five more,[2] and more than one-quarter of all U.S. newspaper circulation took place within the New York City metropolitan limits.

Brown's *Daily News* was neither the tabloid that bears that name today, nor its publication parent.[3] New York papers were overtly partisan and/or niche-oriented. The *News* reflected its Democratic Party loyalties and was also a mainstay among New York's Irish and Irish-American readers. Back then, the *Daily News* was decidedly a second-tier paper within the city; so was the *New York Times*! Joseph Pulitzer's *New York World* was king of the roost—soon to be challenged by the *New York Journal*, which William Randolph Hearst purchased in 1895. Other big papers included the *New York Herald, The Sun,* and the *Brooklyn Eagle.* That's a lot of competition, and the so-called "newspaper wars" of the 1890s had a big impact on both Brown and the newsboys he enshrined.

Newspapers were profitable, but one could easily lose a fortune as well. Fifty-five dailies were a lot, and reader loyalty was fickle. Newsstand sales and subscription services accounted for roughly half of a daily's revenue; the rest came from the newsies, who hit the streets as soon as the papers came off the press. They worked on commission, not a set wage. In sum, newspaper sales relied on an uneasy balance among publisher, circulation manager, and throngs of youthful carriers, most of whom were "badged" (licensed).[4]

The carriers paid for papers up front and kept whatever they earned, including tips. Once they left the agent's window, the newsies owned those papers and had to absorb the cost of any they didn't sell. By the late 19th century, a skilled hawker who sold 100 papers might pocket 33–50 cents for his day's efforts. Needless to say, newsies evolved a host of selling strategies to boost sales—everything from hyping and overhyping the news to concocting sob stories to entice reticent buyers. Their aggressiveness led some middle-class city dwellers to complain that newsies were little more than ink-stained street thugs. Colonel Brown did not agree. In 1895, he graced his summer home of Great Barrington with the statue that stands there today.

Newsies worked long and hard, but they were not without bargaining power. They sometimes formed unions and they knew, as did the circulation managers, that a newspaper's bottom line was dependent on their sales pitches. Brown understood this, but more powerful men learned the hard way.

The entrance of William Randolph Hearst into the New York City market raised alarm, especially when he dropped the price of the Journal from two cents to a penny. Pulitzer had done similar damage to competitors in the 1880s when he began selling the World for two cents, but this time he responded to sagging revenue with an attempt to shore up shareholder value by lowering the margin paid to his street sales force.

The events depicted in *Newsies* are mostly correct and many of the characters in the play/film are drawn from real life. In 1899, newsies organized and struck against both Pulitzer and Hearst, while many of their competitors, including Brown's *Daily News*, kept carrier rates stable. Pulitzer was the first to cave; in two weeks, his daily circulation was scarcely one third of its pre-strike levels.

Good will didn't help the *Daily News*. The paper hemorrhaged money and, in 1900, Benjamin Wood died. His widow—rumored to be both reclusive and vengeful—enacted a coup that removed Brown from management of the paper, and he retired to Great Barrington. Mrs. Wood sold the paper in 1901, which was sold again in 1904. On December 13, 1906, the *Daily News* ceased publication—on the very day Colonel Brown passed away.

The Face of Child Labor

What, though, of our competing views of youthful news carriers? For me, the flip side of Colonel Brown's statue is a 1912 photo by Lewis Hine of begrimed 8-year-old Dante Mercurio working his beat in Washington, D.C., as a well-heeled, plume-hatted matron strides forcefully and disapprovingly by. Young "Danny" earned just eight cents per day, but at least he had shoes. Many of the news hawkers Hine photographed lacked such a luxury. Hine's newsie portfolio included children as young as 6. A St. Louis lad identified as "Little Fattie" was less than 40 inches tall; others were missing limbs or were visibly ill.

By 1900, more than 16 percent of the American workforce—some two million laborers — consisted of children under the age of 16. Most of the child labor force was more like Dante Mercurio than Brown's well-scrubbed towhead. That is, they were of Italian, Russian, Jewish, Irish, and African American heritage — mostly children of poor families whose daily sustenance depended in part on their children's meager earnings. Quite a few were orphans and/or homeless. Individual newsies might have enjoyed their freedom, but kids on the street grew up fast. By 11, many smoked, gambled, fought, and were skilled hustlers.

New York state enacted child labor restrictions in 1886, but such laws were easily circumvented. Despite the efforts of Lewis Hine and the National Child Labor Committee, there was no effective nationwide child labor bill until the 1938 Fair Labor Standards Act (FLSA)—86 years after Massachusetts passed the nation's first child-labor bill in 1852.[5] To be sure, many famous Americans looked back fondly to their newsie days: Louis Armstrong, Irving Berlin, Frank Capra, Al Jolson, the Marx Brothers, and Earl Warren among them. Overall, though, there were more Dante Mercurios among them than future entertainers or Supreme Court justices. The era of the newsies declined less because of moral outrage over child labor than from shifts in the newspaper business and the impact of the Great Depression.

By the 1920s, more newspapers began publishing afternoon editions that came out around 4 pm. This served the dual purpose of having up-to-the-moment news coverage and of making it easier to manage weekly and monthly subscription buyers. During the Depression, adults assumed many of the duties once entrusted to children, and the FSLA greatly thinned the child-labor pool.

Newsies never completely went away—some took up afternoon routes, but only *after* the school day ended. In our own time, we still see the occasional youthful news carrier, but their time is fading. Many newspapers shy away from potential liability issues involved in employing children, not to mention perceptions that many town and city streets are unsafe (traffic, crime) or that children are often unreliable employees. Fewer Americans read physical newspapers these days, and those who do are more likely to be subscribers of morning editions—the industry has come full circle—and expect their papers to arrive shortly after 6 am.

You should visit the statue in Great Barrington. Appreciate the fine sculpture by David Richards, the stone masonry of Mathias Lux, and the casting of Maurice J. Power. Maybe you'll even be inspired to read local historian Gary Leveille's book on it. Admire, but not through rose-colored glasses. The breaking news in front of you is about circulation wars, labor, and perhaps Colonel Brown's backhanded dig at his harder-hearted rivals. The first time I saw it was on a bitter rainy day, a reminder we should not forget that we are gazing into the face of child labor.

1 *The Berkshire Eagle* in Pittsfield covers Great Barrington news on a daily basis. Pittsfield is 20 miles north. A weekly Great Barrington paper, the *Berkshire Courier*, has operated (under several names) since about 1842. (Sources disagree over the *Courier*'s founding date.) The town also briefly had another weekly, *The Berkshire News* (1889–95) and, since 1989 still another weekly, the *Berkshire Record*.

2 Even though the Brooklyn Bridge opened in 1883, Brooklyn remained a separate city until 1898, when it became a New York City borough.

3 Today's *New York Daily News* began publication in 1919, 13 years after Brown and Wood's publication ceased.

4 Historian David Nasaw estimates that about 15 percent of all carriers were unlicensed and showed up hoping a regular was absent, or that they could persuade an agent to allow them to sell papers without a badge.

5 In 1916, Congress passed the Keating-Owen Act to curtail child labor. It was struck down as unconstitutional. A 1924 attempt to pass an amendment to the U.S. Constitution forbidding child labor failed when just five states agreed to ratify it. Existing state laws were seldom effectively enforced.

7
Small Town, Fancy Library: Marshall Field's Gift to Conway

An old adage holds, "You can take the boy out of the country, but you can't take the country out of the boy." That's quite an exaggeration. Lots of young people from rural birthplaces made their mark in the bigger world and even more left the farm and never looked back.

Still, quite a few famous people recall their rural childhood with fondness tinged with nostalgia. Sometimes their travels send them briefly homeward for visits. If the hometown is lucky, the prodigals-made-good leave behind testaments of gratitude. Conway's library is a fine example of that.

There's something about libraries that appeals to the civic virtues of wealthy philanthropists, especially those whose money is sometimes acquired by less-than-charitable means. Andrew Carnegie's

fortune, for instance, endowed more than 2,500 libraries between the years 1883 and 1929, though he never set foot in most of them.

Conway's library, though, was given by Marshall Field (1834–1906), whose philanthropy was generally centered in Chicago and whose best-known public building is the Windy City natural history museum that bears his name. But Field himself picked the site for Conway's Field Memorial Library in 1899, and the building was dedicated in 1901, a little over four years before Field died in January 1906.

Marshall Field Leaves Conway

Though his glory came in Chicago, Field's story began in Conway. In many ways, though, the library reflects the big city, not the town where Field came into the world on August 18, 1834. The first thing that strikes the eye is that the solid limestone building with marble columns and green-patina copper dome is out of place amidst the wooden frame and occasional red-brick structures that surround it. The visual effect is like seeing a shrunken and modest prototype of the (original) U.S. Capitol plopped down in a Western Massachusetts farming community, which is exactly what Conway was in 1901. Today Conway has fewer than 2,000 widely dispersed souls; it had just 1,450 residents when the library opened, having lost about 17 percent of its population between 1890 and 1900.

Hilltown farming had been in decline since his childhood, which prompted 17-year-old Field to seek better oportunities in Pittsfield. By the time he was 18, he was living with his brother in Chicago and working in a large dry goods concern. In 1862, he was a partner in that firm. His first big break came in 1865, the last year of the Civil War, in which he became a senior partner in Potter Palmer and Company. Within two years, Field bought out Palmer and, with Levi Leiter, created Field, Leiter and Company.

In 1881, Field bought out Leiter. This was a decade after the event that made Field a wealthy man: the 1871 Great Chicago Fire, which burned more than three square miles of the city, much of it in the commercial district. The fire left Chicago a physical blank canvas upon which some of the greatest architects, investors, risk-takers, visionaries, scoundrels, and conmen left their mark. Field fell into the risk-taker category, having borrowed more than $1.7 million to rebuild his dry goods business. (That sum would be the equivalent to more than $35.3 million in 2017 dollars.)

Field quickly repaid his loan, but timing was his greatest ally. As Chicago recovered from the fire, its population skyrocketed. It had just under 100,000 people when Field arrived, grew to nearly 300,000 at the time of the fire, and contained over a half million in the decade it was rebuilt. By 1890, Chicago had over a million people, a nearly 110 percent increase in just 10 years, and had swelled to nearly 1.7 million when Field's Conway library opened in 1901.

Field's Chicago was a city of railroads, stockyards, shipping, manufacturing, and retail. Marshall Field was the undisputed king of the last of these. Growing cities meant increased demand for soft goods, home furnishings, and consumer goods. What Macy's was to New York, Wanamaker's to Philadelphia, or Jordan Marsh to Boston, Field's was to Chicago. His Romanesque Franklin Street store—designed by famed architect Henry Hobson Richardson—was noted for its quality, good prices, stunning visual impact, and devotion to customers. Field is often credited with the phrase "the customer is always right." That may be apocryphal, but Field stood out in an age in which *caveat emptor* ("let the buyer beware") was the prevailing ethos.

Chicago was also a city of immigrants, labor strife, pollution, unpleasant odors, and social problems, but Field was insulated from these. In 1890, a time in which the average female clerk at his downtown department store earned roughly $400 per year (about $11,000 today), Field reportedly made $600 per *minute* in profits and was well on his way to the estimated $150 million fortune he amassed before his death on January 16, 1906. His social circle included other Eastern-born evangelicals and entrepreneurs born in the 1830s, including former partner Potter Palmer, meatpacker Philip Armour, financier Lyman Gage, and lumber baron Turlington Harvey. His best friend was sleeping-car magnate George Pullman, and Field also enjoyed cordial relations with evangelist Dwight L. Moody, who also hailed from Western Massachusetts.

A Particular Kind of Christian

Field was a Presbyterian, but during the post-Civil-War era theological distinctions among wealthy liberal Protestants such as Episcopalians, Presbyterians, Methodists, Universalists, and Congregationalists—became less important than a shared worldview. To muddy matters further, many liberal Protestants were politically conservative, Marshall Field among them.

Such Christians were "liberal" in that they tended to see faith, ethics, and experience as personal matters; treated much of the Bible as metaphorical rather than literal; and sought to reconcile faith with science, skepticism, acquisition of wealth, and Biblical criticism.[1] Emphasis on individualism appealed to wealthier liberal Christians, some of whom hoped to construct an earthly kingdom of God in the here and now.

Field's faith factored into his philanthropy. In 1890, he and John D. Rockefeller endowed the University of Chicago, and Field was among the wealthy Chicagoans who invested in the 1893 Columbian Exposition (world's fair), interpreted by many historians as an attempt to display the elevated values of Chicago's Protestant elites. Wealthy Chicagoans viewed the fair's centerpiece, the gleaming White City—a lagoon-side assemblage of monumental buildings and awe-inspiring statuary—as a silent form of evangelical proselytizing.[2] It was no accident that Marshall Field endowed the Museum of Natural History when the fair was still open, or that its first home was the White City's Palace of Fine Arts. (Field's museum moved to its current location in 1921.)

There was also a darker side to some liberal Christians. The non-doctrinal, moralistic, and individualist aspects of 19th-century evangelical Protestantism split into two opposing social visions: the reforming zeal of the Social Gospel movement and the defense-of-the-status-quo response of Social Darwinists. Whereas the first sought to ameliorate poverty and social problems, the second justified them as both natural and divinely mandated.

Social Darwinism was (and is) a highly selective amalgam of Charles Darwin's natural-selection theories and Old-Testament-style judgment. Darwin was a scientist whose theories are associated with biological evolution; Social Darwinism is a social misapplication of his writings—especially the idea of survival of the fittest—as filtered through the writings of thinkers such as Herbert Spencer, William Graham Sumner, and Darwin's eugenicist half-cousin Francis Galton.

When paired with 19th-century evangelical Protestantism, Social Darwinists defended their personal fortunes as stamped with God's approval—rewards for their "naturally" superior intellectual and

moral traits. They also believed there was no such thing as a social problem; poverty, business failure, human misery, and misfortune confirmed the unworthiness, sinfulness, and inferiority of the sufferers. Low wages and squalid living conditions, for example, could be viewed as God's wrath upon the undeserving.

Although he was not among the firebrands, Field was a Social Darwinist. Field's employees were generally paid below retail-industry standards. He despised labor unions and not only sided with George Pullman when his workers struck in 1894, but also encouraged the Illinois National Guard to break the strike with such fervor that the troops were dubbed "Marshall Field's Boys." Field's philanthropy was mainly channeled toward august institutions, not social reform.

Retail Glamour Passed and Recalled

Until 2005, most people associated Marshall Field with the department stores that bore his name. Field's block long, 12-story store at State Street and Madison was not only a Chicago landmark, it was also the world's largest department store when it opened in 1892. Field's brand was associated with both grace and affordable elegance. The State Street flagship sported Tiffany glass mosaics, marble columns, fanciful clocks, a stylish lobby, the first escalator in a retail store, clerks trained in etiquette, and fanciful seasonal displays. By the 1980s, though, Field's was one of the first giant department stores to feel the pinch of globalism and discount retailing. It was first sold in 1982 and underwent several other transfers, but retained the name Field's until 2006, when all Field's stores were renamed Macy's by Federated Department Stores, Incorporated, the retail holding company[3] that purchased Field's latest parent the previous year.

You can still see the mosaics in Chicago, but you can also get an idea of Field's monumental vision by walking into the lobby of his library in Conway. If the dome seems slightly disproportionate from the outside, check out its 20-foot diameter from the inside as it soars 42 feet above the sill and displays its mosaics. Gawk at the Ionic columns, the Brescia violet Italian marble floor, and other architectural wonders. When it was dedicated on July 13, 1901, Field treated an estimated 1,200 people—including most of the town's total population—to a luncheon. He died in 1906, but you can still find his portrait presiding in the library's south reading room. His parents are depicted in the north reading room. Both are vestiges of the country that remained in the boy whose fortune was made in the Windy City.

1 Biblical criticism emerged during the 17th-century Enlightenment. It involves close examination of the Bible, including the origins, authorship, intent, sources, and deeper meaning of Biblical texts. Many who engage in it are people of faith, but they generally view the Bible as symbolic and metaphorical rather than literal. Twentieth-century fundamentalism—whose roots lay in late 19th-century *conservative* Presbyterianism—was partly a reaction to Biblical criticism.

2 Evangelicalism would not be widely identified with fundamentalism for several more decades.

3 A holding company does not engage in direct manufacturing or delivery of services. It is an investment firm that buys controlling interest in the stock of other companies. Federated Department Stores merged retailers than were once independent. The name Macy's is now used for numerous former retail giants, including Dayton's, Field's, Filene's, Hudson's, Strawbridge and Clothier, and Wanamaker's. In 2007, Federated officially changed its name to Macy's Incorporated.

8
Three Men Lost on Florence Road

People often assume that professional historians know about everything that happened in the past. I wish that were true. But I can say something about a question I get asked a lot: "What's up with that airplane statue on Florence Road?" Anyone can read the specifics. On May 13, 1948, a C-54 airplane crashed on the Adams farm, which is located near where the city of Northampton, the village of Florence, and the city of Easthampton merge. Three men died: First Lieutenant Wilford Lavinder, Captain Paul Lonquich, and Staff Sergeant Jack Zaresky. The plane type and the ranks tell us this had something to do with the military. What folks really want to know is: Why a sculpture? None of the men was an Adams or a relation, nor were they locals.[1] Why these three, when more than 419,000 Americans died during the Second World War? The monument's dedication date—June 19, 1999—really confuses newcomers. Why commemorate these men 51 years after they crashed?

Risky Business

Let's start with he fact that the Bay State and the military have a long history. Massachusetts is 10th in the nation as a recipient of Department of Defense spending, more than $12 billion per year. Western Massachusetts is home to two bases: Barnes Air National Guard Base in Westfield, and Westover Air Force Reserve Base in Chicopee. This complicates our understanding of the C-54 Skymaster memorial. Between them, the bases launch an average of 125 flights per day and in tense times, it's a lot more than that.

During World War II, Westover wasn't a reserve center; it was the largest Air Force base in the Northeast. Another reality of life in Western Massachusetts is that air tragedies occur; not many, but enough to remind that flying military planes is risky. There's a monument on Mount Tom in Holyoke that marks the region's worst air disaster. On July 9, 1946, an Air Force B-17G-105 "Flying Fortress" ferrying recently demobilized World War II personnel slammed into the hillside and killed all 25 aboard. So again, why memorialize Lavinder, Lonquich, and Zaresky?

Let's start with the personnel involved in the 1948 crash, as one of the site's virtues is that it honors four men whose names would otherwise be a footnote to history. Yes, I said *four*. That's how many were *supposed* to be aboard. Call it coincidence, luck, or divine intervention, but tragic tales are often accompanied by stories of those spared by fate. On May 13, 1948, First Lieutenant George A. Edge survived because he reported for duty too early.

The doomed C-54 arrived at Westover from Goose Bay, Newfoundland, slightly behind schedule, as the last part of its journey was marked by bad weather. Pilot Dan Russell handed over the craft to command at Westover. Russell reported no problems with the plane, but protocol called for an inspection before the plane could return to service. Because weather delayed the flight from Goose Bay, when Lt. Edge reported for duty, the inspection was still in progress. Since the day was also his 24th birthday, Edge retired to the Officers' Club for an early celebration and left word to contact him when the plane was ready to go.

Someone forgot to do so, and the C-54 took off at 11:10 am. Edge alerted Captain Lonquich by radio of the breakdown in communications and was told the plane would return to base and pick him up. That never happened; at 12:22 pm, the C-54 went down at an 80-degree angle and burst into flames so intense that they damaged several buildings on the Adams farm. The three crewmen died instantly; the crash force was such that plane and body parts were spread across five acres and the craft's engine remains embedded in the ground. Edge called his mother to tell her he was safe, as the plane's manifest listed him as a passenger, hence a presumed casualty.

Edge was born in Roosevelt, Oklahoma, on May 13, 1924, one of eight children born to Claude and Joanna Edge, the latter a substitute teacher at the one-room schoolhouse George attended as a child. He was an excellent wrestler who captained his high school team and enrolled in junior college on a sports scholarship.

Edge was studying aeronautical engineering when the war broke out; he enlisted, and graduated from an Army Air Corps program in January 1944. He was stationed in the Philippines, Okinawa, and Japan after the war, before transferring to the Military Air Transport Service in 1948, a posting that took him to Westover. In 1950, Edge married Jean Graham of Chicopee and they had a son, George Jr. Later that year, he left the military and took a job with the Flying Tiger Line, a cargo service established in 1945 that merged with Federal Express in 1989. The Edges lived in several countries, but had settled in Mountain View, California, when George collapsed after a flight to Narito, Japan. Though he died at just 55 on March 21, 1979, a quirk of fate meant he outlived his comrades.

Captain Paul Lonquich of Yonkers, New York, who commanded the doomed C-54, was 40 when he died on Florence Road. Records indicate he had been born in Germany. Both he and his wife Isle (1907–1984) are interred in the Long Island National Cemetery in Farmingdale, New York—just 40 miles from Yonkers, where Mrs. Lonquich remained until her death on October 27, 1984.

First Lt. Wilfred W. Lavinder of Portsmouth, Ohio, co-piloted the plane, and was probably at the controls when it went down. He was 23 when he perished, and his wife Laura—who was born in Rome—was at home in Ohio preparing to give birth to the couple's daughter,

Grace. Laura met Lavinder when he was stationed in Milan. She recalled that when her husband was commissioned as an officer, "the future looked so bright." Laura had been in the United States only a few months before the accident. She eventually remarried and had two more children, but still vividly remembered her shock when told Wilfred was gone: "I was a vegetable. I thought I was going crazy." The memorial's 1999 dedication was also emotional for Grace, whose closest contact with her father was seeing his name etched in the monument's burnished steel base.

Staff Sgt. Jack Zaresky of Jackson Heights, New York, was 26 at the time of the crash. He too left behind a widow, Jean, who remarried and moved to Florida. She and her son Jon attended the 1999 ceremony. Although he bears his stepfather's surname of Marshall, Jack Zaresky is Jon's biological father.

No one knows for certain what happened on that fateful day in May 1948. All three men had seen combat during the war and had flight experience. The day of the accident found Lonquich supervising Lavinder on a base check and line training exercise, essentially routine checks of his proficiency.[2] All four men were scheduled to leave Westover for Germany the next morning, and this gets us to the significance of the Florence Road memorial. Lavinder, Lonquich, Zaresky, and Edge were slated to take part in the Berlin Airlift. Only Edge lived to do so.

The First Casualties of the Berlin Airlift?

If you know about the Berlin Airlift, you've either had a good history teacher or you're probably at least 50 years old. It was a key moment in the early Cold War and if the Cold War seems like yesterday to you, you've definitely left your school days behind. The Cold War ended in 1991, which means that no current high school or traditional undergraduate student ever experienced it. The Florence Skymaster memorial began life as a way to honor military veterans, but has evolved into an artifact of a bygone age from which lessons can be drawn.

In brief, the Cold War references the ideological competition between Western democracy and Soviet-style communism that gripped the world from 1945 through the collapse of the Soviet Union (USSR) in 1992. Although the United States and the USSR were allies in the war against fascism, theirs was a shotgun wedding that did not survive the end of that conflict. Wars generally leave destruction in their wake and both sides sought to rebuild war-torn Europe in their own image, the U.S. in Western Europe and the Soviets in Eastern and Central Europe. Germany was divided after the war, with England, France, and the United States supporting the new nation of West Germany and the USSR propping up East Germany.

The two blocs also agreed to split the city of Berlin, which was a logistical problem for the West as it lay 100 miles inside communist East Germany. The Soviets agreed to allow 10 trains a day into Berlin, a limited number of trucks, and flights through three 20-mile-wide air corridors. The U.S. announcement of the multi-billion dollar European Recovery Plan—known to history as the Marshall Plan, since General George C. Marshall administered it—alarmed Soviet leader Josef Stalin, who saw it as an attempt to stifle insurgent Western European communist groups. It was, actually, and a successful one at that.

The Marshall Plan touched off a tit-for-tat round of small aggressions; for example, the Soviets stopped food supplies from East Germany to West Berlin, and the U.S. banned industrial supplies to East Germany. Harassment, a crash between a Soviet and British plane, and a US-led effort to introduce a new currency (Deutsche marks) pegged to the dollar led Stalin to up the ante. On June 21, 1948, the Soviets stopped trains bound for Berlin, at a time when the Western sectors had only about a month's worth of food in reserve.

Just three days later the Berlin Airlift began, with generals Lucius Clay and Curtis LeMay[3] playing key roles in coordinating daily flights of coal, clothing, and food into West Berlin. Stalin knew that downing the planes would lead to a broader conflict—and possible American atomic retaliation.[4] Instead, he bargained the airlift would be logistically unfeasible and too expensive, and that the U.S. would abandon West Berlin. Stalin could not have been more wrong. American, British, Canadian, Australian, and New Zealander flyers delivered nearly nine tons of supplies each day. By the time the airlift ended nearly 11 months later, they had made some 200,000 flights in total.

The Douglas C-54 Skymaster was one of the airlift's more successful aerial workhorses. It weighed 39,000 pounds and could carry nearly its own weight (up to 34,000 pounds) in cargo. When Stalin relented on May 12, 1949, General Clay was heralded as a hero and enjoyed a New York City ticker-tape parade. Had Lonquich, Lavinder, and Zaresky lived, they would have joined Lt. Edge in celebrating one of history's most stunning emergency resupply efforts. It bears repeating, though, that military flights can be dangerous; 31 U.S. servicemen died in accidents during the Berlin Airlift, and one could easily count the Northampton four as victims as well.

The Costs of Conflict

The Skymaster memorial is also a reminder of the perilous games of brinksmanship that took place during the Cold War. It was a tense time in world history that wasn't always just a rhetorical cat-and-mouse game. Low-intensity conflicts in Greece, Korea, Egypt, Vietnam, the Congo, Angola, Afghanistan, and numerous other places led to thousands of combat deaths. Moreover, by 1949 both the U.S. and the U.S.S.R. were atomic powers and, after 1952, potential nuclear combatants.[5] Many ordinary citizens feared mass annihilation.

Events such as the Suez Crisis (1956), the building of the Berlin Wall (1961), and the Cuban Missile Crisis (1962) kept global citizens on tenterhooks for decades after World War Two ended. The 1999 statue dedication on Florence Road also commemorates that, luckily, the West won the Cold War, which officially ended in 1991 when the Soviet Union dissolved.

In sum, the Skymaster memorial commemorates four specific individuals, valorizes those who took part in the remarkable Berlin Airlift, and pays homage to all the men and women who have served in the military. If it looks a tad austere and somber, it's because it also reminds us of the toll armed conflict exacts. It is often said that truth is the first casualty of war[6] but that's wrong; it is almost always youth.

1 There are, however, two small plaques, one honoring U.S. Navy Lt. Sam Adams (1912–42), who was killed during World War II. He was awarded a Navy Cross and two Gold Stars. The other plaque pays homage to another Samuel Adams, who served during the Vietnam War.

2 Base checks evaluate a pilot's ability to handle the aircraft in an emergency. Line training usually involves an experienced pilot sitting in an adjacent "jump seat" to mentor a less experienced one. If a problem arises during flight, the jump pilot can take command of the craft. The probability is that Lavinder encountered difficulty and that Captain Lonqvich was unable to stabilize the plane.

3 Curtis LeMay later resurfaced in unfortunate political circumstances. He was the vice presidential candidate during the quixotic and segregationist-based 1968 presidential campaign of Alabama Governor George Wallace. LeMay was said to have advocated bombing North Vietnam "back to the Stone Age." He later claimed he was slightly misquoted and said only that the U.S. had the capacity for doing so, but his remarks appeared intemperate.

4 The Soviet Union was working on its atomic bomb, but it wasn't tested until August of 1949. This was a worrisome event in Cold War history as it meant conflict could potentially bring about atomic warfare in which millions would perish. A key construct of Cold War logic was that mutually assured destruction would deter both sides from employing such weapons—risky thinking that added to global tension and the psychological terrors experienced by untold numbers.

5 The atomic bombs used against Japan in 1945 were fission bombs that involved splitting an atom's nucleus. Though highly destructive, the hydrogen bomb that appeared in 1952 uses a fusion process to produce a weapon that is roughly 500 times more powerful. For that reason, nuclear weapons are regarded as weapons of mass destruction with the potential for annihilating most, if not all, human life on the planet. Small wonder that children doing duck-and-cover drills during peak tension moments of the Cold War often suffered from anxiety and nightmares.

6 No one knows for certain who first said this, though Senator Hiram Johnson (1918) often gets credit.

9

Mount Greylock: A Whale of a Mountain?

Some things are big and impressive all on their own, like Mount Greylock. At approximately 3,491 feet, it is the highest peak in Massachusetts.[1] Was it also the inspiration for Moby Dick, the great white whale? As in all things related to novelist Herman Melville, the answer is complicated. Maybe we should start by acknowledging that reading *Moby Dick* generally has one of two effects on those forced to read it—and "forced" is the right verb—in high school. For some, the book sparked an epiphany that instilled a lifelong love of literature; others occasionally awake from nightmares in which they were hurled back in time to their high school English class on Melville. Depending upon which camp you're in, Mount Greylock is to be thanked or cursed.

Posthumous Fame

Melville is a famous individual today, and *Moby Dick* is considered by many literary critics to be a candidate for the elusive Great American Novel. Neither was the case when *Moby Dick* was published in 1851. Melville (1819–1891) is the reverse of people you'll encounter in Section III, in that he is much more famous now than he was in his own lifetime. Aside from a fruitful period between 1845 and 1850, when Melville produced five novels —*Typee, Omoo, Mardi, Redburn,* and *White-Jacket*—so little of what he wrote resonated with the general public that most folks considered him a second-rate writer and he thought himself a failure.

And so he was, if measured in financial terms. His father had fallen into bankruptcy and Herman was just one step ahead of insolvency until near the end of his life. He was known for fits of melancholy and

Herman Melville's view from his window

depression, his marriage was rocky, and even his closest friends and associates found him egocentric, unstable, and treacherous. Melville once wrote a withering critique of his friend Nathaniel Hawthorne because he needed the money—the ultimate hack job—complicated by the fact that he was also exceedingly jealous of Hawthorne. Biographer Edwin H. Miller called Melville a "social isolate" for much of his life.

Fame is always externally conferred and, today, Melville is considered one of the literary giants of the 19th century. This is largely on the strength of *Moby Dick* and the posthumously published *Billy Budd*, as few of the novels favored by his contemporaries are read today.

Our question is one of inspiration. Was the curved silhouette of Mt. Greylock a model for Moby Dick? That is a story often told by teachers, park rangers on the Mt. Greylock Reservation, and docents at Arrowhead Farm. Arrowhead—in Pittsfield near the Lenox line—is where Melville wrote the bulk of the novel for which he is best remembered.

Moby Dick the Mountain?

It sometimes surprises people that Melville, a man so associated with the sea, wrote *Moby Dick* in the land-locked Berkshires. Prior to 1850, Melville had lived close to the Eastern seaboard. Visits to his uncle Thomas' home in Pittsfield enamored Melville of the beauty of the Berkshires, but it was the city's moment as a bookish epicenter that convinced him to relocate. By 1850, the area's literary circle included Hawthorne, Fanny Kemble, James Russell Lowell, Catharine Maria Sedgwick, and Oliver Wendell Holmes, Sr. That year, the 31-year-old Melville moved to Pittsfield with his wife, Elizabeth née Shaw (1822–1906), to whom he had been married for just over two years, and their infant son Malcolm. With a $3,000 loan secured from his father-in-law, Lemuel Shaw, chief justice of the Massachusetts Supreme Judicial Court, Melville purchased a farm on Pittsfield's outskirts from Dr. John Brewster. He dubbed it "Arrowhead", shown below, when he unearthed Native-American artifacts while plowing. This would be Melville's off-and-on home for the next 13 years, though they were seldom happy or profitable.

They were, however, productive ones. Melville worked feverishly on *Moby Dick*, starting early in the morning and often neglecting to eat until four or five o'clock in the afternoon. His wife "Lizzie," pregnant for a second time, disliked Pittsfield, Arrowhead, and winter in the Berkshires, but dared not disrupt her husband or even enter his study unless invited to do so. Melville's writing desk faced north and got only morning light, but it looked across a field toward Mount Greylock, which loomed in the distance.

Did Melville gaze upon its snow-covered slopes during the winter of 1850–51 and imagine a white whale? Nathaniel Hawthorne thought so, and claimed that Melville first discussed *Moby Dick* with him and Oliver Wendell Holmes, Sr. while waiting out a storm in a Mt. Greylock cave, their spirits buoyed by a bottle of champagne. Later Hawthorne wrote of Arrowhead, "On the other side of Pittsfield sits Herman Melville, shaping out the gigantic conception of his 'white whale,' while the gigantic shape of Greylock looms upon him from his study window." Subsequent biographers followed Hawthorne's lead. Typical are the comments of the authors of *Critical Companion to Herman Melville*. Of Mount Greylock, they write, "…the view of the white, rolling shape of the mountain as seen in winter from Melville's writing desk at Arrowhead doubtless contributed to his masterwork…."

The mercurial Melville's own comments are more enigmatic. In *Moby Dick,* he described the white whale as "one grand hooded phenomenon, like a snow hill in the air." He also described his study as having "a sort of sea-feeling," from which he looked out, "as I might out of a port-hole of a ship in the Atlantic. My room seems a ship's cabin; and at nights when I wake up and hear the wind shrieking, I almost fancy there is too much sail on the house and I had better go up on the roof and rig the chimney." Anyone standing on the north side of Arrowhead on a clear winter's day and gazing toward Adams, where Greylock sits roughly 15 miles distant, is certainly impressed by the mountain's bulk and its distinctive double-humped profile. But is it mere coincidence that the back of a sperm whale also has a large hump sided by smaller ridges? Melville enjoyed outings to Greylock and dedicated his next novel, *Pierre* (1852) to "Greylock's most excellent majesty." Still, other local writers, especially Holmes, commented more on Greylock than Melville.

It makes a great story to equate Greylock with the white whale, but author A. Robert Lee was doubtless correct when he suggested that *Moby Dick* was "an imperial act of imagining." Literary scholars have mined the novel for its various inspirations–The Bible, Shakespeare, Milton, Cervantes, Emerson, and Dickens–but insofar as the white whale is concerned, several more direct sources stand out. First, history records several terrible incidents in which sperm whales stove in and sank whaling boats. Melville was quite familiar with the 1820 sinking of the *Essex* and of the account *Narrative of the Most Extraordinary and Distressing Shipwreck of the Whale-Ship Essex*, written by Owen Chase, one of only eight survivors. There were other accounts of whales sinking ships, including that of the *Ann Alexander*, which went down in the South Pacific as Melville was writing *Moby Dick*.

More pointedly, an 1839 Jeremiah N. Reynolds article for *The Knickerbocker* magazine related the tale of "Mocha Dick," an albino sperm whale slain in 1838 off the coast of central Chile near the island of Mocha. Reynolds described Mocha Dick as a monster and claimed his back was festooned with myriad harpoons from past battles. The Mocha/Moby parallels seem too obvious to be accidental. Moreover, white whales, though rare, were hardly a Melville invention; albinism occurs in most species. Nor were stories of hardship and tragedy at sea rare, as Melville discovered during his 18 months aboard the *Acushnet* in 1841–42. Melville was one of 15 members of the 26-man crew to cut short a four-year stint at sea, after finding his experiences more rigorous and dangerous than romantic.

It is important to remember that, by the 1830s, the United States was the number one whaling nation in the world. Whale oil was used to light homes and, more importantly, provided lubricants for the nascent Industrial Revolution. Sperm whales were especially prized for the rich spermaceti deposits in their skull cavities. They tended to be found, however, in deep waters far from the coastline, and the open-boat harpooning methods of the day made hunting whales especially perilous. One estimate claims that between 14,000 and 20,000 whalers lost their lives between the years 1750 to 1920.

Fanciful sections of Melville's tale notwithstanding, much of *Moby Dick* was more rehashed journalism than imagination. This is especially true of the long descriptions of whale processing that many modern readers skim or ignore altogether.

The Unimpressed Reading Public

We may never know how much Herman Melville modeled his whale after Mount Greylock. Available evidence is suggestive, but not definitive. What we do know is that Melville had more success enjoying nature than with making money. Today *Moby Dick* is regarded as a masterpiece, but as Gavin Jones observes, it was such a flop at the time that Melville's "reputation was in free fall." So was his health. He collapsed during an 1858 speaking tour and, four years later, suffered a broken shoulder and rib injuries when thrown from a wagon.

In 1863, Melville sold Arrowhead to his brother Allan for a price that barely covered his debts and moved into Allan's former home in New York City. For the next several decades, Herman tried his hand at lecturing, poetry, and work as a customs inspector. By most accounts, he was a morose man, perhaps suffering from clinical depression. His eldest son, Malcolm, committed suicide in 1867; newer studies claim that Melville drank heavily and may have been physically abusive to his wife.

Some sources claim that Herman Melville was a forgotten writer by the time of his death in 1891. That's an exaggeration, but he was by no means viewed as a major literary figure until decades later. In

Melville's lifetime, *Moby Dick* sold just 3,215 copies in the U.S. market—numbers that would have yielded lifetime royalties of under $1,000, or roughly $27,688 in 2017 dollars. To put that in perspective, in 1851, journalist Horace Greeley estimated that it took around $539 per year for a family of five to survive in penury, let alone try to sustain a property such as Arrowhead. *Moby Dick* sold another 500 copies in Britain, but insofar as sales were concerned, the novel was a bust. Seven years later, Melville stopped writing novels altogether, except for the unfinished *Billy Budd*, which didn't see the light of day until 1924.

As for Mt. Greylock, its connection to Moby Dick may be wishful thinking based on Melville's resurrected reputation in the 20th century. Still, the book has thrilled so many readers since Melville's death that there's no harm in standing in Greylock's shadow and letting your imagination run. True or not, Greylock is a whale of a mountain.

1 There is disagreement over Greylock's exact elevation. See next chapter.

10
I Can See for Miles and Miles: 25 Unique, Easy-to-View Places in Western Massachusetts

Baseball legend Yogi Berra is credited with remarking, "You can see a lot just by looking." Maybe he did, or maybe it's a case of—as only Yogi could have put it—"I never said half of the things I said." No matter who uttered it, there's whimsical wisdom in those words. The routines of everyday life often induce tunnel vision. Details whiz by us on the periphery while our eyes are focused straight ahead. Sometimes we have to get up high to appreciate the magnificence of Western Massachusetts.

There are lots of places to do that. The Appalachian Trail runs through the region, along with hundreds of other mountain and hill trails, but let's concentrate on places that don't require sturdy hiking boots, hours of trudging, and youthful calves to appreciate.

Since I'm setting the rules, I'll just give a nod to those so well known they're in all the guidebooks, such as Summit House at Skinner State Park in Hadley where, on a really clear day, you can gaze downward at UMass, Northampton, Hadley, Holyoke, Springfield, and skyscrapers in downtown Hartford, Connecticut. Or Mount Sugarloaf State Reservation in South Deerfield, where you can see how the Connecticut River carved the valley below and look down upon Sunderland, which looks like a toy village from your lofty vantage point.

There are also dozens of fire towers plopped across the region—including ones in Cheshire, Goshen, Ludlow, Savoy, and Warwick—but I'm skipping them as well as some are off-limits to climbers and because they're basically just Erector sets on steroids. Let's talk places that are unique.

A small disclaimer: Don't be surprised if some of the elevations I cite don't quite match with those quoted on websites or printed on topographical maps. Maybe it's New England contrarianism, or perhaps it's a matter of who did the surveying and when, but I found lots of discrepancies about the height of various peaks and overlooks.

Poet's Seat

Greenfield has a tower on Longview Summit that advertises a three-state view. It's been closed for years now, but the town has another overlook with a better pedigree: Poet's Seat Tower (Mountain Road near Maple Street). It sits atop a rock face and looks like a watchtower seeking the rest of its castle. Three sets of stairs take you to an arched-window terrace—a nice framing device for photos—and a final set of spiraling metal stairs goes to the very top. In all honesty, the backstory of Poet's Seat is more romantic than the view. The sandstone edifice we see today was built in 1912 to replace a wooden tower that went up in either 1873 or 1879, depending on whether you believe the on-site plaque or printed records. Never mind. Poet's Seat was named for a reclusive local poet, Frederick Goddard Tuckerman (1821–73).

You won't find his work in most anthologies, and scholars generally don't think much of his verse, but he had oddball quirks that add charm. He was Boston born, but in his 20s he chucked Harvard, his law training, and the city itself to move to Greenfield. There his major pastime was indulging his love of nature by gardening and collecting plant specimens. He was a contemporary of Emily Dickinson and the two families knew each other, but there's little to suggest that Frederick and Emily ever met. Apparently Tuckerman was something of a recluse in his own right. He is said to have named the ridge Poet's Seat because he liked to go there to be alone and write. Subsequent dreamers have followed his example.

Scott Tower

Scott Tower in Holyoke (18 Scott Tower Road) has better views, if you're up for a grittier experience and a sadder tale. It is named for Colonel Walter Scott (1861–1935), a Montreal-born son of Scottish parents who made his mark in the wholesale trade, in Scottish fraternal organizations, and through philanthropy. His title of colonel was honorary. Because Scott was a big supporter of police in the U.S. and abroad, the Republic of Ireland awarded him a Medal of Valor. He, in turn, endowed the Walter Scott Medal for Bravery, which is still given to police and firefighters. Although he spent most of his life in Boston and New York, his daughter Edna Scott Magna lived in Holyoke. Scott's philanthropy was broad and deep, and included serving as a trustee of Northampton's Clarke School for the Deaf and endowing scholarships at Smith College and American International College.

Scott Tower was built in 1942 as the centerpiece of Holyoke's Anniversary Hill Park, a late Works Projects Administration effort. Anniversary Hill Park—whose name was quickly changed to Scott Field, since it didn't actually commemorate the anniversary of anything in Holyoke—was briefly a picnickers' paradise appointed with tables, fire pits, sweeping paths, a brook, and a pine grove. Boosters drew comparisons to New York's Central Park.

Such analogies were a bit grandiose, but Scott Field was a pleasant place for a few decades. The construction of Interstate 91 in the 1960s isolated the park, though, and both attendance and upkeep declined. Despite rehab efforts in the 1970s and ongoing efforts to restore the site, trash, decay, and lack of maintenance make Scott Tower a place you'd not want to visit after dark. During the day, though, you can check out the tower's impressive street art graffiti and climb to the top. The once-graceful tower has lost its conical red cap and it's hard not to compare its appearance to the smokestacks of abandoned Holyoke factories, but there's nothing shabby about the view of Mt. Tom or the Holyoke Range. To find it, use Cherry Street, park at Community Field Park, and stroll about a mile—under I-91 and past a cell-phone tower. The experience is worth it.

Stafford Hill

If you prefer a more genteel experience, try the Stafford Hill Memorial in Cheshire (Stafford Hill Road). It affords glimpses of the surrounding Berkshires, though overall the spot is more contemplative than spectacular. By now you know I'm a sucker for a good back-story, and Stafford Hill fits the bill.

The 25-foot tower[2] was designed and built by Newton C. Bond in 1927. It is a replica of a field stone structure in Newport, Rhode Island, that lots of folks have speculated was built by Norse settlers in the 12th century. Others say travelers as diverse as medieval Portuguese, post-Crusades Knights Templar, or 15th-century Chinese explorers erected it. Actually, the Newport original is the base of a 17th-century windmill owned by the grandfather of Benedict Arnold.[3] Rhode Island connects to Cheshire in other ways as well.

Cheshire was originally called New Providence Plantation, its original 1766 settlers hailing from Providence and Coventry, Rhode Island. Shortly thereafter, Joab Stafford (1729–1802)[4] bought 400 acres of land in New Providence. During the Revolutionary War, Stafford led a militia known as the Silver Grays[5] into the pivotal 1777 Battle of Bennington, which historians see as paving the way for a major Colonial victory at the Battle of Saratoga.[6] Stafford was wounded at the Battle of Bennington, which actually took place in Walloomsac, New York, 10 miles from the Vermont town that takes the credit. (History gets messy sometimes!)

After independence, Stafford lived near Albany, New York, before returning to New Providence. He deeded Stafford Hill to the town, which was renamed Cheshire in 1802, the very year Colonel Stafford died. He is now buried on the hill bearing his name, though Stafford was originally interred in the Baptist graveyard on Windsor Road. When a group called the Pioneers and Patriots of New Providence commissioned Stafford Tower in 1927, they dug up old Joab and placed his remains in a new tomb inside the tower. But maybe you don't want to think about that when you're having a convivial picnic and keeping your eyes peeled for critters in the adjoining Stafford Hill Wildlife Management Area.

Children's Chime Tower

High places and clanging bells like those of Children's Chime Tower on West Main Street in Stockbridge can help clean out a busy mind. If you get lucky during the summer carillon season, you might get to climb about a third of the 65-foot tower, which will take you into a room full of levers that looks like someone is deconstructing a giant piano. These are actually the pulls for the tower's 11 bells. But you can metaphorically soar even if you don't leave ground level.

Guess what? There's a story behind the tower. It's also called the Dudley Field Memorial Tower, as David Dudley Field II (1805–94), a wealthy New York City lawyer, gifted it in 1878. Lots of rich folks hit the Berkshires in the summer, but Field's philanthropy was driven by the fact that his father (1781–1867) had been the town's Congregationalist minister. The tower sits in front of a church on what is reputed to be the site of Stockbridge's first meetinghouse (1739). That's more or less a rough guess, but the handsome fieldstone shaft capped by a stick-style clock tower really does play children's music, in keeping with its patron's wish to honor his grandchildren.

Quabbin Observation Tower

One of the grandest views is that from the Quabbin Observation Tower (See p. 71). The official address is Ware, but it's accessed from Quabbin Hill Road, which is closer to Belchertown than to Ware. The Quabbin Reservoir story is equal parts glory and heartbreak. As early as 1895, planners realized that Greater Boston would soon exhaust local fresh water sources. A bill to construct a dam and aqueduct in Western Mass passed in 1926, grading began the next year, and by 1930, a dam rose to capture water from the Swift River and several smaller streams. The project took nine more years to complete because first, four towns had to disappear—buildings, cemeteries, people, and all. By 1939, though, the Worcester County settlement of Dana, and the Hampshire County towns of Enfield, Greenwich, and Prescott were gone from Massachusetts maps.

As you might expect, a great deal of heartbreak was involved in disinterring 7,500 dead, and forcing 2,600 people to move elsewhere. In addition, construction accidents took the lives of 26 workers. The reservoir filled in 1946, and today the Quabbin's aqueduct system delivers water to about 2.5 million people in and around Boston. The reservoir's 412 billion gallons are so pure that they are unfiltered.

The Quabbin has also become a major corridor for wildlife reinvigoration of species as small as salamanders, as iconic as bald eagles, and as large as moose. Not to mention that the vistas are drop-dead gorgeous. The first you'll come to is the Enfield Lookout. Further on, there are signs for the Quabbin Observation Tower. You'll find a large parking lot and steps to what looks like a landlocked lighthouse. You can climb the 84-foot tower for dazzling gawks at much of the

39-square-mile reservoir and distant hills. It's so awe-inspiring that for a moment it's easy to forget the sorrows that brought the Quabbin into existence. That is, unless you know someone who lives in Western Mass. They'll be happy to remind you that just three small towns in Western Mass get to drink any of the Quabbin's pure water; nearly all of it is piped 65 miles to the east.

Mohawk Trail Vistas

The Mohawk Trail (Route 2) shows up several times in this book for good reason. Some claim it was America's first scenic highway, though there were no such official designations until the 1960s. However you label it, a westward jaunt on the Mohawk Trail takes motorists from the Deerfield Valley to the foothills and mountains of the Berkshires. Once you start climbing beyond Charlemont, you'll get bird's-eye views and find several jaw-dropping pullovers. The highest point is Whitcomb Summit (2,272') near the incongruously named town of Florida, where you can see into Vermont and New Hampshire. A statue of an elk and a summer retreat center mark the spot.

A little further west is Eastern Summit, where there's a snack bar/gift shop that seems to be perpetually in and out of business, but there are great views from its parking lot. It's officially located in the village of Drury, which is part of the town of Florida. (Good luck trying to locate the actual village. It has a population of 72 souls and apparently you drive through the heart of it when you're 1.2 miles from Florida.)

Once you pass through Florida, you'll come to a place that can take away your breath in more ways than one, the hairpin turn at Western Summit (2,020') that's the gateway to a steady descent into North Adams. That turn is nicknamed "Dead Man's Curve" and you should take seriously the 15 mph speed-limit sign unless you want to add to the legend. A better idea is to ease into the Golden Eagle Restaurant at the crest and take in the sight of North Adams and the Hoosac Range in a survivable manner.

Veterans War Memorial Tower

We've already mused a bit over Mount Greylock, so let's climb to the top of the Bay State's first land preserve (1898). There's some disagreement about its official height; the peak is said to be 3,489 feet high, but surveyors often claim it's a few feet taller. But if someone says you can't go any higher in Massachusetts, they're wrong. The Veterans War Memorial Tower at the summit adds another 93 feet. Or is it 105? Depending on whom you ask, the tower is officially in either Lanesborough or Adams. Detect a pattern here?

The tower's appearance is what you'd get if you took an ancient world beacon-style lighthouse and adorned it with an art deco eagle; the latter motif was popular when Civilian Conservation Corps workers built the tower in 1931–32. The beacon really works and, when illuminated, can be spotted 70 miles away. As the tower name suggests, the facility is dedicated to Commonwealth citizens who served in the armed forces, its honor court a reminder of those who fell in combat. From the tower's observation level you get a 360-degree panorama of the Taconic Mountains, the Berkshire Hills, and the surrounding countryside. You really can see a lot just by looking and, as you might expect, Wi-Fi coverage is pretty good up there.

1 This chapter borrows its title from a song recorded by The Who in 1967.
2 Some sources say it's 23 feet. I didn't measure it!
3 The grandfather's name was also Benedict Arnold.

4 Some sources say Stafford lived from 1728 to 1801. Stafford was born in late November of 1728, which partially accounts for the first discrepancy, as his birth occurred before calendars were adjusted in 1752. His birth occurred in what is now called the Old Style Calendar, when the Gregorian calendar replaced the Julian calendar. Why some sources give his death date in 1801 and others a year later remains mysterious. His tomb says 1802, which is the date I used. While we're on mysterious ground, Stafford's first name is variously given as Job, Joab, and Jorab.

5 This regiment's name is also sometimes spelled Silver "Greys."

6 One of the key Colonial commanders at Saratoga was, ironically, Major General Benedict Arnold, just before he switched sides and took a commission in the British army. As previously noted, America's most infamous traitor was the grandson of the man who built the Newport, R.I., tower that was copied in Cheshire.

Do you know me? I was famous once.

Section III

Famous Long Ago: People and Things Forgotten

This section's title borrows a delicious phrase from Raymond Mungo, a prolific Los Angeles-based writer. Mungo has Massachusetts roots; he was born and raised in Lawrence, attended Boston University, and lived in southern Vermont and western Massachusetts during the height of the countercultural 1960s. The title of Mungo's book *Famous Long Ago* is satirical and self-deprecating. In a way, though, Mungo gets it right; fame is often a fleeting thing. How often have you walked up to a gravestone or a statue, read the inscription, and remarked, "Who?" A lot of folks resting in the earth or standing high upon pedestals were quite famous in their day, veritable household names, yet are little-known now.

Americans are notorious historical amnesiacs. The speed of change in American society can be so dazzling that it seems as if today's cultural icons, technological wonders, styles, and obsessions are thrown out with tomorrow's trash. Who watches a movie set in the 1970s and thinks, "Wow! I really love the clothes and hair styles?" Who remembers Lorena Bobbitt, Heidi Fleiss, Bob Packwood, Dan Rostenkowski, or Milli Vanilli? I hear they were big back in the 1990s!

This section features three people who were famous, but are now overlooked. Each was local, and two—Edward Bellamy and Dwight L. Moody—were world-famous. The third, Erastus Salisbury Field, was seen mostly as a local eccentric but his work still sparks discussion among art collectors.

There's a reason why New England has more colleges and universities than any other region: it was the intellectual capital of England's North American colonies. That legacy continued after independence, as did the tendency for intellectual inquiry to go hand-in-glove with outputs of art, literature, philosophy, political theory, and creative pursuits of all sorts. Samuel Adams dubbed Boston "the Athens of America," a grandiose claim, though Massachusetts was indeed a seedbed for the intellectual flowering of the colonies. He was dead wrong to confine it to Boston.

In the realm of letters alone, Western Massachusetts has produced such literary giants as William Cullen Bryant, Emily Dickinson, W.E.B. DuBois, Will Durant, Helen Hunt Jackson, Jack Kerouac, Robert Parker, Theodore Geisel (Dr. Seuss), and Edith Wharton. More recently, it has been home to Augusten Burroughs, Martin Espada, Tracy Kidder, Suzanne Strempek Shea, Anita Shreve, Mo Willems, and Jane Yolen. Kurt Vonnegut, Jr. used to hang out here because his artist daughter Nanny lives in the region and is married to another acclaimed artist, Scott Prior. But don't get me started on famed artists, musicians, and performers who have holed up in the region, or we'll be here forever.

You can't declare yourself famous. That great amorphous mass called the "public" decides whose art, books, ideas, music, and so on are works of "genius." It also decides how long those folks get to wear their crowns and when they become forgotten.

Historians have studied how this became more complicated in the age of mass and popular culture. In the past, "character" determined social reputation. In the early 20th century, new phenomena such as mass-market journalism, radio, movies, and commercial entertainment shifted the focus from character to personality and ushered in the age of celebrity. In 1968, artist Andy Warhol quipped that in the future everyone would be famous for 15 minutes. Perhaps that was flippant, but popular culture thrives on the principle that what is famous and desirable now cannot be so for long.

The second part of this section takes an unusual leap. It stands to reason that if we forget famous people, we forget what the past looked like altogether, or we rebuild our concept of it based on a few remnants. Buildings and places that were once the site of dramas that captured nationwide attention are torn down or altered, and with those changes, the memory of those events fades. I will show this by discussing a humble factory in North Adams that, in 1870, hosted a conflict with national implications.

Nostalgia is another response to the past, especially to those physical reminders of bygone times that can be viewed as "quaint." Forget about obviously fake things—like the legions of "olde" colonial taverns and inns that are rich in ambience, but flunk the authenticity test, or commercial attempts to cash in on the past. Samuel Adams really was a brewer, but I can assure you he'd not recognize the beer that today bears his name! Instead, we will look at how nostalgia causes us to misremember what town greens were. I will also discuss covered bridges, some of which pass the authenticity test while others don't.

Some of my professional history colleagues get worked up about "fake" history— especially things that deliberately evoke nostalgia. I have nothing against nostalgia. A lot of it is fun, as long as we realize that what we experience is sanitized. You can, for example, learn much by visiting Old Sturbridge Village; just don't believe for a second that you've just experienced New England life between 1790 and 1830. The evidence lies at your feet and in your nose; you are not walking among unwashed bodies or upon filthy unpaved paths befouled by mud, manure, and night soil. Nor do you smell those odors. Let's just say that few tourists would wish to visit a for-real 1810 village.

That's the thing about nostalgia; it gives us a *taste* of the past, but it can't tell a detailed story. That's the job of historians, and this one salutes nostalgia for getting folks interested in the past. But it's my job to set the record straight.

II
Utopia Began in Chicopee Falls

A Bible passage from Luke (4:24) contains this remark from Jesus, "Truly I say to you, no prophet is welcome in his hometown." That certainly applies to Edward Bellamy (1850–98), whose home in Chicopee Falls stands so forgotten that when I asked at the Police Department directly across from its 91–93 Church Street location when the building was open, no one knew that it *was* Bellamy's home or who he was. "I know there's a Bellamy Elementary School, but I never knew who it was named after," said one officer. This is sad commentary for a man whose 1888 novel *Looking Backward, 2000–1887* is the single-most-important utopian vision the United States has yet produced. Bellamy remains famed abroad, yet in his own backyard, his Chicopee home struggles to keep its doors open.

Armchair Utopia from an Unlikely Setting

Although the small city of Chicopee (55,991) has its charms, it's unlikely that a first-time visitor would associate it with utopia. In a sense, that's logical, as locals have had other things on their minds. A key lies in the town's name, which local tradition claims derives from the Nipmuc words *chekee* (turbulent) and *pe* (waters). Chicopee is located where the smaller Chicopee River joins the broad Connecticut, and Bellamy's home is just blocks from where the first river has been dammed since he lived there. The rivers made Chicopee a prime industrial site, and the central town in a Springfield-to-Holyoke triad that made all manner of goods, including beer, bicycles, brass, firearms, iron, paper, and textiles. Automotive pioneers Charles and Frank Duryea once had a shop in Chicopee, as well as one in Springfield.

Edward Bellamy was born in Chicopee, where his father was a Baptist minister. Edward spent most of his life there. A brief stint at the *New York Post* instilled an interest in journalism that he parlayed into a return homeward and a post at the *Springfield Union* newspaper. In his spare time, Bellamy penned three failed novels, though his fourth, *Looking Backward,* became a roaring success. *Looking Backward* is generally regarded the 19th century's third-best-selling novel, trailing only Harriet Beecher Stowe's *Uncle Tom's Cabin* and Lew Wallace's *Ben-Hur*. Only Stowe's book was timelier.

It's About Time

Looking Backward is a time-travel book. Its protagonist, a bourgeois insomniac named Julian West, retires to a soundproof underground chamber, is hypnotized, and sleeps through a fire that destroys his Boston home. He is awakened 113 years later when a physician, Dr. Leete, unearths the subterranean chamber during home renovations. West revives to find the United States operating under democratic socialist and utopian principles. Money, competition, and inequality have been abolished, thereby vanquishing poverty and crime. The nation is now the sole owner of all goods, services, and property. Each citizen is paid in credits that can be converted as wished, though the lack of competition or opportunity for accumulation operates as a natural check on inequality. All citizens are required to enter the Industrial Army at age 21 and to retire at 45, and each receives exactly the same number of credits based on the nation's collectively produced aggregate wealth. The only distinction among jobs is that those with less desirable tasks work shorter hours. (The job of the educational system is to determine what job is best suited for each person.)

Bellamy's novel was prescient in many aspects. He anticipated such things as the invention of radio, credit cards, shopping malls, and e-commerce. His view of women, though constrained by Victorian notions that men and women were inherently different, was bold for his day—and his vision of nationalized childcare, cleaning services, and communal kitchens went beyond those of most Victorian-era feminists.

His was a democratic socialist vision—citizens voted for the utopia—but his society was also more realistic than those of other 19th-century utopian thinkers. Bellamy took the view that a good society protected individuals from their own base instincts; hence his utopia tied national interests to individual desires. Economic planning was centralized and rationalized.

Bellamy was not a gifted prose stylist. *Looking Backward* is mostly a series of questions posed by Julian West, for which he received lecture-style answers from Dr. Leete that contrasted the values of West's world with those of the 21st century. Some of the book's success was due to the contrived (and often mawkish) romance between West and Dr. Leete's daughter Edith, which attracted middle-class readers.

Mostly, though, Bellamy's book appealed because he offered an evolutionary path to a socialist future that looked more like a big cooperative community effort than anything Karl Marx imagined. For 19th-century readers, Bellamy's peaceful road to reform was a hopeful counterpoint to the capital/labor strife and violent upheavals of the day. Bellamy's economic visions—based in equality and a planned economy—also appealed to those who had seen the American economy grow, but at such an uneven rate that recessions had occurred roughly every seven years since the end of the Civil War. The recessions—called "panics" in their time—of 1873–79 and 1893–97 were surpassed in severity only by the future Great Depression of the 1930s. Working-class readers longed for a world in which economic and labor disputes were resolved without discord and violence. *Looking Backward* was found on most shelves of Knights of Labor reading rooms, the Knights being the largest labor federation of the period.

Enduring Impact

It is hard to exaggerate the novel's impact. Reformers were so taken by it that they formed more than 160 Nationalist Clubs[1] across the United States, each dedicated to bringing Bellamy's fictional world to life. Bellamy was hailed as a visionary and was solicited for his views on social issues of all sorts. Legions came to see Bellamy's utopian novel as a blueprint for real-life social change. He was even persuaded to pen a sequel, *Equality* (1897), to answer questions about and objections to his utopia, as if the original book was a political platform rather than a work of imagination. *Equality* faltered, though, because it lacked romance and was turgidly written.

Bellamy died of tuberculosis in 1898, but the legacy of his imagined world lived on. *Looking Backward* was cited as influential by numerous Progressive Era and New Deal reformers. It was even more popular abroad, where it inspired various reforms, including those of New Zealand's Liberal Party politicians, who enacted reforms that predated the New Deal by 40 years. It was also popular in Europe, where views of social democracy are generally more accepted by citizens accustomed to seeing socialism in many different varieties, as opposed to citizens in the United States, who have been indoctrinated to lump all left-wing politics into the same ball of wax.

Though it made some of my colleagues cringe, I used to tell students that political ideals such as socialism, democracy, and libertarianism are like ice cream, just a general category. To know whether or not you admire or dislike a particular set of politics depends upon whether you mean vanilla, chocolate, raspberry swirl, or some blend of objectionable ingredients.

As a person who did not believe in violent revolution or compelling citizens to accept things they didn't choose, Bellamy's socialist views were on the mild end of the socialist spectrum and more like liberal democracy. This explains why both Progressive Era and New Deal reformers adapted some of Bellamy's fanciful ideas in more pragmatic forms such as anti-poverty campaigns, educational reforms, consumer protection laws, regulation of business abuses, and protective labor legislation.

Those who fail to recognize that Bellamy was a utopian novelist, not a political leader, went on to make wildly misleading claims that help explain why Bellamy's star faded. Some hardcore conservatives, for example, equated Bellamy's Nationalism with fascism, simply because Nazism translates as "National Socialism." Bellamy actually used the term Nationalism–meaning government control of production and the economy–because he knew that many feared the word socialism, but the Nazism parallel is nonsense; the latter is a right-wing philosophy in which there is no democratic input.

Even sillier, because Edward Bellamy was cousin to Francis Bellamy, who wrote the Pledge of Allegiance in 1892, some far-right groups demonize both men as proponents of dangerous one-world ideals. Attacks such as these have done little to change the fact that *Looking Backward* remains the premier work of American utopianism and it has never been out of print. The novel inspired numerous imitators and touched off a small boom of time-travel and utopian novels, but its far-reaching success has yet to be duplicated.

Faded Hometown Glory

Alas, neither the author's U.S. fame nor his house in Chicopee has fared as well. The home—built by Edward's father in 1852—passed out of family hands in 1905, and had two other owners before 1974, when a local historic-preservation group was able to buy it. The purchase was substantially underwritten by community development grants that (barely) survived Great Society programs fashioned in the 1960s, but never provided enough seed money for the house to become a full-fledged Bellamy museum.

The Edward Bellamy Memorial Association has shared the space with a host of other associations and city boards, and is now open to visitors only by appointment. As seen today from Church Street, the right-hand side is an addition to the house from Bellamy's time. The home's interior has been only partially renovated and contains period furniture, but the only furnishing remaining from Bellamy's time there is a small oak cabinet that once contained his chamber pot!

Like Bellamy's, Chicopee's fortunes have fallen. The city is an ex-

ample of what happens when the economy shifts. By the time Bellamy's home passed into the hands of history enthusiasts, factories were closing that once provided thousands of jobs and tax revenue that could have generated operating funds for a Bellamy museum. The closing of a large Uniroyal Tire plant in 1980 removed still another major employer, and today's median family income in Chicopee is more than $17,000 less than the Commonwealth average. The city enjoys a reputation as a center of Polish culture, including the production of kielbasa, but its largest local employer is now the Westover Air Reserve base, and many of its civilian employees live elsewhere.

Considering Bellamy

As an educator, I often assigned *Looking Backward*. To this day, Bellamy's novel yields admirers, detractors, and skeptics–exactly the sort of disagreement that makes for spirited classroom debate. Skeptics are by far the largest group, the common refrains being that equality is "unnatural," or that a utopia is "impossible." When my students said these things, I gently reminded them that equality is allegedly a touchstone American value. I also prodded them to consider the many millions who have mused over *Looking Backward* and asked whether people in the past might have had superior imaginations to those today. It remains worthwhile to read *Looking Backward,* drive to Chicopee, and stand in front of the house to ponder the city's forgotten prophet.

When I was in New Zealand as a Fulbright scholar, I often showed my new friends and colleagues a map of where I live. Some had heard of or even been to places such as Amherst, Northampton, or the Berkshires, but invariably Chicopee sparked excitement. *They* knew what most Americans, including many in Western Mass, did not: that it was the home of Edward Bellamy. When I told them the sad tale of his homestead, they were incredulous and wondered how this could happen to one of the most famous people of all time.

I met with similar astonishment in Australia and Western Europe. Clearly fame is fleeting and prophets often wear out their local welcomes. It would be nice, though, if folks in Western Mass would do more to make sure Bellamy is remembered and his ideas debated. As in my classroom, it's fine to disagree, but Bellamy challenged us to think about what makes a good society. Surely that is an idea worth discussing.

1 They were called Nationalist Clubs because the word Nationalism was used to describe Bellamy's economic system in which the collective "nation" owned all resources. It was a synonym for state-owned socialism and is now an archaic use of a noun associated today with either nation building, or a form of hyper-patriotism in which individuals see their nation as superior to all others in a xenophobic way.

12
Dwight L. Moody: Northfield's Man of the Moment

Northfield isn't a small town compared with some of its isolated neighbors dotting the hillsides of Western Massachusetts' northern border, but it's not a large one either. The town proper is a single long street that ends at the New Hampshire line, a border so skinny that if you make a right turn off of Main Street/Route 10 and drive a few hundred yards up Moody Street, you're technically in East Northfield, which shows up as Gill on some GPS systems. Dwight Lyman Moody was born at #32 on February 5, 1837. The home is still there and the Moody Center is developing a museum there. These days, the name Moody doesn't ring as many bells as it used to. Like Edward Bellamy, "D.L." Moody—as he liked to be called—was once internationally famous.

The Awakening of D.L. Moody

In 1862, Samuel Clemens famously "lit out for the territories." That was three years after Moody lit out for Chicago. Everyone remembers Mark Twain, Clemens' *nom de plume*, but in the late 1800s, Moody was as famous as Twain, if not more so. Moody's words certainly touched more individuals. Unlike the Missouri-born Clemens or his Conway-born contemporary Marshall Field (see chapter 7), who also made his reputation in Chicago, Moody spent a lot of time in his hometown. He centered major parts of his missionary work in Northfield, and died there on December 22, 1899. His grave and that of his wife grace a small knoll on the campus of the former Northfield School, a short walk from the back of his homestead. That school (now a Thomas

Aquinas College campus) and nearby Northfield Mount Hermon are part of Moody's legacy.

It took effort to spend time in Northfield, as Moody was constantly on the move. Some biographers see Moody as the template for modern evangelism, a prototype for Billy Graham, though Moody's politics were more progressive. He was the most famous figure of the Third Great Awakening and his presence was much in demand.

Religion scholars often argue that Christianity matters more in the United States than in Europe. That's debatable, but what's not is that American faith has been rekindled more often by widespread, long-lasting outbursts of revivalism labeled "awakenings." The First Great Awakening (c. 1730s–43)[1] also involved a Western Massachusetts man, Northampton's Rev. Jonathan Edwards, whose sermon "Sinners in the Hands of an Angry God" moved congregations to tears, gyrations, and other emotional responses.

Moody, though, was cut more from the cloth of Charles Grandison Finney, a key figure of the Second Great Awakening (c. 1790–1840s), whose message was less stern and more hopeful.

Moody's birthplace suggests middle-class comfort, but that was not his formative experience. He was born into a large family and his father died when he was just 4, leaving his mother with 9 children to raise. As was common at the time, D.L. was sent into domestic service and worked for food and lodging. All told, he received only about five years of formal education. Even as a child, though, Moody demonstrated interest in spiritual matters.

At 17, Moody moved to Boston to work in his uncle's shoe store. He regularly attended the Congregational Church of Mount Vernon pastored by the Rev. Dr. Edward Norris Kirk, who acted as Moody's mentor, guided his spiritual conversion, and welcomed Moody into the church (on his second try). Dr. Kirk was an evangelist, a term with different associations then than today.

In the decades before the Civil War, Northern evangelicals were often reformers as well as proselytizers. Like evangelicals of the First Great Awakening, they focused on personal sin, but also on how sin was made manifest in unredeemed society. Evangelicals were often the backbone of abolitionist, temperance, and other moral-reform movements.

Quite unlike earlier evangelicals who preached predestination, those coming out of the Second and Third Great Awakenings held out the possibility of "moral perfection"; they believed that individuals could redeem themselves in God's eyes. Moody immersed himself in the Sunday school movement and recruited young boys with the dual purpose of converting them and saving them from the corrupting influences of the streets.

For many working-class children, Sunday schools were forums for religious instruction and substitutes for formal education. By the end of the 1870s, though, many states mandated school attendance and Sunday schools generally confined themselves to religious lessons. Moody, however, was among those who saw the secular and religious worlds as inseparable, a view he maintained in mission work, his association with the YMCA, revivals, Bible conferences, and involvement in educational efforts ranging from tract societies to the founding of several schools.

In 1858, Moody relocated to Chicago and, two years later, devoted himself to full-time religious work. He was a conscientious objector[2] during the Civil War, but did mission work among Union soldiers.

In 1862, he married the former Emma C. Revell, a Sunday school teacher, with whom he eventually had a daughter and two sons. Revell was the daughter of a rich shipbuilder, and Moody's marriage to her led to increased physical comfort and personal refinement.

From Ashes to Fame

Moody's work in Chicago was dramatically interrupted by the 1871 Great Chicago Fire, which destroyed his church, his local YMCA, and his home. Necessity drove him onto the missionary road. Although he was not the first urban evangelist, Moody raised the performance bar.

Just four months earlier, Moody had met Ira Sankey, a superb singer, hymn writer, and publisher. The two joined forces, and for the next 28 years, Sankey and Moody had an on-again/off-again friendship, but steadfast evangelical chemistry. Congregants flocked to hear Moody's powerful homilies and fervent prayers and to hear Sankey's rich baritone vocals. The press found the pair irresistible; Moody revivals seldom failed to attract attention from newspapers in the cities where they took place.

In 1875—the same year he crossed the continent leading revivals—Moody purchased land in Northfield. Four years later, the Northfield Seminary for Young Ladies opened its doors to 25 students. That was triple the number of anticipated students, but was nonetheless a humble beginning for a campus that went on to educate hundreds of young women until 2005, when it closed and operations were consolidated with those of the Mount Hermon School for Boys, which Moody founded across the Connecticut River in Gill in 1881.[3]

Moody's schools embodied a personal trait I label "anti-modernist modernism," a term that demands explanation. In the 20 years between the founding of Northfield Seminary and Moody's death in 1899, he warned against the unholy allure of theaters, saloons, amusement parks, and Sunday entertainment. Yet Moody did not hesitate to preach in bars, vaudeville halls, sports venues, midways, or at circuses. He fretted over the unholy allure of consumer society and materialism, but used popular culture gimmicks to enhance his evangelical crusades. These included decorated carts featuring colorful tableaus that formed graphic backdrops named things such as Little Hell Wagon and Gospel Wagon. Moody also broadened his base by softening remarks on issues that troubled him personally, such as mass immigration, labor unrest, biological Darwinism, Social Darwinism, and women's suffrage.

Northfield School was the quintessence of anti-modernist modernism. The campus was (and is) stately and inspirational, but also steeped in the romantic landscape and cottage architecture of Andrew Jackson Downing, and the grandiose visions inspired by Frederick Law Olmstead. In short, it was an odd mix of evangelical fervor, romanticism, and egoism.

Northfield trained female missionaries, which sounds quite genteel, except Moody also believed all young women should be well educated and immersed in nature. Both views were considered unorthodox at the time. Moreover, some students were Native Americans and the daughters of slaves, exceedingly radical additions. At Mount Hermon, Moody defied convention by salting the campus with poor boys from urban areas—those considered throwaway dregs by Gilded Age elites—but made certain their sweeping rural vistas were supplemented with both academic training and farm work. An anti-modern modernist indeed!

The Man Who Went Away, but Never Left Northfield

Such rural/urban and traditional/modern fractures were basic to Moody's own nature. His mission was urban, but his large summer Bible conferences were held in sylvan Northfield. An organization eventually called the Moody Bible Institute was founded in Chicago, but many of its administrative details were hammered out in Northfield.

Moody's dual nature was dramatically on display at the 1893 World's Fair. Moody befriended the fair's movers and shakers—including Marshall Field—and readily took part in revivals on the fairgrounds. He preached to as many as two million people there, but objected to the fair being open on the Sabbath.

Nonetheless, his center of operations was not Chicago, but the nearby town of Harvey, Illinois, the utopian vision of real estate speculator Turlington Harvey. That town was more Northfield than Chicago. It sported fraternal organizations, prohibition societies, churches, and a Young People's Society of Christian Endeavor. Its shops were shuttered on Sundays.

In both Chicago and Harvey, Moody found receptive audiences when the Panic of 1893 led to soaring joblessness, though he was saddened when local voters in both places allowed liquor sales. Everyone agreed, though, that Moody was a spellbinding preacher. He was known for slowly building drama, spicing his sermons with parables, and moving to emotional climaxes in which he implored the assembled to change their hearts.

One of Moody's ardent supporters called him a "great advertiser" for evangelical Christianity. He meant it as a compliment, though Moody probably would have blanched at its commercial implications. Still, Moody's style and his willingness to use secular popular culture tools for spiritual crusades have parallels in the way advertisers use ends to justify means.

Indeed, Moody's ideals had an indirect influence on one of America's greatest advertisers, 1907 Amherst College grad Bruce F.

Barton (1886–1967). Barton was a co-founder of the powerful BBDO advertising agency and the author of *The Man Nobody Knows* (1925) in which the parables of Jesus are compared to the campaigns of advertising pitchmen.[4] Barton was raised in the Chicago suburb of Oak Park, where his father William was a Congregationalist minister and Moody's contemporary.

More directly, Moody's preaching style found expression in baseball-star-turned-evangelical Billy Sunday (1862–1935), whose public ministry began in 1891, but soared shortly after Moody's death. Moody and Sankey were said to have preached to a total of over 100 million, and their influence reached across the Atlantic thanks to an 1873–75 preaching tour of the United Kingdom.

Their legacy was broader still if one considers the missionaries trained at Moody conferences, those reached by Moody Institute branches, and the fervor of Moody converts, including one of his sons, Paul Dwight Moody (1879–1947), who headed a Congregational Church in St. Johnsbury, Vermont, before serving as president of Middlebury College from 1921 to 1943. He was a great booster of his father's style of evangelism.

Moody was conservative theologically, but had a keener sense of social justice than Billy Graham. Moody would not fit comfortably in today's evangelical world, in which emotional preaching has become entwined with materialism and fundamentalism. Moody did well materially, but took pains to insulate himself from charges of hucksterism or personal gain. American fundamentalism first crystallized in 1878, but was not a potent force until the 1920s. It's doubtful that the ecumenical Moody would have found comfort in it.

Time has faded Moody's fame. His schools began moving toward a more secular and modern academic curriculum in the 1930s[5], summer Bible conferences have grown smaller, and mainstream Protestant mission work has fallen from fashion. The Moody Institute remains, scholars still show up annually for the Northfield Conference, and a

Christian college has taken over the vacated Northfield School campus.

Perhaps time will redeem Moody's faith, a non-dogmatic mix of personal redemption and moral social reform. Until then you can drive by his home and contemplate the life and times of a famous man who traveled the world but—symbolically speaking—never left Northfield.

1 The First Awakening continued in the South until around 1753, though it is usually (and inexplicably) said to have ended in 1743.

2 My use of "conscientious objector" is somewhat anachronistic, as it wasn't widely used in Moody's day. Technically, Moody compared his views to those of Quakers who, along with other Pietistic Anabaptist religions, were recognized for their pacifist beliefs.

3 The two schools officially merged in 1971, and since 2005 Northfield Mount Hermon has operated on just the Gill campus. It is now a prestigious coeducational preparatory school.

4 BBDO stands for Batten, Barton, Durstine & Osborn, still an advertising giant.

5 The move to modernize the curriculum led also to an unsolved Western Mass murder mystery. In 1934, Mount Hermon Head of School Elliott Speer was shot to death in his campus home. Speer was at the fore of educational modernization efforts, and clashed with opponents. Some have theorized he was a victim of the fundamentalist surge that arose after the Scopes Trial, but this remains speculative.

13
Erastus Salisbury Field: A Yankee Who Thought Big

An old proverb holds that a rolling stone gathers no moss. Maybe it gathers something bigger. There's a house on Pleasant Street in Ware that claims to be the home of artist Erastus Salisbury Field (1805–1900), but there are places in Hartford, New Haven, Boston, New York, North Amherst, Sunderland, and Leverett that can make similar assertions.

A settlement known as Plumtrees that's now part of Sunderland might have the best claim of all. Leverett, the town of Field's birth, is perched above and slightly east of the Connecticut River; Plumtrees lies along the river on the way to Sunderland and it's where some of Field's best work was done.

But for long stretches of his life, Field was indeed a rolling stone. To complicate matters even more, if the measure of a man's life is his masterwork, Springfield can be said to be Field's abode.

Erastus Who?

Erastus Salisbury *who*? Within the grand sweep of things, Field was a local eccentric who made few ripples. Folk artists seldom do. But anyone who has stepped into the Blake Court of the Museum of Fine Arts in Springfield comes away impressed. It holds Field's most (perhaps only) famous painting, *Historical Monument of the American Republic*. If ever the phrase "you can't miss it" applies, it's to this painting. After all, it's more than nine feet tall and 13-plus feet wide. Even if you have a decent wide-angle lens, it's hard to capture it in a photo without tilting the camera.

The original is nine feet by 13 feet!

If the size doesn't impress you, the composition will, if it doesn't short-circuit your brain first! A figure from ancient Mesopotamia dressed in American patriotic garb? At first glance, it looks as if the Tower of Babel sired a city block's worth of children. But look up; there are steam locomotives running through the air along a skyward loop connecting the main tower complex with six adjacent ones. How would a passenger even board such an improbable train? Who are those pillar-topping flag-bearers that no human eye could have seen, and why do some reach into the sky above?

The canvas depicts a dizzying assemblage of tableaux, niches, bas-reliefs, sculptures, friezes, and words. There are puzzling details galore: a winged demon, eagles and less rapacious birds, farm animals, ships, carriages, soldiers from various historical periods, black figures and white ones, tranquil scenes and those with violent bloodshed, and columns bearing the cryptic initials T.T.B. After a while you wonder if the artist was heir to the spiritual vision of 16th-century Dutch painter Pieter Bruegel the Elder, or maybe the grandfather of surrealist Salvador Dali.

Child of a New Nation

What was Field trying to tell us? The best way to "get" this gigantic mishmash is to view it and Erastus Field as products of a new nation. He and a twin sister, Salome, were born in Leverett on May 19, 1805, a time in which the Treaty of Paris (1783) that recognized American independence was not yet 23 years old. Field family members[1] had deep Colonial roots, but were otherwise like most locals: yeomen farmers with little formal education and not much need for it. From an early age, though, Field was fascinated by art, American republicanism, and religion.

The early rumblings of the Second Great Awakening were underway by the time Field was born and he eventually gravitated to evangelical Congregationalism. He was on the cusp of his 10th birthday when Colonel Andrew Jackson's great "victory" at the Battle of New Orleans touched off an explosion of American nationalism[2] that cemented American identity.

Field shared nationalist excitement with his Leverett neighbors, but they weren't much help in nurturing his art; there were very few trained art teachers to be found outside of cities such as Boston or New York. For that reason, Field journeyed to New York City in 1824 for his first known formal instruction—with Samuel F. B. Morse (1791–1872). I'll bet that name resonates. Morse is now best known for his claim to have invented the telegraph, but art was his first vocation and Morse was praised for his portraits and paintings of historical scenes. Field was thrilled to be present in the studio when the Marquis de Lafayette posed for Morse.

Field returned to Leverett in 1825, and spent much of this time as a limner, a term used for an itinerant portrait painter generally thought to be less skillful than academically trained or apprenticed painters. Limners worked on commission and volume—often simply painting as reasonable a likeness as they could of a person's head and face and inserting it onto a pre-painted figure.

Field doesn't appear to have done that, but his earliest portraits are stiff, disproportionate, and rendered with little background detail; in all, the sort generally labeled folk, naïve, or primitive art.³ Field was a quick study, though; in less than a decade, his portraits became more sophisticated and detailed.

In 1831, he married Phebe [sic] Gilmur—the surname probably an alternative spelling of Gilmore—of Ware, and their only child, Henrietta, was born the next year. The Ware house identified with Field belonged to Phebe's family, and the couple lived there from time to time—to the degree that they were settled anywhere. Over the next 17 years, Field also lived in New York, Connecticut, and numerous places in Western Mass. He even purchased land in nearby Palmer, but was constantly on the move in search of commissions.

Field made a decent living, but by the time he came back to Sunderland in 1848 to manage his father's farm, he knew that his days as a limner were numbered. Today we'd say that his job was a victim of technological change. In 1839, his mentor and friend Samuel Morse returned from France with a Daguerreotype camera. Sometime in the 1840s, Field even posed for and hand-tinted his own portrait. He quickly concluded that Daguerreotypes—an early form of photography—would supplant the kind of painting he did: full-sized portraits he sold for four or five dollars each, and miniatures that cost a dollar and a half.

An Artist in the Antebellum North

If you can't think small, think big. Field did so both socially and professionally during a period of history that encouraged it. His religious faith deepened just as Northern reformers were soaking in evangelical brine. Like quite a few folks in Western Mass, Field concluded that slavery was sinful, and he became an ardent abolitionist. His fervor was such that it dismayed him deeply that his friend Morse continued to support human bondage.

As Field's ideals deepened, his artistic vision grew bigger, both figuratively and literally. Literary transcendentalism inspired numerous artists to see nature as a spiritual canvas. This was especially the case for the Hudson River Valley painters, who were labeled luminists because their works seemed to glow with an inner light. Field probably knew of Thomas Cole's much-praised 1836 painting *Oxbow*, a bird's-eye perspective of the loop in the Connecticut River near Northampton. He personally knew Albert Bierstadt, a leading luminist who painted enormous canvases imbued with transcendentalist symbolism. Later, Field hired Bierstadt's photographer/engraver brother Edward to make images of *Historical Monument of the American Republic*.

Field probably wasn't skillful enough to render nature like the Hudson River painters, but he took cues from the spiritual and historical qualities that inspired luminist and realist painters.[4] Field never completely abandoned portraiture, but from the 1840s on, he also painted canvases featuring Ulysses, the Garden of Eden, God's plagues on Egypt, the flight of Jews into the wilderness, The Last Supper, the Taj Mahal, ancient-world scenes, and American political icons.

Decoding *Historical Monument*

Nothing, however, compared in ambition, detail, or sheer size to *Historical Monument*. It's pretty obvious that the canvas is an allegory, but of what? It's not glib to say, "just about everything." It is indeed a monument to the American Republic, but also to its prehistory, other artists, and what Field saw as the Old and New Testament underpinnings of the Republic.

There are 10 towers—two main buildings plus eight adjoining spires—130 panels, and countless figures. Two temple-like wings flank the central tower, one of which contains a flood of words proclaiming the Bible's centrality in all things, especially in creating the American Republic. Those initials T.T.B. stand for "The True Base," meaning the foundations of the U.S. Constitution. Some of whose words are carved into the towers, but God's revelation is the true base Field really intended. Field linked many of his scenes to Bible tales and verses, even though most of what we see depicts Colonial and United States history.

By "history," I mean pretty much everything that happened in English North America from the 1607 English settlement at Jamestown through the 1867 impeachment of Andrew Johnson. There's so much going on in the painting that, in 1876, Field hired Amherst printer H. M. McCloud to produce the 11-page *Descriptive Catalogue of the Historical Monument of the American Republic* that decodes the scenes tower by tower and level by level.

The central tower gives us insight into Field's aims. Three levels up, a seated President Lincoln is flanked—as the viewer sees it—by John Wilkes Booth to his left and George Washington to his right. Lincoln's assassination is a sort of apotheosis (deification) with Lincoln the Emancipator completing the Republic that Washington began. That winged demon sitting on a column upon the leftmost tower from Lincoln is Satan.

The same tower depicts slavery; the black figures are slaves in flight, and the white ones their pursuers. Field usually located things he saw as good on towers to Lincoln's right—The Boston Tea Party, the Continental Congress, the Constitutional Convention, Washington's inauguration—and placed wars, massacres, slavery, the seeds of secession, and other troubling things to the left. But Field wasn't entirely consistent; after all, it's hard to cram in about 260 years of history, even if you do have a nine-by-13-foot canvas.

Field was earnest about his creation; he even tried to answer objections that his towers were Babel-like follies that could never be built. He argued—very improbably even if your grasp of physics is rudimentary—that his towers could stand if parts were filled with stone or concrete. How those suspended tracks were supposed to bear the weight of locomotives is anyone's guess. So too is the question of why anyone would want to build such things. But Field clearly had deeper things on his mind.

An Abiding Obsession

It was once thought that Field hoped to display his painting at the 1876 Centennial Exhibition in Philadelphia. We now know that was Plan B. Field began work on *Historical Monument* as the Civil War was ending, and had completed much of it by 1867. His first idea was to tour the country and give lectures with his painting as a backdrop. For reasons unknown, that never transpired. Perhaps he still mourned his wife, who died in 1859, or maybe he found the logistics daunting. The most likely explanation is that he was preoccupied with other projects during a productive period of his career. He did submit a different proposal for the 1876 Centennial Exposition in Philadelphia—a world's fair—but it was rejected.

Field continued to add to *Historical Monument* until 1888, by which time he was elderly. The painting had long ago grown too big for his humble studio shed, so he worked on it in a neighbor's barn. By the mid-1880s, he doesn't seem to have done much else. Field easily slipped into the role of the bent, bearded, tight-lipped, self-reliant Yankee. He voted in a state election in 1900 and passed away on June 28 of that year, having just turned 95.

Historical Monument disappeared in the early 20th century, and its very existence was first an oral legend, then forgotten. In 1933, it was found in the attic of a house once owned by his brother Phineas' son, only to be lost again. Field's grandniece, Madeline Ball Wright, is said to have rescued it from a storage shed behind a pigsty in the 1940s. In 1960, it made its way to the Springfield Museum of Fine Arts, where it dazzles and perplexes.

As you gaze upon the *Historical Monument* today, think of Erastus Salisbury Field— once famous locally and now a name known best to just a handful of art historians. Yes the painting is odd; but it's also the life's work of a man who literally grew up with the American Republic, saw it tested by division and war, and passed away shortly after doing his civic duty by casting a vote not far from where his journey began.

1 It doesn't appear that the Field line of Leverett was related to the Field family of Ashfield that spawned Marshall Field.

2 Jackson famously routed British forces in a series of battles that concluded on January 18, 1815. Spontaneous celebrations broke out to commemorate American victory in the conflict now known as the War of 1812. Actually, a peace treaty had been signed in Ghent, Belgium, on December 24, 1814, rendering the Battle of New Orleans tragically moot. Had not Britain been preoccupied with defeating Napoleon, it would have made short work of the fragile American Republic. The Treaty of Ghent was basically an agreement to return to prewar conditions, hardly a justification for the loss of thousands of American, British, and Native American lives. One noteworthy consequence was that Britain promised to return runaway slaves removed to Canada, but never kept that pledge. Another result, though, was that Americans celebrated *as if* they had won the war. The wave of nationalist enthusiasm that roiled the nation into the late 1830s helped define the nascent Republic. Shortly thereafter, the United States began to fracture along the sectional lines that led to the Civil War.

3 These terms sound demeaning and, originally, were. Today they are used mostly to reference the work of informally trained artists. Ironically, folk, naïve, and primitive art frequently fetches high prices from museums and collectors.

4 As noted, luminism takes its name from the use of light in landscape paintings that often cast the illusion of glowing from within. Realism is a style of painting that seeks to avoid artistic "tricks" and portray subjects naturally—even if the subjects and events are fanciful.

14
North Adams and Its Chinese Drama: Behind the Brick Wall

It's not just people who are forgotten. History begins as the shared experiences of people caught up in events that others recorded—or not! Much of the past is quickly forgotten, unless it is unearthed by relatively small numbers of sleuths such as local-history buffs, antiquarians, and academic historians and their students.

Historical "sites" also mislead us. Not only are we highly selective about what we choose to remember, we sometimes badly misinterpret what we do select. For example, Salem's witch trial displays and Northampton's "gallows' hill" falsely represent events that took place elsewhere.[1]

Then there are sites that were nondescript in their own day, were briefly the center of a great drama, and then slip back into obscurity. Such a place is now an ancillary building at the Massachusetts Museum of Contemporary Art (MASS MoCA).

Big Drama in a Nondescript Building

As you walk toward the museum entrance from the Marshall Street parking lot, you see a slope-roofed, redbrick building sporting a giant MASS MoCA sign. What once was a factory is small by the standards of the museum's 24-acre campus, but in 1870, it was the site of a mighty capital/labor controversy that captured nationwide attention: the first known use of Chinese strikebreakers east of the Rocky Mountains. Believe it or not, your morning glass of orange juice is an offshoot of what transpired.

Shoe manufacturer Calvin T. Sampson once owned the unremarkable building we see today. He was a Vermonter by birth and a self-made entrepreneur who parlayed peddling shoes into investments that allowed him to open his own shop on Eagle Street in North Adams in 1858. Sampson's business prospered, he married well, and in 1868, he moved his operation into a solid new factory on Marshall Street, the one that we see today. Although Sampson's factory produced nearly 300,000 pairs of shoes per year, three challenges stood in his way: unstable economic conditions, technological change, and a labor union: the Knights of St. Crispin.

Great fortunes were made following the Civil War. Outwardly, North Adams was thriving. Sturdy factories like Sampson's dotted the town and its 1870 population rose to 12,090, a 57 percent increase in just a decade.[2] The national economy, however, resembled a roller coaster ride in which short booms were followed by steep busts. This instability was among the reasons Mark Twain dubbed the post-Civil-War period the "Gilded Age." He and co-author Charles Dudley War-

In 1870, the center of labor conflict; today, part of MASS MoCA

ner saw American posterity as surface glitter that, like a cheap picture frame, was ugly when you scratched the surface. The same forces that propelled the growth of the American economy often discarded workers like worn machine parts. December 1867 marked the end of a recession that had lasted for two years and eight months. In September 1869, another bust occurred when attempts by robber barons Jay Gould and James Fisk to manipulate the nation's gold supply precipitated a downturn that stretched into December 1870.

North Adams was not immune from such economic fluctuations. Sampson's profits fell, though his plight was slight compared to the fates of his Irish and French-Canadian workers, who faced lay-offs, wage cuts, and increasingly long hours. They and shoe workers nationwide also faced challenges associated with technological change. Technology is good, right? Perhaps, but there's a reason we have the adage, "Timing is everything."

The timing of the 1869–70 downturn hit skilled shoemakers especially hard. They were already reeling from earlier introductions of machines that punched holes, lasted, and stitched.[3] Each automated improvement reduced the need for workers at a time in which employment in the industry was dull and times were hard for North Adams shoemakers.

Male shoemakers, though, were represented by the Order of the Knights of St. Crispin (KSC), a union named for a martyred 3rd-century Roman shoemaker/evangelist considered the patron saint of cobblers. Founded in 1867, the KSC was probably the nation's largest trade union, with some 50,000 members. In 1868, the Crispins forced Sampson to dismiss a non-union employee and the next year, held a brief strike. Sampson responded by firing most of his 150 workers and dispatching his superintendent, George W. Chase, to recruit scabs from nearby North Brookfield. That did not go well; KSC leaders massed at the local train station, convinced the scabs to go home, and forced Sampson to relent. In April 1870, the Crispins demanded a reduction of their 10-hour work day and a raise in their pay rate of $1.70 per day. That very day, Sampson sent Chase on a longer journey: to San Francisco.

The Chinese of North Adams

The purpose of Chase's errand was revealed on June 13, 1870, when 75 young Chinese males disembarked at the North Adams rail station. "Young" was the operative word. Other than the English-speaking foreman, Charles Sing, Sampson's recruits were (probably) aged 14 to 24.[4] Aside from Sing, few of the arrivals had an inkling that they were writing a new chapter in the capital-labor wars; they represented the first known case of importing Chinese strikebreakers into a labor conflict east of the Rocky Mountains.

Police expected trouble and ringed the station; George Chase reportedly packed a six-gun. These measures weren't needed; the town's initial response was curiosity, as most people in North Adams had never before seen a Chinese person. Tensions arose when it became clear that the "Celestials," as local papers dubbed them, were scabs. Under the terms of a three-year contract, Chinese laborers worked 11-hour days in exchange for $23 a month for the contract's first year, and $26 a month for years two and three, barely half of what Sampson's unionized workers demanded.

The arrival of the Chinese split North Adams, with some residents supporting Sampson's "experiment" and others seizing upon the era's anti-Chinese hysteria and accusing the shoe magnate of bringing "barbarians" into their midst. Newspapers near and far, but especially on the East Coast, divided along the same lines. This time, not all editorialists took their customary anti-union or pro-labor positions. Unions had long railed against imported contract labor, and warned that such practices would drive down the wages for all workers. Nearly everyone realized that Chinese laborers in the East upped the ante, and North Adams seemed an affirmation that some employers were indeed driving wages below market rates. Several customarily anti-union papers went so far as to side with the KSC in seeking to ban the Chinese.

The Crispins organized rallies in numerous cities, with one in North Adams drawing as many as 4,000 protestors. Rumors circulated of plots against Sampson's life and a planned arson of the Marshall Street factory, but the worst that came of any of this was that Sampson was ostracized by some townspeople.

For their own protection, the Chinese were housed in an unused part of the factory and eventually in nearby quarters. Given that most of the workers knew no English when they arrived, were far from both home and San Francisco's Chinese enclaves, and were unaccustomed to New England's harsh weather extremes, one can only imagine the isolation these young men experienced.

Sampson, however, was delighted to learn that production was up and that his profits had increased by nearly $40,000 in the first year. He duly imported 95 more Chinese workers. After that tense first year, passions cooled. The Crispins offered to take a pay cut and pondered the wisdom of organizing Chinese workers. Neither plan got off the ground as the KSC was decimated by the Panic of 1873 and eventually merged with the Knights of Labor.

Other Eastern industrialists–most notably a laundry in Belleville, New Jersey–also imported Chinese strikebreakers. Yet by 1880, there were but 19 Chinese left in North Adams, and Eastern employers ceased using Chinese labor scabs.

Chinese labor was never a serious threat in the East, but the nationwide tide of anti-Chinese sentiment led to restrictions on Chinese employment and, in 1882, Congress passed an outright ban on Chinese immigration to the United States. Not that the Chinese were clamoring to come to North Adams.

Local middle-class women of a religious bent—a group that included Sampson's wife, the former Fannie Burlingame, the daughter of a local industrialist—provided rudimentary educational, language, and religious instruction to the Chinese. Most of the Chinese were homesick, and Western Mass winters proved dispiriting. Nearly all departed for San Francisco when their contracts expired. (At least seven died in North Adams.)

Oranges and Lue Gim Gong

Lue Gim Gong (1854?–1925)[5] was not among the exiles. He left China when he was about 12 years old, a self-selected victim of wanderlust, and was probably 16 when he came to North Adams. He became a favorite of Fannie Sampson, who tutored him and converted him to her Baptist faith. Lue continued to work as a shoemaker until felled by tuberculosis; Fannie is said to have personally nursed him back to health. He briefly returned to China in 1885, but returned to San Francisco shortly thereafter. In 1889, Lue contacted Fannie, and she helped him relocate to DeLand, Florida, where the Sampsons wintered. Fannie even adopted Lue, who dabbled in the family gardens and greenhouses using skills he learned as a boy in China.

When "Mother Fannie" died in 1903, she left her Florida estate to Lue. He proved himself a brilliant horticulturalist and an inept dealmaker. When a 1904 frost wiped out much of Florida's orange crop, Lue spent several years developing the "Lue Gim Gong Orange," one resistant to frost because it ripened in summer rather than spring.[6] He used the same technique to develop heartier apples and grapefruit.

Lue would have made a fortune, except he signed a deal with a nursery that promised to pay royalties on every Lue Gim Gong orange "tree" it sold. Instead, it swindled Lue by selling seedlings. He was forced to sell his estate and was nearly bankrupt, even though he had won several awards for his horticultural skills and some began to dub him the "Luther Burbank of citrus."

Luckily, Lue made still another discovery: a technique for grafting orange blossoms onto budwood. In 1911, his skills attracted the attention of auto manufacturer Ransom Olds. Olds hired Lue as part of his development plan team for the new town of Oldsmar, Florida. Lue applied his talents with such aplomb that the Pinellas County town sported a Gim Gong Road.

Lue died in 1925, but don't look for Gim Gong Road if you ever find yourself in Oldsmar; in 1944 the name was changed to Commerce Boulevard. Don't look for his name on your orange juice either; it's usually just called the "Valencia" orange now, though Lue's hybridized version probably saved it from extinction within Florida.[7]

Ponder the 1870 drama the next time you visit MASS MoCA. Who knew all of this happened in a building so humble that it has been relegated to a sign holder? Exit the parking lot and walk beneath Route 2, where you'll encounter a clever diversion: the city's "harmonic bridge," support tubes that channel noise from the traffic above and convert it into musical tones. Several of the tubes are painted with images of workers. It would be just if someone painted Chinese faces on one of the pillars.

---

[1] For the record, there is little within Salem that directly relates to the witch trials. By the time of the 1692 trials, Salem was split between Salem Village and Salem Town. Today's Salem mostly occupies the Salem Town boundaries, which was where merchants, shopkeepers, and people engaged in commerce lived.

Most of the witchcraft drama took place in Salem Village, which is today's Danvers and its environs. No one knows where the victims were buried. See chapter 5 for the story of Northampton's faux gallows' hill.

[2] This population figure includes the town of Adams. North Adams was not a separate town until 1878.

[3] Shoemaking was once a skilled job in which an artisan cobbler handmade shoes from soles to laces. Technology such as improved cutting, punching, and sewing machines allowed for assembly-line production. The term lasting may be unfamiliar. It refers to shaping the outside of the shoe and was done with forms in the hands of skilled lasters. Each time a new machine was introduced, the need for skilled shoemakers—sometimes called cordwainers—declined.

4 Sources generally agree that 75 Chinese arrived in 1870, though a few say 95, a number I suspect confuses the first arrival with the second. There is also disagreement concerning the ages of the first Chinese arrivals. Some sources say the youngest workers were 14 and that at least one might have been as young as 12. Census data give an array of ages from 14 to 38, with the bulk claiming to be between the ages of 14 and 18. We will probably never know the precise ages of many of the Chinese as few of them were armed with birth certificates. Insofar as we can infer, translator/foreman Charles Sing, who was said to be 22, probably would have seemed a mature adult to many of his charges. Lue's date of birth is variously given as 1854 or 1856.

5 Lue's orange was a cross-pollinated Valencia and Sweet Mediterranean, which he perfected in 1909, after several other variants failed to satisfy Lue.

6 There is a bust of Lue Gim Gong in Oldsmar, and he often shows up on murals in the area.

15
Hadley:
It's Not Easy Being a Green

In the next two chapters, I want to highlight how nostalgia alters our views of the past. Some of the best history lessons speak in whispers rather than shouts, so let's look at a few of the more humble Western Mass remnants of the past that are probably different from what you imagine.

The Scoop on the Town Commons

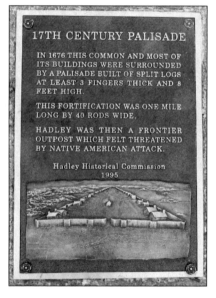

We all know what a "typical" old New England town looks like, right? Maybe you conjure something akin to Amherst: a sylvan green circled by a college, a handsome inn, a solid church, an august town hall, and rows of shops. You imagine the town common as the focal point of Colonial life, a place where cattle grazed, where firewood and nuts were available to anyone who wished to collect them, and where people gathered for important town meetings.

If that's what you think, you've been the victim of the greatest rebranding campaign of the 19th century. New England town greens are picturesque, but most claims to a long historical pedigree are pyrite trying to pass for gold. Peruse Frederick Hitchcock's 1891 *Handbook of*

Amherst and you'll find his remark that, prior to 1880, Amherst Town Common was an "unsightly swamp."

Maybe you've noticed that I've used the terms "common" and "green" interchangeably. That's part of the problem, as is inconsistency over whether to use the singular "common" or the plural, "commons." But let's first consider a large greensward in Hadley, three plus miles west of Amherst.

Route 9 through Hadley is named Russell Street in honor of the Rev. John Russell Jr., who, in 1659, guided nearly five dozen families that left the Hartford/Wethersfield, Connecticut, area in disgust, and founded the new settlement of Hadley, Massachusetts. It's hard to miss Hadley Town Common, which forms a median strip along West Street. Circumnavigate it and you will have walked, biked, or driven nearly two miles. A quick glance might suggest it's not worth the effort. It's big, it's green, and it's mostly empty except for some non-photogenic utility poles along its perimeter and elderly sugar maples on its south side. There is, however, the small marker pictured on page 116 that alerts us that we're treading upon some for-real historical sod.

Let's go back to the terminology problem. In New England, a town common was often also a village green, but we have to be careful, as quite a few village greens are fakes that are no more Colonial than a child's toy musket. But even a legitimate town common was seldom the same thing as land called "the commons." Huh?

It's easy to be confused because of the inconsistency in how things get labeled. The basic difference is that a "common" was a bit like our romanticized view of the village green, a central focal point of a settlement. It was, however, usually the smallest of all "common lands" to which village settlers had access. Most of what is (usually but not always) called the "commons" (plural) consisted of much larger tracts of land away from the village center that helped sustain settlements whose economy depended upon collective agricultural output. That is to say that the village green/town common played a lesser role in the local economy.

English settlers to North America brought the concept of village greens with them, but New England offered opportunities that departed from those of Old England, not the least of which was a lot more available land. New settlements were often "nucleated," a fancy way of saying that homes clustered around some sort of center. "Some sort" is an important qualifier. Hadley's West Street is long and linear. The first road was 20 rods in length, expanded to 40, and had houses on either side facing the town common.[1]

Because settlers were agrarian people, the economic center of Hadley was neither the common nor the houses; it was the eight-acre farm lots that lay behind and beyond the home lots. A December 12, 1661, order stipulated that Hadley should be enclosed by a four-foot-high, five-rail wooden fence sunk into a three-foot ditch, an effort that initially required about 16 miles of fencing. Rails and gates marked the entrance into Hadley, but very little else was enclosed by a stockade until the 1670s.

Hadley Town Common was a very small part of the overall common lands. How could it be when it took roughly two acres of grazing meadow to feed a single pair of milch cows? Neither were the actual commons purely "common." We like to think of common lands as open to anyone who wanted to graze animals or forage for wood, nuts, and berries. But although some open-farming patterns occurred, common lands were closely regulated.

Beginning in 1670, Hadley *apportioned* grazing and woodland rights and made grantees responsible for controlling animals and limiting wood harvests. This reduced conflict and was also for the good of the community. Call it early land management.

Over time, four separate commons areas emerged: Forty Acres Meadows to the north, Great Meadow west of the Connecticut River, Hockanum Meadow to the south, and East Meadows, the last of which is today part of Amherst.[2] Hadley Town Common only operated as a temporary commons during times of warfare. Put aside romantic notions of bustling village life and neighborly relations. Bends in the Connecticut River defined Hadley, with common lands splaying out four to five miles from the original homesteads as dictated by the river's course. A true "center" of town was also problematic given that Hatfield was originally part of Hadley, and it lies on the opposite bank of the river from today's Hadley.[3] Hadley probably had a tavern along West Street by the late 1660s, though none shows up in records until 1688. Maybe that's because shepherds, fence inspectors, and hog reeves were far more important than tavern keepers.

Bickering Puritans

By now you're probably wondering what villagers shared on Hadley Town Common. This gets us to the original purpose of most inside-the-town-greens; they were "meeting house lots," the place where the church stood. That's commemorated in Hadley by the small marker pictured here, which sits north of the green's center of the green. Hadley Town Common was not the economic, geographic, or social center of Hadley, but it was its spiritual hub.

One of the lessons we learn from Hadley's origins is that New England's European forbearers were often more pugnacious than pious. Village life often featured disputes, power struggles, and pique. Massachusetts Puritans were a hybrid of ill-fitting beliefs. Unlike the Separatist Pilgrims, Puritans never quit the Church of England (Anglican). They didn't care for official Anglican doctrines and practices, so they adopted non-approved ideas from dissenting Protestants. They agreed with the Calvinists' strict doctrines of election and predestination,[4] and took from Anabaptists the view that only adults who underwent a spiritual conversion could be baptized and accepted as church members. In most of Colonial New England, only white men who were both church members and property owners could vote or hold political office. It wasn't easy to determine those God chose to save, but Puritans adopted the somewhat shaky idea of "visible saints," the idea that outward success, piety, and stellar character *might* portend God's favor.

Problems emerged in the second and third generation, when children and grandchildren of visible saints failed to have timely conversion experiences. In a society in which there was no separation of church and state, this meant that some offspring of the founding elites couldn't vote or hold office, a threat to the social and political might of powerful families. Some more worldly Puritan leaders developed the idea of a Halfway Covenant. It allowed the blood kin of visible saints to join Congregational churches as "halfway" members that could be baptized on the assumption they would undergo a future conversion.

This wasn't officially put into place until 1662, but the very discussion of it was enough to drive devout traditionalists such as 32-year-old Rev. John Russell Jr. (1627–92) and his followers out of Connecticut and into Massachusetts. To them, the Halfway Covenant was little more than a blasphemous power grab, and they were certainly correct about that. In Hadley, there was no Halfway Covenant; Russell and his followers were serious individuals. They named their new town for a place in Sussex, England, and set about the stern task of living as they felt God demanded.

Plans were made to build a meetinghouse 45 feet long by 24 feet wide, with six-foot lean-tos added on each side. Services were held in homes until the church was completed in 1670.[5] Far from being an eye-catching site, Hadley's meetinghouse lot sported a crude, unpainted building with simple wooden benches and a loft that held a call-to-worship bell. It did not have a steeple, an ornament Puritans thought frivolous and ungodly. There probably was also a small outbuilding stable for horses, and one of the meetinghouse wings would have been used as a "nooning shed," a place to rest and eat, as services routinely lasted three hours or longer. An official road bisected the green, as did myriad ruts and divots from horses, carts, and wagons. The "green" was often more mud and manure than grass.

Hadley Town Common served a few more purposes. Militia drills took place there, and it was partially fortified. King Philip's War (1675–77), a conflict with Native Americans, sparked a wave of palisade building in the Connecticut River Valley. In 1677, Hadley voted to fortify the meetinghouse lot as a temporary refuge for livestock, women, and children during warfare. But because the village escaped direct attacks such as those that led to bloodshed in Hatfield and Hockanum, records suggest that Hadley only partially completed the fort on the green.

Hadley had just four pastors in its first 152 years of existence. Its first meetinghouse lasted 47 years (1670–1717) before it was deemed too small. A new church arose and stood on the same spot until 1808. By then, disputes had led to splits and several breakaway congregations met elsewhere. A third meetinghouse was built on West Street, but in 1841, 23 years after Massachusetts ended state support for Congregationalism, two smaller groups merged and the church moved to Middle Street. With that move, Hadley Town Common ceased to be Hadley's center in any sense. As the 19th century unfolded, graceful elms grew along the old common and made it look more like the postcard image of a town green.[6]

Inventing the White Village

Today, Middle Street looks more like that village postcard, especially with its white Congregationalist Church, whose steeple is topped by a striking weathervane. As historians Dona Brown and Joseph Conforti have noted, New England was the first region to imagine itself as unique. It did so in the decades before and after the Civil War, by which time trade, industrialization, immigration, and agricultural decline had transformed the region. Rather than celebrate ingenuity, industry, and intellect, writers such as Harriet Beecher Stowe, Jedidiah Morse, Joseph Wood, and Timothy Dwight; engravers such as John Barber and Alice Morse Earle; and scores of village-improvement societies, antiquarian groups, Colonial Revival devotees, painters, and folk art collectors created an imagined New England past, sometimes intentionally and sometimes naively.

Conforti notes that the reinvention of the region was marked by a lot of pure *invention*, a history defined by Pilgrims[7] and Yankees living in an "orderly central village." You might notice that the bickering Puritans were moved to the back pews in favor of the Separatist Pilgrims. Mostly, though, in Dona Brown's delicious turns of phrase, New Englanders put "dilapidated buildings and grass-grown streets to work" for tourists and travelers seeking "quaint bygone places … [and the] imagined serenity and grace of a more stable class order."

Things untidy and unsightly gave way to what scholars have called "white villages." Surviving nooning sheds came down, neat inns and taverns arose, and meetinghouse lots were repurposed as tranquil greens. In many cases, greens were created in towns that never previously had them. These makeovers conveyed the impression of genteel, centralized village life, comforting images for middle-class minds, but not reality as experienced by Colonial settlers and yeomen farmers. You've seen the white village in countless movie establishing shots: those handsome white clapboard buildings framed with black trim that evoke New England, even if they were fashioned in a Hollywood back lot.

There is a lot of history to be learned from Hadley's humble greensward; it's just not the kind you'd acquire from romantic writers, dreamy artists, tourist brochures, glossy magazines, or movie directors. It is nice, though, to have open spaces in which to muse and to roam. These days, Hadley Town Common actually serves as a gathering place for fairs, parades, and celebrations. Among its other roles, it's where the town's annual asparagus festival is held, and I will broach no argument over my assertion that its local crop is the finest ever turned onto a plate.

1 A rod is about 5½ yards.

2 Amherst was known as East Hadley until it was incorporated as a separate town in 1759. Forty Acres stretched toward what is today North Hadley. Hockanum was located between present-day Hadley and South Hadley; the latter was incorporated in 1779.

3 For very practical reasons, Hatfield was recognized as distinct in 1670.

4 In brief, predestination holds that God has preordained how history will unfold, the roles individuals will play in bringing about that plan, and who will be saved and who will be damned.

5 It does not appear that those additions, also called leantors, were ever built.

6 Alas, Dutch elm disease devastated New England and, by the 1970s, Hadley lost most of its elms.

7 The Puritans were downplayed as intolerant, hidebound, and narrow-minded—a fanciful way of doing history given that they absorbed the Pilgrims, not vice versa!

16
You Don't Have to Go to Vermont to See Covered Bridges

Covered bridge in Conway

Who doesn't love a covered bridge? For a lot of folks, covered bridges are like sugar maples in autumn: symbols of New England itself. For those wishing to engage in nostalgia or wax rhapsodic, the covered bridge embodies New England's past and its ingenuity, a symbol of simpler times and efficient adaptation to long, hard winters. According to guidebook writer John S. Burk, Massachusetts built at least 270 covered bridges after 1840, including ones in Montague and Northfield that were sturdy enough to carry railroad traffic. At last count, there were only 13 covered bridges left in the Commonwealth and one of those, the Dummerston Bridge at Old Sturbridge Village, was moved to the museum from Vermont. Several others aren't really bridges at all; they were built as landscape features. The good news is that nine of the Bay State's covered bridges lie west of Worcester, and six of them have links to the past.

Think "covered bridge," and Vermont first pops to mind. To be sure, its 104 survivors make it the covered-bridge king of New England, followed by New Hampshire with 54, Maine with 14, with Massachusetts, Connecticut, and Rhode Island trailing behind.

Covered, Uncovered, and Recovered Bridges

Let's address nostalgia and our current love of covered bridges by beginning with the question of why bridges were covered in the first place. The answer is obvious: New England weather. The roof gave protection from the elements to the decking that crossed streams and valleys. In the past, just as today, bridges were generally more difficult and expensive to build than roads, so you wanted bridges to last as long as possible. Still, they were (and are) mostly wooden structures that do not last forever. If going over a covered bridge evokes a frisson of going back in time, you have fallen prey to an illusion. Or maybe not. Journalist Howard Mansfield posed a terrific historic preservation conundrum in his 2001 book *The Same Axe Twice.* He told of a farmer who claimed to have used the same axe his entire life, though he had replaced the handle three times and re-forged the head twice. Is it the same axe? That's probably a matter of how you choose to view it. If you live in a house originally built in the early 1700s that's had clapboards replaced, chimneys rebuilt, foundations repaired, and modern amenities added, do you live in a "Colonial" house?

Technically, though, there's no such thing as an original covered bridge. The same wooden roof that preserved from New England weather the wooden decking—which lasts longer than most of today's asphalt and steel spans, by the way—eventually succumbs to the elements and requires refashioning just like the farmer's axe. So is such a bridge "old?" Six of the nine Western Mass covered bridges began their lives in the 19th century, but none of them would still be here without drastic alterations. That's especially the case for those that carry automobile traffic, such as the Conway bridge pictured at left.

Cars also help answer the question of who doesn't like covered bridges. Answer: more people than you'd imagine. Not many covered bridges were like those in Montague and Ashfield; most were light-weight remnants of the horse-and-carriage era. When the age of automobiles took off in the 1920s, covered bridges weren't "quaint"; they were impractical. According to Burk, Franklin County once had 69 covered bridges, with 30 in Colrain and Greenfield alone. Berkshire County had 46, Hampden County 43, and Hampshire County 18. Whenever towns and counties could, they dismantled covered bridges and replaced them with steel bridges that could support automobiles.

Floods also took their toll. Some bridges perished in the disastrous 1927 flood or the rising waters associated with heavy rains in 1936. A 1938 hurricane carried away scores more. When waters receded, residents generally clamored for old eyesores to be replaced with "modern" spans. Arsonists torched some of the covered bridges that survived; maybe a few of the felons thought they were speeding the pace of progress.

Covered bridges might have disappeared altogether were it not for the combined efforts of tourism marketers and passage of stronger historic preservation laws in the 1960s. Coincidentally, the same reputational upgrade for covered bridges also led to three fake Western Mass spans: the covered footbridge built in Westfield's Stanley Park in 1965, and two small structures in Ashfield, one built by a property owner in 1985, and the other erected in 1994 to cross a freshet on the site of the former Gray's Sugarhouse. But let's look at the six with longer pedigrees. Franklin County has four of them. The three clustered closest together lie in Charlemont, Colrain, and Conway.

Bissell Bridge

At just 60 feet in length, Charlemont's Bissell Bridge (pictured) doesn't take long to traverse, but it has a lovely setting. It crosses a narrow gorge across Mill Brook where a small waterfall spills across a ledge. It currently stands as a "through truss" bridge[1] whose interlacing diamond-shaped side braces connect to top beams. Today's structure is quite different from the original 1880 structure. That bridge was badly damaged during a 1938 hurricane, was condemned, and com-

pletely rebuilt in 1950–51. The remodeled bridge carried traffic until 1995, when a new rehab took place. The current structure has been in service since 2005, and is a popular diversion for Mohawk Trail (Route 2) travelers.

Conway Burkeville Bridge

The 1870 Conway Burkeville Bridge pictured at the opening of this chapter also has a picturesque setting. It crosses the South River near a historic Roman Catholic Church and is supported by a modified Howe truss, a distinctive inverted v-shaped internal frame. It takes its name from Nicholas Howe, a Massachusetts millwright who patented his design in 1840. For sticklers, the Conway Bridge is a "multiple kingrod" structure, meaning that iron verticals support the Howe truss. The bridge has taken its lumps. It was damaged during 1938, and heavy snow collapsed the roof in 1975, both episodes necessitating repairs. Ten years later it was deemed unsafe and closed, but it reopened to traffic in 2013 after extensive rebuilding.

Arthur Smith Bridge

Travel and Leisure named the Arthur A. Smith Bridge off Lyonsville Road in Colrain as one of America's "most beautiful" covered bridges. Maybe you have to be a preservationist to appreciate its beauty. I found it forlorn. It sits along a dirt road flanked by cornfields, is closed to traffic, and the North River is mighty puny where the bridge crosses it. Nonetheless, the bridge is quite historic. It opened in 1869, and is the only Burr truss covered bridge in Massachusetts.

That design, patented in 1817, was the brainchild of Theodore Burr, a cousin of infamous Vice President Aaron Burr. These bridges, most of which are not covered, use an arch and multiple king posts—angled support braces—to give support and strength. That design and the fact that metal supports were added in the 1920s are probably what saved the Smith Bridge. It was badly damaged by an 1878 flood and was abandoned until 1896, before being rebuilt and moved to a section of Lyonsville Road named Smith Flats. It weathered the 1938 hurricane and was in service until 1991, when it was closed and moved once again. More renovations were completed in 2007, but the bridge was mildly damaged by Hurricane Irene in 2011. It's on the Historic Register, so I hope it has brighter days ahead.

Pumping Station Bridge

Hurricane Irene absolutely clobbered the Pumping Station Bridge in Greenfield. There really is a pumping station nearby, complete with a small spillway on the Green River. The current bridge embodies the "same axe twice" scenario. The first bridge was built in 1870 and underwent numerous renovations. Whatever was left of the original was torched during an arson in 1969. Up went a new span with an added walkway that opened in 1972. Trucks violating weight limits caused the deck to warp, and the bridge was closed again in 2003. It reopened just in time for Hurricane Irene to bash in its sides and dislodge it from its abutments. After a million dollars worth of repairs, it reopened in 2014. Is it the same bridge?

Locals sometimes call it the Eunice Williams Bridge as it connects to Williams Road. Her story tops the bridge's drama. Seven-year-old Williams (1696–1785) was taken hostage by Mohawk raiders during the 1704 Deerfield Massacre. She was taken to a Kahnawake Mohawk settlement near Montreal, where she forgot English, learned Mohawk and French, converted to Roman Catholicism, married a Mohawk man, and birthed three children, all to the chagrin of her Puritan family. When they sought to ransom her, Eunice refused, and lived out her days as a Mohawk. Few covered bridges can top a tale like that!

Sheffield Upper Bridge

In Berkshire County, the town of Sheffield refused to allow itself to be without a covered bridge. It once had two across the Housatonic River: Lower Bridge and Upper Bridge. Both probably date from 1854, though local stories claim the bridges were built as early as the 1830s. Lower Bridge lasted until 1952, was replaced the next year, and dismantled in 1987.

Sheffield Upper Bridge (pictured) is the last one standing, though it's more of a covered-bridge park, as the span no longer carries traffic. The original was made of pine and used a "Town truss" for support. The style bears the name of Connecticut builder Ithiel Town, who developed it in the 1820s. This kind of truss gives some covered bridges a checkerboard-like appearance. Upper Bridge was once a post road that connected Boardman Street to the village on the other side of the Housatonic. Vehicles were banned from using it in 1974. A rebuilt bridge appeared in 1981, but disappeared 10 years later, another victim of arson. The current structure dates from 1998.

If you walk across it you'll come to a UFO monument. Yes, you read that correctly. In a pleasant small park you'll find a 2½-ton granite marker that proclaims America's "first off-world/UFO incident," which might surprise folks in New Mexico who are convinced a UFO crashed in Roswell in 1947. Never mind.

On September 1, 1969, Thom Reed reported that he, his brother, mother, and grandmother crossed the Upper Bridge and saw a light rise out of the Housatonic River. Suddenly all four were transported out of the car to a hangar-like facility, where they allegedly saw insect-like creatures. Just as quickly all were back in the car. In case you think the Reeds got into some LSD that night, 40 other residents reported seeing strange lights and a saucer in the sky that evening.

I walked across this bridge and—given that the Housatonic is only a few feet deep there—the idea of a reported 20-foot high by 30- to 40-foot diameter ship reflected in the water seems far-fetched. But what do I know? Reed passed a polygraph test with flying colors. Hurry if you want to see the monument. I gather there is rising sentiment to move it. In any event, maybe its fanciful back-story tops the Pumping Station Bridge tale.

Gilbertville Bridge

The 1886 Gilbertville Bridge provides a good setting to imagine days when a covered bridge marked the outer boundary of village life. This 137-foot Town truss bridge crosses the Ware River and connects Ware in Hampshire County with Gilbertville in Worcester County. Gilbertville is an unincorporated village that's part of the town of Hardwick. Small textile, paper, and manufacturing mills—most of them now defunct—dot the region. Today, Gilbertville has a faded mill town feel, but one can also imagine the village in more prosperous times when villagers made their way to shops and work. A walk or drive across the bridge frames homes and buildings as one ascends a short hill toward Route 32A.

Maybe gauzy imaging of a sylvan past is why we've come to love covered bridges. Historians often remind that the past was just as complex as our own time. After all, people in all periods of history spent most of their days focused upon the same things: themselves, their families, making a living, and hoping for happiness.

Still, I'll look the other way if you want to daydream. I also promise not to tell anyone if you slip across the border to Bennington, Vermont, the next time you're in the Williamstown area. There, you'll find an entire museum devoted to covered bridges to enlighten you.

1 Technically, it's a variation of a Long truss, a style developed by Stephen H. Long in 1830.

Chainsaw carving in Orange

Section IV

Follies, Choices, and Causes

We often pass by things that puzzle us because they seem odd, eccentric, dreamy, or from another time. This section is devoted to undertakings that challenge our ideas of the ordinary. They are windows into other ways of thinking. Despite their mind-boggling appearance, though, there is usually more logic to perceived oddities than meets the eye.

Western Massachusetts contains many impressive homes, monuments, gardens, architectural details, and public buildings. This chapter, though, is devoted to the ones that stop us in our tracks. Such places are often labeled "follies," a loaded term that implies that the people who conceived and built them were a bit reality-challenged.

This is especially the case when a constructed site contains features that seem to serve no useful purpose—like a concrete miniature lighthouse sitting by the roadside a hundred miles from the sea, a wooden well that draws no water plopped onto a suburban lawn, a whimsical chainsaw carving, or a grandiose fountain adorning a summer home. We are especially prone to hurl the "folly" label at something so elaborate and expensive-looking that we suppose it must have impoverished its owner.

Without a doubt, big investments sometimes yield much bigger losses. By 2016, Stewart Prestley Blake (1914–2021) had spent over $7.7 million to build a home on the East Longmeadow/Somers, Connecticut, line that is a replica of Thomas Jefferson's Monticello. Two years later, it was auctioned for $2.1 million.

Is it a folly? Blake didn't think so. He insisted he built it as a matter of civic pride to pay homage to Jefferson, a person he had admired since childhood. From Blake's point of view, he got what he wanted. And it hardly dented his bottom line; Blake co-founded Friendly Ice Cream Corporation and, in 1979, sold it to Hershey Foods for $164 million. Moreover, he was 102 when he offloaded his Monticello look-alike.

Blake certainly fared better than the owners of some of the big Berkshires mansions you see in Lenox and Stockbridge; quite a few were sold at a loss due to bad financial investments, divorces, or—most common of all—impossibly high upkeep costs. As many so-called great families in Britain discovered, a castle can easily exhaust a fortune. So too can sprawling country estates. Yet no one calls those buildings "follies."

Words such as "oddity," "weird," and "folly" are external judgments. Owners of non-functioning lawn wells or carved pigs think of their objects as decoration and presumably like the aesthetics. Maybe we ought to call such things choices rather than follies. Similarly, distinctive buildings—no matter how oddly they strike passersby— appeal to the folks who erected them, and some once served now-forgotten purposes.

Folly is a synonym for foolishness, and it has always struck me as unfair that architects and art critics have appropriated it to refer to grandiose and "impractical" visions. Is there anything inherently more folly-ridden about a person of means squandering money on an offbeat vision than someone of limited resources taking out mortgages they cannot pay on cookie-cutter 800-square-foot ranch houses? Pragmatism is, at best, a shaky standard.

There are loads of unique artist's homes, unorthodox DIY shelters, off-the-grid dwellings, and other such break-the-norm homesteads, gardens, and landscape designs across Western Mass. I'll highlight three.

Western Mass also has monuments to movements some would call quixotic, perhaps even as utopian as Edward Bellamy's vision of the future. In my mind, being "unrealistic" does little to diminish the good intentions of activists of any time. When it comes to past movements, quick judgments yield convenient but shallow labels that tell us nothing about intentionality, legacy, or ongoing efforts. This section also features two causes, the failed temperance movement and the quest for peace.

17
Henry Kitson's Santarella:
Here Is Where I Laugh

The Berkshires' hamlet of Tyringham isn't on the beaten path, but those who find themselves on its main drag—which is pretty much the *only* drag—inevitably slow down to stare when they pass Santarella. There's a "No Trespassing" sign, but even from across the road you see an odd roof, unusual angles, and sandcastle-like drip structures. You imagine yourself in the presence of something out of the ordinary. And you're right, sort of.

Santarella was the brainchild of Henry Hudson Kitson (1863?–1947)[1], a name now known mostly to art historians, but once as well regarded in the world of sculpture as contemporaries such as Daniel Chester French (1850–1931), Gutzom Borglum (1867–1941), Gaston Lachaise (1882–1935), and Augustus Saint-Gaudens (1848–1907). Saint-Gaudens, especially, was an occasional collaborator, sometimes friend, and periodic rival to Kitson.

"Minute Man" in Lexington, MA

Many people know Henry Kitson's iconic sculptures, if not his name. Images of a statue in Salem, Massachusetts, are often reproduced as the quintessential depiction of Puritan sternness, though it's actually the colony's founder Roger Conant. Kitson's "Puritan Maiden" monument is much beloved in Plymouth, as are statues of Robert Burns and General Nathaniel Banks in Boston. Perhaps his best-known public work is the "Minute Man" statue on Lexington Green, though much to his consternation, Daniel Chester French's "Minute Man" in adjacent Concord is more famous still.

From England to America

Kitson's year of birth is disputed, but we know that he was born into a large English family of comfortable means in Huddersfield, West Yorkshire. Four sons, including "Harry," as Henry was known in his youth, eventually pursued careers in architecture, sculpture, and painting. Harry's oldest brother John, who went by his middle name of William, blazed what became a family career path in the arts.

William and partner Robert Ellin created the architectural sculpture firm of Ellin, Kitson, and Company, to which Harry was apprenticed, as were his brothers Samuel and Robert. When work took the firm to the United States, Harry landed in New York City in either 1877 or 1878. His initial time in America was brief. With William acting as patron to his younger brother, Harry was sent to Paris in 1882, to study sculpture at the École des Beaux-Arts under the noted Jean-Marie Bonnassieux. While in Paris, he also took classes at the School of Decorative Arts.[2]

From Harry to Sir Henry

In 1884, he returned to New York and worked with his brothers. Two years later, he struck out on his own in Boston, where he dropped the diminutive "Harry" in favor of his birth name and established himself as an independent sculptor. In addition to early commissions, Kitson opened a popular sculpting school. Shortly thereafter, he began mentoring the gifted 15-year-old Theo Alice Ruggles (1871– 1932). In 1893, the *Boston Sunday Globe* celebrated their marriage as a "tale of art and love" that some thought existed "only in story books." Both won lucrative commissions that placed them within Boston's fashionable social set. By 1895, the Kitsons were listed in the *Boston Blue Book* and entertained lavishly at their 334 Church Street residence— when they were there, which wasn't often.

For a time, the Kitsons were a late Gilded Age power couple, with successful sculpting careers and bohemian sensibilities. In 1893, Alice exhibited at the Columbian Exposition in Chicago and two years later, became the first woman admitted to the National Sculpture Society. In 1902, Henry became "Sir Henry," when he was knighted by Queen Elisabeth of Romania as a reward for a bust of her that he sculpted in 1900. The Kitsons eventually had three children: Theo, John, and Dorothy.

The pair thrived during a period of muscular nationalism that engulfed the United States from the late-19th to the mid-20th century. The end of Reconstruction (1865–1878) saw interpretations of the Civil War (1861–65) shift from a conflict to preserve the Union and end slavery to the fact-challenged notion that it had been a crucible that purified American democracy. Civil War commanders were commemorated in story and stone, with the Kitsons winning numerous commissions to fashion heroic renderings of military leaders, Union and Confederate alike. Vicksburg National Battlefield in Mississippi has many works by both Theo and Henry.

This particular spin on American democracy coincided with the nation's rising industrial might, its entry into the age of imperialism, and the perils of two world wars. In short, the Kitsons rose in lockstep with desires to see American greatness commemorated in symbolic, large-scale public monuments.

Kitson Moves to Tyringham

The storybook romance of Theo and Henry fell apart in 1909, and they separated. Each had business ties in Boston, hence Theo moved to Framingham and Henry to Tyringham. The latter choice baffles some Kitson scholars, but that's because the couple's children, who sought to sanctify their parents, censored the *Kitson Papers,* an archival collection now held by the New York Historical Society. Henry went to Tyringham because he was romantically involved with a local, Marie Louisa Hoborn (d. 1947), who became his second wife in 1938, three years after Theo's death. Long before then, Marie was frequently misattributed in print as Henry's wife and was referred to as "Lady Kitson."[3]

Marie's father, Benjamin F. Hebron, owned the land upon which Santarella eventually took shape, having purchased it from the caretaker who inherited it from its first owners, the Kopp family. Kitson was living there by 1916—most likely with Marie—in a 12-room frame house built in the 1860s. Kitson originally planned to use the adjacent barn as his studio, but the very size of the monuments on which he worked required renovations. From there, obsession took over and Santarella eventually drained his sculptural income faster than he could carve out more.

The first drain came from his desire to construct a thatch-covered cottage as his primary dwelling, something reminiscent of his West Yorkshire boyhood. At his behest, local farmers grew rye grass, which promptly rotted in the Berkshires' climate. Kitson then fashioned faux thatching from asphalt and imported craftsmen from England to install it. It took 12 years and untold thousands of dollars to cover a 45-foot roof with 80 tons of shingles piled 20 inches deep, each piece individually fashioned.

Locals suspected that Kitson was "titched in the head" when he asked them to haul stones from their fields and dump them on his land. From these, however, he built formidable chimneys that one biographer dubbed as akin to "the grottoes of Europe." Others he used as makeshift flying buttresses for the 50-foot long by 30-foot wide barn that he retrofitted with heavy beams to support the heavy monuments he carved.

Kitson was said to have supervised the placement of each stone, each shingle, and each detail of the property, including two porches, three chimneys, an ornate library, stained glass windows, a silo moved onto the property to use as a smaller studio, and a six-foot brush fence that walled off the outside world from the ongoing construction site. Santarella even included a Japanese summerhouse and a dream-like garden with exotic plants and a re-routed stream. To tend to this elaborate and exacting landscape, Kitson employed an actual Japanese gardener: Awoki.

What was Kitson Thinking?

These transformations, many of them prompted by spontaneous ideas, gave rise to all manner of speculation. Santarella has been variously called a "storybook house," the "gingerbread house," the "witch house," something from Grimm's fairy tales, and "just plain weird." In 1944, biographer Eloise Myers speculated that Kitson simply "needed to live in an [artistic] atmosphere …" and that many of his "ideas augured well the examples of modern art."

I doubt modern art was on his mind. The name "Santarella" gives us a clue. It's a Neapolitan dialect word that loosely translates as either "goody-goody" or "little saint," and has ironic meanings that convey a puckish sense of being carefree, perhaps even reckless—sort of like calling a rambunctious child a "little devil."

Kitson almost certainly borrowed the name from Italian writer Eduardo Scarpetta's 1889 farce *Na Santarella*, a reworking of the French play *Mademoiselle Niouche* that he and Theo might have seen in Paris during one of their European jaunts. Scarpetta's home is located on a street in Naples still nicknamed Santarella, and the house bears a nameplate reading: *Qui rido io*–"This is where I laugh."

Is Tyringham's Santarella a singular folly? Not exactly. It's odd for the Berkshires, but it's not out of keeping with early-20th-century "storybook houses" inspired by Hollywood film sets. Others in the same vein include fantasy homes built in California by architect W. W. Dixon, L. Frank Baum's Ozcot, and William Randolph Hearst's San Simeon estate. The difference, though, was that Baum and Hearst could afford to indulge their whims and Kitson could not. Especially as he got older, his energy flagged, and public taste in monuments shifted.

Santarella Fades and Rises Anew

Although Kitson's children vehemently denied it, he was nearly broke by the time of his death on June 26, 1947, just weeks after Marie passed away. Months before he died, a bank in Lee from which he routinely borrowed money politely suggested he try a rival institution. By then, Santarella was in need of urgent care, shown by the fact that its 1947 asking price, including four acres of woodland, was only $11,000 (roughly $122,764 in 2017 dollars). By his death, most locals viewed Kitson as an eccentric, or—as some put it—"temperamental, uncouth" and "a scary old man." By then, both he and Awoki sported long unkempt beards that made it easier for locals to view Kitson as a crank rather than a former local patron. It also did little to encourage viewing Santarella as the center of Kitson's artistic vision; it became a "folly."

Santarella's new owner was Donald Davis, who purchased it for just $8,500—nearly 25 percent less than the asking price and less than today's equivalent of $95,000. Davis converted Santarella into an art gallery, which was moderately successful, though not enough so to justify its upkeep. In 1996, Davis sold it for $295,000—about $469,000 in 2017 dollars—to a couple that planned to open a B & B. They quickly determined that renovations were more extensive than they hoped. In 2004 they flipped it to current owners Denise Hoefer and Dennis Brandmyer for $895,000—about $1.18 million currently, which is far less than one might think such a unique property would bring. At this writing, Santarella is used for special events and vacation rentals, but it is also for sale once more.

Victorian novelist Elizabeth Gaskell (1810–65) once observed, "Sometimes one likes foolish people for their folly, better than wise people for their wisdom." We are amused by physical follies as well, but most uses of that particular "F-word" are applied *ex post facto* to people or places with agendas and meanings never intended for the bemusement of observers disconnected in time or temperament. We should imagine Santarella though the eyes of the past. Henry Kitson could easily fit into this book's "Famous Long Ago" section; at the height of his career, those who knew anything about sculpture would have known his name. Like many famous artists, Kitson indulged his tastes and exercised his artist's eye in his home and its furnishings.

It's ironic that most people today only learn about Kitson if they stumble upon Santarella and wonder who built such a strange house. If you keep your eyes peeled, though, you'll spot Kitson's work throughout New England and further afield. It seems he always thought big!

1 Kitson's birth date is variously given as April 9, 1863, 1864, or 1865.

2 The French name of the school is *École nationale supérieure des arts décoratifs*.

3 Kitson's children so thoroughly controlled their parents' reputations that it is hard to find solid information about Marie. Her name is variously given as Mary Louisa, Marie Louisa, and Maria Louisa. The surname should be given as Hobron, though it is often mistakenly rendered as Hebron. Many sources fail to mention that the Kitsons separated, or that Henry married for a second time. The *Kitson Papers* have scattered references to Marie, but seldom as Henry's paramour or second wife. There is a small, undated obituary in the collection and a note that Marie's body was cremated when she predeceased Henry by less than two months.

18
Montague Castle: A Wizard's Vision

John Lennon once remarked, "I believe in everything until it's disproved. So I believe in faeries, the myths, dragons. It all exists even if it's in your mind. Who's to say that dreams and nightmares aren't as real as the here and now?" His words are a good way to appreciate both an ongoing project known as Montague Castle and Brian McCue, who has been working on it since the late 1970s.

Montague Castle is a remarkable place, one McCue describes as his "moon, stars, angels, and faeries" house. There are also dragons, prisms, whirligigs, butterflies, rainbows, and all manner of other fanciful and vivid details. The one thing that's lacking is a grand plan; what gets added is mostly a matter of intuition, inspiration, sweat equity, and available free materials.

The official address is 240 Greenfield Road in Montague Center,[1] but your GPS will only get you most of the way there, as both the Greenfield and Montague ends of the road terminate a few hundred yards from the Castle. The wooden bridge crossing the nearby railroad tracks is now for pedestrians and bicyclists only. Get out, walk, gawk, and prepare to have your mind blown.

Brotherhood of the Spirit

Metaphorically speaking, McCue has long lived on a separate island amidst, but not part of, the mainstream. If the Castle looks as if it's a vestige of the 1960s, it is. In the cheap shorthand that often passes for conventional wisdom, the '60s are "dead." Except that's not the way history works. It generally leaves behind building blocks upon which new visions arise, and trails from which new paths are forged. The past doesn't die; it mutates. When you gaze at Montague Castle, you see the remnant of a remarkable and controversial experiment: the Brotherhood of the Spirit movement, which began in 1968 and officially dissolved in 1988. Unofficial vestiges remain.

The Brotherhood, which underwent several metamorphoses, was an experiment in communal living and New Age spiritualism. Western Massachusetts and adjacent Southern Vermont were such a hotbed of alternative lifestyle experiments in the 1960s and 1970s that no one actually knows how many communes were attempted. By the early 1970s, there may have been more than three dozen utopian experiments in the 35 miles between Amherst, Massachusetts, and Putney, Vermont. Most were short-lived, but lest one be tempted to label their inhabitants naïve or reckless, historical judgment also renders foolish the mean-spirited opposition to the youthful dreamers who sought new ways of living.

The Brotherhood of the Spirit was far more than a group of kids sharing a house and growing their own food. It took shape when Leyden-born Michael Metelica (1950–2003) returned from having spent 1967 participating in San Francisco's "Summer of Love" rather than his original idea of joining the Hell's Angels. In 1968, Metelica convinced a Leyden blueberry farmer to let him build a tree house in which he could meditate. He was soon joined by a handful of friends, all of whom received spiritual guidance from psychologist Charles Hapgood (1904–82) and psychic Elwood Babbitt (1921–2001).

The Leyden tree house was burned by fearful locals in 1969, but by then Metelica's reputation as a spiritual teacher was such that the burgeoning commune relocated, first to temporary places in Guilford, Vermont, and Heath, Massachusetts. In 1970, the commune moved to Warwick, Massachusetts, where an ever-expanding building and 26 acres of land eventually accommodated more than 150 people. Brian McCue was among the early arrivals at Warwick.

The Warwick group seriously explored New Age spirituality, a catchall term that embraced everything from investigations into Eastern religions and meditation to Earth-based and neo-pagan religions such as Wicca and Druidism. Through a combination of meditation, spiritual exploration, self-criticism, spartan living, self-sufficiency, and Metelica's teachings, commune members sought to attain higher levels of consciousness. Members vowed to avoid drugs, alcohol, and sexual promiscuity. The Brotherhood expanded into Northfield in 1970, had its own rock band (Spirit in Flesh), a recording contract, and a membership that swelled to more than 300 by 1972.

That same year saw the Brotherhood incorporate, take over a swath of decayed downtown properties in nearby Turners Falls, and launch business ventures including a greeting-card company, a magazine, a music shop, several eateries, a grocery store, and a tour-bus company.

Worldliness led to shifts that ultimately clashed with spiritual values. In 1973, the community changed its name to the Metelica Aquarian Concept and Renaissance Community. At that point, critics began to denounce the community as a cult. Some former members to this day blanch at the cult label, but what's indisputable is that the community both reached its apex and then eroded.

Depending on one's perspective, the period between 1973 and 1976 was either an attempt to bring needed structure to the experiment or the beginning of Michael Metelica's descent into megalomania. In 1973, critics charged that Metelica demanded absolute control over the community, its finances, and its ideology. Metelica's view was that, "People trusted me to be a god, not a man who believed in God." In an infamous rally held in Greenfield, some members held aloft signs reading, "Know God, Know Metelica."

Some members meant that literally; in 1974, the Aquarian Concept became the Renaissance Church and Renaissance Community, a formally recognized and tax-exempt religious organization. That same year, Metelica changed his name to Rapunzel, a nod to the fairy tale of a long-haired, mellifluous-voiced young woman locked in a tower awaiting a rescuer. Folklorists link this story to older myths of confined goddesses of light whose rescues illumine the world, especially at summer solstice.

A Dream Dissolves

Alas, the new Rapunzel veered toward materialism and egoism. Many members lived in poverty, while Metelica acquired fleets of automobiles, state-of-the-art recording equipment, buses, and even an airplane. He also proved vindictive, especially toward those who questioned his hedonism or his newly acquired habits of smoking and drug use.

Some members were banned from Northfield and exiled to Warwick, which was falling into disrepair; many others quit the community. For a time, Renaissance businesses thrived, and Metelica was flush enough to sponsor rock festivals and other events. Numerous community members took jobs helping mentally challenged patients at the Belchertown State School; others engaged in charity work. About 50 children were born in the community after Rapunzel decided they were needed for the future health of the community. Locals in job-starved Turners Falls often ended up on the payroll of the Renaissance Community.

In 1975, the Renaissance Community purchased an old hotel in Gill that Rapunzel dubbed the "2001 Center." Activities shifted across the Connecticut River from Turners Falls to Gill. Brian McCue was part of the Gill building crew, but also began work on his house in Montague Center.

The 2001 Center pioneered in its commitment to sustainable energy and technology, but after 1979, things went downhill quickly. By 1980, only the Noble Feast Restaurant and Renaissance Greeting Cards remained vital, and those associated with latter quit the community and moved the business to Maine. As more members pushed back against Rapunzel's authoritarian control and decisions such as bringing guns onto community property or inviting locals to hold drunken parties, the Renaissance community split, leaving Rapunzel with a core of devotees said to number around 70 adults and scores of children.

Still another battle in 1984—over control of a silk-screening business—further reduced membership. The end came in 1988, when remaining members expelled Rapunzel and bought him out for $10,000. Most of the properties became privately owned.

Ashes and Rebirth

Was it the end? Not really. Even as the community lurched toward dissolution, former members stayed in contact, held reunions, and discussed ways of revitalizing the Brotherhood's original spiritual ideals. Five members still lived together as late as 2007. Michael "Rapunzel" Metelica's 2003 cancer death softened resentment and piqued interest in his earlier ideals.

Montague Castle is testimony to the better angels of the Brotherhood of the Spirit. New Age spirituality is ubiquitous on McCue's property. McCue laughingly says, "I am the Renaissance Community these days," and that's only a slight exaggeration. Since 1997, he has hosted an annual "Renaissance Costume Ball" heavily populated by former community members. There's also a communal sauna on Sundays, open meditation on Saturdays, a well-used fire circle, a room with musical instruments left by others who drop by to perform, and 50,000 electric lights that illuminate the woods on summer nights.

McCue is never sure who will drop in to stay overnight or rent a room longer term, nor does he care. The house is quirky—filled with Buddhas, gemstones, mobiles, artwork, mystical symbols, scavenged bits of nature, and shards of glass. It's also true to both the DYI ethos of the community and its prescient environmentalism. A five-flue central chimney delivers heat with maximum impact at minimal cost and, as McCue puts its, "Only the shingles, copper, and roofing are new; everything else is used, recycled, or found." He's had helpers, but he has built or overseen every square inch of a rambling home that looks a bit like a Victorian plucked from the Summer of Love.

Is Montague Castle a marvel, a folly, or an eyesore? Town officials have thanked him for developing the property, an indication that locals no longer worry about unorthodox people in their midst. As for aesthetic judgments, McCue says people often pass by, gaze at the house, and say either, "That is so cool," or "What is *that*?" Either one is fine by him. Like me, McCue distrusts the word folly. "It's just a term people use for what they don't understand," he says.

Besides, he likes to maintain an air of mystery. His business card lists him as the owner and president of the Renaissance Painting Company, but he has another one for his creative consultancy work on which he's identified as "Brian the Wizard." Others conferred that title upon him, and he smiles coyly when asked if he means it in a Druidical sense: "I guess that one is on a need-to-know basis," says he.

When asked about Metelica, McCue just shook his head and said, "Ah, Michael." But it's hard not to notice that there's a round tower on the front of his house, a blond mannequin at the window, and long tresses hanging out the window. To which I say, until idealism is disproved, who's to say it's not real?

[1] The location of "Montague" confuses those who don't know the area. It is actually a cluster of five villages—Montague City, Montague Center, Millers Falls, Lake Pleasant, and Turners Falls—that collectively make up the Town of Montague. More than half of the town's 8,400 people live in Turners Falls.

19
Good for What Ails You (Even if Nothing Does): Goshen's Three Sisters Sanctuary

In the Middle Ages, those fleeing prosecution, enemies, or a troubled past could take refuge in a church or monastery and remain free from consequences or harm for as long as they remained on the grounds. The English word for this was modified from Old French: sanctuary.

Back then, sanctuaries were consecrated ground, thus not subject to earthly rules and customs. We still think of sanctuary as a place beyond convention, a space where everyone from wilderness lovers to hermits, fugitives, and undocumented immigrants can find succor. But these days we have also personalized sanctuary to include refuges where we can escape from ourselves, even if just for a short time. Yoga centers, nature preserves, writing retreats, art workshops, spas, and farm stays are among the places likely to use the word sanctuary in their names and mission statements. In other words, we view individual healing as a form of sanctuary.

The Making of an Artist

If something ails you, Goshen's Three Sisters Sanctuary and its magnificent gardens could certainly serve as a healing place, but you can be right as rain and go there simply because it is creative, quirky, tranquil, and unique. When I say unique, I mean it literally, not in the sloppy way marketers apply it. This is the sort of place where discoveries lie around each twist—some of them profound, some of them inspiring, and quite a few just flat-out fun.

The Three Sisters Sanctuary lies along Route 112, just beyond the center of Goshen. Its appearance from the highway intrigues, but gives a false impression. The first thing that catches the eye is the 16-foot-tall "Tin Man of Goshen," which suggests offbeat advertising akin to that of the Whately's giant milk bottle. (See chapter 4.) Indeed, the Good Time Stove Company resides in the weathered building to the Tin Man's left. But if you slow down, everything else you see—in the shop and in the adjacent gardens—will confound and amaze you. You could visit a hundred times and not exhaust its wonders.

Welcome to the artistic vision of Richard M. Richardson, who was born in New Jersey in 1948, but fled soulless suburbia for the Berkshires foothills town of Goshen in 1971. He's now so acclimated to tranquility that he gets edgy when he visits a "city" like Greenfield (17,456) or Northampton (28,483). Richardson now calls himself an "environmental artist," though he admits that he has no formal artistic training and that what you see is an ongoing journey sparked by joy, grief, healing, and experimentation.

The stove shop has been on site since 1973, but Richardson did not fashion the Tin Man; he traded for it. It probably dates from the 1950s and it fronts a crowded showroom of antique stoves in various states of restoration. Most of them date from the 19th century, including potbellies, log and box shapes, parlor designs, Franklins, and Victorian and country ranges. Richardson's middle daughter, Sara—jocularly nicknamed "the Stove Queen"— now manages the shop.

The building's contents are works of art in their own right, but the grounds and shop's exterior will definitely stop you in your tracks. It's what you might get if you threw some Amish folks, hippies, and random objects into a blender. There is an arbor and arch titled "Hermit's Last Ride" fabricated from bicycles left behind by a deceased Bernardston loner. The arch, various masks, birdhouses, smaller tin men, brightly painted metal decorative motifs, wooden tracery, old tools, plumbing parts, and assorted oddities suggest you have stumbled upon a folk art supply house.

Inspirational Gardens

Then you enter the gardens. Many religious traditions go to great lengths to express in physical form the passage from the "profane" (earthly) realm to the spiritual. You are supposed to experience a frisson when entering an ornate church, temple, mosque, or synagogue.

Richardson's gardens do this in elemental ways, and those elements hark back to Classical Greece, when the philosopher Empedocles (495–444 BCE) imagined that the universe consisted of earth, water, air, and fire. Both Aristotle and Hindus added ether, the void above the air. The Chinese also saw wood and metal as basic elements, but the common ideal is that nature and humankind are linked. A whole host of spiritual and philosophical traditions—including animism, Druidism, Shaktism, Shinto, Taoism, and Zen Buddhism—go so far as to say you can't find happiness or contentment unless you harmonize with nature.

Don't fret; you won't need to learn Sanskrit or read a philosophy book to enjoy Richardson's gardens. You pass through a portal adorned with whimsical flourishes, and enter a tranquil space of flowing water, graceful statuary, ornamental grasses, stone, and wood. The experience of moving from the droll folk art outside to the serene collaborations with nature beyond the barrier is analogous to going from a carnival funhouse into a church. The "Water Garden" sets the mood for what inspired it all.

Richardson insists, "I did not begin this garden; it began me." Its genesis came in conversations with his brother, who was terminally ill with cancer and died in December 1994. The first garden was a way for Richardson to honor his brother and work through grief. As it took shape in 1995, he moved from grief to joy and dubbed it the Three Sisters Sanctuary to honor his three daughters: Tina Marie, Sara Wenona, and Megan Elizabeth. He is quick to credit them for teaching him how to be creative and encouraging him to continue building. Nearby the "Water Garden" sits the "Tina Marie Sanctuary." She died of a brain aneurysm in 2004, and her ashes reside in a cairn topped with a small glass ball. It, too, is a place of contemplation and healing.

If all of this seems a bit too mystical, rest assured that plenty of offbeat treats lurk within the four-acre garden complex. The formality of the "Water Garden" and "Tina Marie Sanctuary" give way to other gardens, visions, and playfulness.

Some installations match the whimsy of the stove shed, but in different ways. There is, for example, the "Grounded Treehouse," a skeletal structure adorned with psychedelic female mannequins representing earth, fire, and water, and presumably each daughter is one

"Grounded Treehouse" detail

of these. Richardson jokes that he built in front of a tree rather than in it because he's afraid of heights. Or you might want to try your luck by spinning the "Wishing Wheels," spoked wagon wheels framed in panels.

Richardson also indulges in what is often called hardscaping, the use of stones to create functional spaces and/or art. There is what he has labeled the "Energy Garden" on the grounds. It sports a seven-foot stone ringed by smaller ones set at 45-degree angles and topped with crystals, as well as a tiered stone theater used for concerts, community events, weddings, and other occasions. In 2019, a labyrinth was completed—a standing stone composition of several large quartz pieces, some weighing over 22,000 pounds —bordered by smaller ones. It is the first of three planned entanglements Richardson calls "Dragon Labyrinth," and symbolizes the passage of life from conception to death.

If you prefer nature in a less scaped form, the gardens back up to a 3,700-acre protected wetland adorned with wildflowers, drowned trees, verdant vegetation, and passing wildlife. Blown-glass panels and sculptures edge the path and afford intriguing views. Nearby is a butterfly garden with statuary and plants that attract actual butterflies.

Embracing the Dragon

If you're like most folks, though, the *piece de résistance* is "Mosaic Fire Dragon," a singular delight that must be seen to be fully appreciated. Observe carefully, as the only complete photograph you'll snap is in your head; the angles, scale, and detail are beyond what a camera can capture in a single image. Steel, chicken wire, concrete, and a swirling line of stone, rock, and cement form the dragon's tail and body, which direct you toward an open fire pit under the dragon's raised head. A recent addition makes the dragon breathe fire.

As for the scales and details of the dragon's body, you name it and it's somewhere: shards of colored glass, ceramic tiles, cacti, tin cups, shells, tiny toys, metal links, recycled objects, even gnomes. Like the gardens, you could explore the dragon every day and discover something new. It fascinates, and you will be keenly aware that the whole thing would be a gigantic silly mess in the hands of someone lacking artistic sensibility.

Richardson modestly claims not to have any clear vision; he prefers to work in an organic way that prevents over-planning from getting in the way. When he and son Jamie LaBonte work with excavators to move large rocks, the stones are often relocated numerous times until the placement "feels right." After all, feeling is linked to healing whatever you're missing in life: a loved one, inspiration, creativity, emotional connections ….

You can stay at the sanctuary for various retreats, or just drop by to unwind. Each year, the grounds also spotlight other regional artists. Because the gardens are ever evolving, no two visits will yield the same experience. I'm not sure you could ever absorb all of the visual stimuli. But here's my best advice: If you're ever driving down Route 112 toward Ashfield, spy a 16-foot tin man, and speed by it, you need to turn around. His big red heart signals that he's offering sanctuary—and mirth.

20
Pouring Cold Water Over Alcoholism: Lee's WCTU Fountain

Drivers leaving the Massachusetts Turnpike at Exit 2 often pass straight through Lee via Route 20 (Housatonic/Main Streets). They should pull into the Town Park Village Green parking lot beside City Hall and visit Chief Konkapot. He is enshrined in marble and has water bubbling from his mouth into a trough.

Konkapot was a real person and was probably the primary chief (sachem) of the local Mohicans (aka/ Mahicans, from the Eastern Algonquin *Muh-he-con-ne-ok*, "people of flowing water.") Konkapot and another leader, Umpachenee, spearheaded a 1724 treaty that ceded much of modern-day Berkshire County to English settlers.

By then, the Mohicans were in decline and their culture on the cusp of change. Ten years later, Konkapot made another fateful decision; he asked local Mohicans to convert to Christianity and embrace English-style education as a way of surviving amidst white settlers. In 1738, Puritan missionaries led by the Reverend John Sergeant (1710–49) established a mission in nearby Stockbridge that converted so many Native Americans that they were known colloquially as "praying Indians." The Rev. Sergeant—whose meeting with Chief Konkapot was later depicted by Norman Rockwell—was said to have baptized Konkapot in 1735, several years before the mission opened.

But It's Not About Native Americans

If the lichen-stained Konkapot fountain fails to impress at first sight, look more carefully. It was carved by Daniel Chester French (1850–1931), who made his home in Stockbridge, from whence he produced such iconic pieces as the statue of Abraham Lincoln in the Lincoln Memorial and the Minute Man statue in Concord.

French's Lee fountain is humbler, but observe the graceful wiggling fish on the monument's reverse side, a metaphor for the Housatonic River that meanders through Lee. The fountain originally stood at the junction of Main and Railroad Streets, quite near where Route 20 crosses the river today.

The back of the fountain informs us that this fountain is not dedicated to Chief Konkapot. The inscription reads:

This Fountain Was Begun By The Loyal Temperance Legion
Under the Leadership of Amelia Jeanette Kilbon
And Was Completed By Other Friends
As a Tribute To Her Memory
1870 – 1897

Kilbon was a Lee native who graduated from the local high school in 1887. She attended Smith College and graduated in 1892, but seems to have been a quiet presence there. She graduated with C's in all of her subjects—the modern equivalent of a B average[1]— having taken more courses in art, rhetoric, and Greek than in other subjects.

Kilbon's obituary states that she was active in the Congregational Church and was an "ardent worker in all church societies and particularly organizations for the training of the young." The Loyal Temperance Legion (LTL) was an arm of the Women's Christian Temperance Union (WCTU), which developed temperance lessons for children, aged 6 through 12. Kilbon's death from consumption at age 26 shocked locals, who admired her piety and devotion.

Temperance as a Noble Experiment

Of all American social movements, attempts to curtail alcohol use are the most likely to be labeled "folly." Temperance is forever tied to America's failed attempt to legislate sobriety through a constitutional amendment: Prohibition, passed in 1919 and repealed by the 21st Amendment in 1933. So spectacular was its demise that, to this day, the 18th Amendment is invoked as "proof" that banning any vice is an

exercise in futility. Additional fallout lies with the fact that temperance gets conflated with prohibition, though the two are not necessarily the same thing.

Popular culture hasn't helped the public image of the temperance movement. Few have heard of Amelia Kilbon, but lots of people have seen caricature images of an axe-wielding Carry Nation (1846–1911) on her way to smash saloons. Or they've viewed 1933 photos depicting jubilant Americans hoisting legal glasses of booze after the repeal of the 18th Amendment.

Comics from vaudeville days to the present have gotten laughs at the expense of anti-alcohol advocates. Maybe you could do your own standup act in the Berkshires. All you need to know is that a "pot" (285 ml.) was once common parlance for an earthenware container that held just over a half pint of beer, and that "konk" is an alternative spelling of conk, as in "conked out" from over-indulgence.

Perhaps that's a stretch, but so is the popular perception of temperance, which was far more than the misguided attempt of busybodies to suck the life out of parties. Both temperance advocates and prohibitionists sought to curtail alcohol abuse, but the very word temperance suggests differences. Many temperance supporters used moral persuasion to convince tipplers to exercise self-control and moderate their alcohol intake. Not all approved of legislative actions seeking to ban all booze.

Second, though temperance advocates might have been overly optimistic about human nature, it is equally naïve to believe that the alcohol-drinking public was self-regulating. Temperance was an unsuccessful response to social problems caused by alcohol abuse, but many of its crusaders were like Kilbon—reformers on a noble mission. They also tried creative ways to get Americans to abandon booze.

This brings us back to the fountain in Lee. It provides insight into a forgotten phenomenon: the building of temperance fountains. The

WCTU and similar organizations once hoped that public fountains would banish alcoholism by converting Americans to the virtues of cold water. There were once hundreds of temperance fountains in the United States. At least 75 WCTU fountains survive, including seven in Western Massachusetts: Ayer, Conway, Hadley, Lee, Leominster, Orange (See p. 158), and Amherst, though the last is currently boarded over.

An Alcoholic Republic?

Temperance and prohibition advocates faced long odds. Historian W. J. Rorabaugh argued that the American fondness for alcohol was so deep that ours was an "alcoholic republic." Maybe you think of English settlers as dour and serious. Actually, our Colonial ancestors consumed copious amounts of beer, hard cider, and rum. The Puritans deplored drunkenness, but they drank weak beer—called "small beer"— throughout the day for a simple reason: as Eric Burns put it, water was "dangerously dirty."

Short of boiling, there was no sure-fire way of purifying water. Dirty water contributed to frequent outbreaks of cholera, dysentery, typhoid, and yellow fever. By virtue of being brewed or distilled, alcohol was far safer. No wonder the American Revolution was plotted in taverns!

Alcohol consumption remained high after independence. One of President George Washington's first crises was the Whiskey Rebellion, a revolt of Pennsylvania farmers upset about a tax on distilled alcohol that cut into their sale of grains. But Americans' taste for alcohol far exceeded the health benefits derived from boiling water. Workers drank on the job, soldiers got rum allotments, toasts marked every social occasion from christenings to funerals, school children were dosed with drops of whiskey, and beer, wine, cider, rum, and sherry flowed freely. By 1830, the per capita consumption of whiskey surpassed five gallons annually.

Attempts to Cork the Bottle

Alcohol always had detractors, including Founding Father Dr. Benjamin Rush (1746–1813), but the 19th century saw organized opposition to intoxicating beverages. The religious revivals of the Second (1790–1840) and Third (1850–1900) Great Awakenings sparked reform movements, including those seeking to address alcohol-related social problems. The American Temperance Society formed in Boston in 1826, and within 10 years secured more than 1.25 million abstinence pledges. Temperance was easily the largest social reform movement of pre-Civil-War America and was especially popular on college campuses. For example, a stunning 76 percent of all Amherst College students took temperance pledges between 1830 and 1861.

Reform efforts also led to discord. Anti-alcohol groups quarreled over whether drinking should be a matter of self-control (temperance) or government ban (prohibition). In addition to the millions of personal pledges, numerous states outlawed booze. Maine went dry in 1851, a full 68 years before the passage of the 18th Amendment. Massachusetts followed suit in 1852, and 13 states banished alcohol before the Civil War. Relaxation of those laws during and following the war had the ironic effect of revitalizing future temperance and prohibition agitation.

Evangelical women were very active in these movements, which is understandable, as they and their children were often the victims of alcohol-fueled abuses such as domestic violence and family income lost to the tavern from missed workdays and firings. A Women's Crusade against booze was declared in 1873, and the Women's Christian Temperance Union formed the next year.

The WCTU's broad reform agenda under the presidency (1879–1898) of Frances Willard made it an ever-present force in American society. The WCTU also pushed for woman's suffrage, labor reform, peace, public funding for kindergartens, Sabbath-keeping, and many other issues. By 1920, it had over 300,000 members.

Other temperance societies included the Knights of Father Mathew [sic], the United Society of Christian Endeavor, the YMCA, the YWCA, the Good Templars, and the Knights of Labor. The most successful of all was the Anti-Saloon League, whose lobbying arm prompted Congress to draft the 18th Amendment. In short, the movement to limit or ban alcohol consumption was a mass movement, not the domain of a few moralists, prudes, and fanatics. Prohibition's passage was initially greeted as an enlightened and progressive reform.

The Problem with the Cold-Water Movement

WCTU water fountains ended up as remnants of the shortsightedness of temperance reform. A spate of elaborate drinking fountains emerged after 1880, often built by temperance groups. San Francisco dentist Dr. Henry D. Cogswell designed and funded 51 across the nation, and the WCTU paid for hundreds more. Cogswell ran afoul of critics who found his fountains so garish that they were often vandalized. Artistic taste wasn't the real issue, though; cold water was not yet a reliably safe drink. The earliest fountains featured a chained community cup for those wishing to quench their thirst. These, of course, made fountains small germ factories far more medically dangerous than alcohol. MIT professor William Sedgwick launched a national "ban the cup" movement and, between 1909 and 1912, most states did away with them. Paper cups appeared in some places after 1907, but led to litter problems.

An early water-jet spigot appeared in 1900, but it wasn't until 1920 that the design of slanted "Benson bubblers" lessened the likelihood of disease transmission. Even then, safety was assured only if the water was treated. No American city chlorinated water until Jersey City did so in 1902, there were no federal regulations for drinking water until 1914, and human waste wasn't widely treated until after World War II.

Today, WCTU fountains are curiosity items for some, a testimony to waylaid idealism for others, and monuments to folly for the less charitable. Still, Amelia Kilbon thought she was acting nobly when she campaigned for a fountain in Lee, and her early death saddened the community.

The next time you're there, honor her by paying Chief Konkapot a visit. Reflect upon the area's Native American history and muse on the temperance movement. Should you happen upon a water bubbler to quench your thirst, thank Ms. Kilbon. She and the WCTU were ahead of their time, but they are a major reason why you're seldom distant from a cold sip of water.

1 Oddly, back then the Smith College grading scale was nearly a reverse of that of today. The highest mark one could receive was a D and the lowest an A.

21
The Peace Memorial of Orange: All We Are Saying, Is Give Peace a Chance

The official state peace statue is in Orange. You didn't know Massachusetts had such a memorial? You're in good company.

Western Massachusetts is home both to two military bases—see chapter 8—and it's a seedbed for antiwar activism. That might not be as contradictory as it sounds. We can debate whether a particular war is necessary, but few would argue that armed struggle is a good thing. I've yet to speak with a war-tested veteran who thinks bloodshed is preferable to peace.

A Current Sense of Loss

Maybe you don't know about the Massachusetts peace memorial because you've never been to Orange, a town of 7,606 people located near Route 2. The word "near" is important. Route 2 is an east-west artery connecting Cambridge with Williamstown, but those towns west of Concord—the "Northern Tier"—are often far less prosperous than the rest of the Commonwealth. Route 2 is partly to blame. It was constructed *near* Franklin County towns between 1957 and 1960, but it often bypassed town centers such as that of Orange.

Deindustrialization came early to the Northern Tier. It began during the Great Depression of the 1930s, and was hastened by post-World-War-II developments such as robotics, global trade, aging factories, and changing consumer tastes. There is, however, no doubt that the decline of railroads—coupled with the decision to build Route 2 away from, rather than through, most of the towns west of Concord—isolated many Northern Tier communities.

Orange is one of them. This Millers River community was once a humming industrial center that produced everything from mechanical pencils and Minute Tapioca to dam-flow gates and New Home sewing machines. Now it struggles with job loss, median family incomes considerably below the state average, and poverty rates more than 25 percent higher.

Does this make Orange an odd location for the Commonwealth's official peace statue? I don't think so.

A Past Sense of Loss

In 1934, Orange residents had a different kind of loss on their minds. Thirteen locals died in "The Great War," now known as World War I. In that year, the town honored its dead by unveiling a 10-foot bronze statue rendered by Joseph Pollia (1894–1954).[1] It shows a returning war veteran engaged in earnest conversation with a schoolboy, though his message is not about duty, honor, or sacrifice. The monument also bears a shrouded figure bearing the poignant decree: "It Shall Not Be Again." There are also 13 stars on the monument, one for each local who perished in the war.

In his day, the Sicilian-born, Boston-based Pollia was one of America's best-known designers of public memorial art. He produced numerous Spanish-American War monuments—including one in nearby Greenfield—as well as those honoring Civil War figures. A contemporary of Henry Hudson Kitson—see Chapter 17—

and Augustus St. Gaudens, he followed in their footsteps by producing monuments that glorified war heroes. His most famous work is of Confederate hero Thomas "Stonewall" Jackson that, despite recent protests, can still be found at the Manassas National Battlefield in Virginia.[2]

Pollia's statue in Orange is glum, because World War I was not a popular conflict. When bloodshed broke out in Europe in 1914, most Americans viewed it as just another European war. Woodrow Wilson campaigned under the slogan "He Kept Us Out of War" in his successful 1916 presidential reelection campaign against Republican challenger Charles Evan Hughes. Nonetheless, on April 2, 1917—just five months later—Wilson asked Congress to declare war against Germany. The president proclaimed, "The world must be made safe for democracy," and pledged that the United States would dedicate itself to human rights, not the pursuit of vengeance or material gain.[3]

Initial skepticism ran so high, however, that the administration set up the Creel Committee, a propaganda agency, to sell the war to a wary public. Congress enacted the Espionage Act of 1917 and the Sedition Act of 1918 to stifle dissent. Antiwar protestors and conscientious objectors were roughly treated; nonetheless nearly three million never registered and 338,000 draftees refused induction. Another 64,693 men filed for conscientious objector status despite the animus against them, and untold thousands simply disappeared into the American countryside.[4]

U.S. entry in the war lasted just 18 months, but 116,516 Americans lost their lives and another 204,000 were wounded. Wilson's idealism was dealt a rude blow; not much good came of the war. A communist revolution transformed Russia, and the Versailles Peace Conference was a disaster. Victorious European powers rejected most of President Wilson's peace initiatives and a disgusted U.S. Senate refused to ratify U.S. participation in the League of Nations, the centerpiece of Wilson's hopes.[5]

In 1918–19, an influenza epidemic brought by returning vets killed 675,000 Americans, including at least 45,000 in Massachusetts. At its height, 100 soldiers per day perished at Fort Devens, located just 41 miles east of Orange. A domestic "Red Scare" bloodied American civil liberties during indiscriminate crackdowns against radicals, labor unionists, reformers, and suffragists.

By 1920, the consensus view was that U.S. involvement in the Great War had been a terrible mistake. Quite a few Americans would have nodded in agreement with Pollia's "It Shall Not Be Again" sentiment. American isolationist views remained strong until fascism's rise and the 1941 bombing of Pearl Harbor.

A Movement Gathers

The Orange monument wasn't declared the Commonwealth's official peace statue until 2000, 66 years after it was erected.[6] This means, of course, that its status had much to do with grassroots lobbying and politics. But it's too pat to think of the Orange memorial as the by-product of countercultural refugees from the 1960s, even though Western Mass was indeed a hotbed of antimilitarism and draft resistance during the Vietnam War.

The litany of post-World War II American military conflict is distressingly long: Korea, Vietnam, the two Gulf Wars, Afghanistan, and smaller military engagements in the Dominican Republic, Grenada, Haiti, Kosovo, Lebanon, Libya, Somalia, and the ongoing war on terrorism. Since World War II, more than 100,000 Americans have died in overseas wars, nearly as many as perished in World War I, the conflict that inspired Pollia's statue.

Perhaps you think the quest to end war is quixotic, but akin to the temperance movement—see chapter 20—most of those who devote themselves to peace movements view themselves as part of a noble cause. The very outbreak of war portends a breakdown in policymaking, and the cost of this is steep. It bears repeating that few combat vets glorify war; they know it's the young who pay the price in blood.

Maybe there isn't a contradiction between Western Mass military outposts and antiwar groups. After all, most peace organizations now work with veterans' groups. There are quite a few peace groups in Western Mass. Since 1978, activists at the Traprock Center for Peace and Justice in Deerfield have worked to advance the cause of preventing war specifically and, more generally, promoting nonviolent conflict resolution. So too have those affiliated with the American Friends Service Committee in Springfield and Northampton, the Berkshire Citizens for Peace and Justice in Pittsfield, and the Center for Peace through Culture in Great Barrington.[7]

Traditionally pacifist religious groups such as the Quakers and Unitarian Universalists (UU) proliferate in Western Mass, and there are various Jewish, Catholic, and interfaith organizations devoted to peace work, not to mention non-Western religious groups such the Zen Peacemaker Circle of Western Massachusetts.

The Zen Peacemaker Circle adds an ironic footnote to the Orange peace statue. If you conducted a public quiz and asked people to name the Commonwealth's official peace monument, many would cite the Peace Pagoda in Leverett. That's a good guess, but that stunning structure is actually the *New England* Peace Pagoda. It stands on the grounds of a community of Nipponzan Myōhōji Buddhist monks that have made Leverett their center since 1985.[8]

Nichidatsu Fujii (1885–1995) founded this offshoot of 13th-century Japanese Buddhism in 1917. He was a contemporary of Mahatma

Gandhi, who guided him toward pacifism. Nipponzan Myōhōji Buddhists have been building peace pagodas since 1947 as part of their response to tragedies such as the Holocaust and the atomic bomb destruction of Hiroshima and Nagasaki. They echo the plea in Orange, "It Shall Not Be Again."

1 The statue itself is five feet two inches in height, but it sits on a base that is nearly five feet tall.

2 The Stonewall Jackson monument was defaced in 2017, during backlash against Confederate monuments.

3 Contrary to popular legend, Wilson did not promise the conflict would be "the war to end all war," a phrase that actually comes from a 1914 H. G. Wells essay.

4 Of the 64,693 conscientious objector applications, 56,830 were granted. The Army imprisoned 500 individuals and court-martialed 540 men, some of whom received lengthy prison sentences. There are Western Mass legends of young men hiding in caves when recruiters came to their villages.

5 The League of Nations was a representative international body that sought to resolve conflicts without war and promote cooperative global projects. It is now viewed as a forerunner of the United Nations, which was formed after World War II.

6 The statue in Orange was informally recognized as a peace memorial years before, but it awaited enabling legislation before it was designated as the Commonwealth's official peace monument.

7 Don't be surprised if you look for one of these groups and find it exists under a different name. The ones listed are accurate as of this writing, but organizations often merge and change their names when they do so.

8 The peace pagoda in Leverett was the first one Nipponzan Myōhōji Buddhists built in the United States. Since then, new ones have arisen in San Francisco, Grafton, New York, and Newport, Tennessee.

Section V

Sports

When it comes to sports, Western Mass residents tend to be participants rather than spectators. That's partly because the region's largest city, Springfield, has just over 154,000 people, which is on the small side even for minor league professional sports.

The city does have an American Hockey League franchise, the Springfield Thunderbirds, and (until recently) the Springfield Sting, a semi-pro team in the American Basketball Association, but no other town or city fields a professional team in any of the major sports (baseball, basketball, football, ice hockey, and soccer). There has been talk of bringing minor league baseball to Springfield, though talks have bogged down over where a stadium would be built and who would pay for it. Besides, with the Eastern League Hartford Yard Goats playing in a sparkling new stadium just 30 minutes away, and a contraction of minor league baseball, a Springfield franchise seems unlikely.

It's pretty easy, though, to find diehard Patriots, Red Sox, Celtics, and Bruins fans in Western Mass. This makes for a strange disconnect, as many folks who root hard for those teams often like little else about Boston. As noted in this book's introduction, Boston is often viewed as a sponge that siphons Western Mass tax dollars into Boston boondoggles such as the "Big Dig," a massive-cost-overrun project that was supposed to cost $2.8 billion, but whose actual tab was closer to $15 billion. A lot of local repairs were put on hold to pay for that! So Western Mass has a strange breed of cat: the Patriots Superfan bedecked in NFL gear on Sunday who cusses up a storm about all things Boston on Monday!

But, like I said, we tend to play more than pay. In the summer, there are tons of summer softball and baseball leagues, from Little League and Babe Ruth Leagues to recreational teams at all levels. We are particularly fond of mixed-gender softball teams. There are summer sports camps galore, and the rivers, lakes, and mountains are filled with enthusiasts ranging from recreational canoeists and kayakers to daredevil white-water rafters, and casual hikers to steel-nerved climbers of Great Barrington's Monument Mountain.

Fall is the season for cross-country competitions and basketball leagues, but the region also fosters an inordinate number of rugby teams whose unofficial motto is: The worse the weather and the muddier the playing field, the better. Autumn is also football season, but the sport's profile is lower here than most parts of the country. High school matches often feel like throwbacks to the 1950s, not the big-time hype of the NFL, televised college football, or even high school matches in states such as Texas or Ohio. Out this way, games draw in the hundreds (or fewer), not in the thousands.

As of 2021, UMass is in year eight of its attempt to upgrade its program to Division I Football Bowl Subdivision status and thus far, the results are so mixed that many people think it's an act of folly to imagine UMass as a big-time gridiron power. Its teams struggle to break five digits for home attendance, and you'd have to go back to 1972 to find a time when 20,000 people attended a game in Amherst. In truth, the real "big game" in Western Mass is between Amherst and Williams. The two colleges compete with each other in just about everything, including recruiting top students. In 2021, *US News & World Report* ranked Williams the number-one liberal arts college in the nation; Amherst was number two. Football clashes between the two archrivals can make the Hatfields and McCoys look like a lovefest.

New England has lots of winter, and folks in Western Mass take advantage of it: cross-country and downhill skiing, snowshoeing, snowmobiling, and skating as singular pursuits; basketball, ice hockey, and ski teams for the organized set. Lots of high schools have hockey programs and those puck wizards are often the most popular kids in the school, not the gridiron players.

Spring brings a few things that are particular to New England. Lacrosse is played in other regions too, but it originated among the Iroquois and caught on in the Northeast before 1900, where it remains a passion. UMass lacrosse matches routinely draw enthusiastic fans, while the stands are empty for home baseball games. There is also street hockey, which is usually played in a boarded outdoor rink with players wearing in-line skates or scurrying about on foot in a form akin to floorball. Track and field, baseball, volleyball, and tennis can be found at most schools.

But instead of writing more about the ordinary, I will take a look at four things that tell a tale or are unusual in the region. How about if we look at big baseball bats, sun-drenched ballparks, candlepin bowling, and curling?

22
Not Entirely Red Sox Nation

It sits just northwest of the center of Williamsburg on Route 9—an eight-foot-tall wooden baseball bat. The Williamsburg thumper is alongside a driveway, and was placed there by homeowner Russell Richardson to display his lifelong team loyalty to the New York Yankees.[1] That's *right*, a Yankees fan in the heart of Red Sox Nation. Massachusetts mythology notwithstanding, he's not the only one.

Boston vs. Western Mass

As noted in this section's introduction, folks in Western Massachusetts hold what can politely be called an ambivalent attitude toward all things Bostonian. Sometimes rooting for Boston sports teams is the *only* thing about the city that induces fondness. Most of Western Mass is at least two hours from Boston, and many folks in Western Mass have a bee in their bonnet about Boston because political power is largely monopolized within the metropolitan area located east of I-95/Route 128.

Boston is the state capital, and you can't go too much further east without dipping your toes in salt water or battling traffic headed for Cape Cod. Sometimes the psychic distance between Eastern and Western Massachusetts is far greater than what's posted on official road signs. Many Western Mass folks feel as if they're an afterthought at best, or perceived as bumpkins at worst. They are not entirely wrong. In 1858, Oliver Wendell Holmes called the Massachusetts State House dome, "The Hub of the Solar System," and residents of The Hub—one of Boston's nicknames—can be pretty smug at times. I have a few Boston-based friends and colleagues whom I chide for treating an outing to Western Mass as if they've just signed up for a farm stay.

There's history behind why Boston dominates the Commonwealth that goes deeper than its larger population. Eastern Mass was where 17th-century Pilgrims and Puritans first settled. Those who ventured into the Connecticut River Valley and the Berkshires were true pioneers; they relocated far from European centers of power, commerce, and ports such as Boston, Salem, or New Haven.

Massachusetts was one of the few states that kept its capital on the seaboard instead of moving it to a more central location that would give politicians a broader view of the states they pledged to serve. It's intriguing to imagine how Bay State politics would have played out if the capital had moved to Worcester or Springfield, instead of rooting itself in architect Charles Bullfinch's Beacon Hill edifice (built in 1798). Western Mass residents push back with snippiness and pique when they feel slighted. If one had to identify the most popular *unofficial* sport in Western Mass, complaining about Boston would be a contender. To hear locals tell it, Boston is a reverse Robin Hood that takes from the poor (Western Mass) to fund inside-Route-128 development, subsidize Boston's subway system, pay for its roads, and maintain an old-boys network of machine politicians, philanderers, and panderers. Any unfilled pothole or delayed construction project in Western Mass can produce a diatribe against the Beast to the East.

Like a lot of New Englanders, those in Western Mass can work themselves into a righteous lather, the facts be damned. It's inevitable the lion's share of revenue will end up in Boston; after all, 4.7 million of the state's 6.83 million people reside in Greater Boston. The moral of this digression is that it's hardly a surprise that some folks in Western Mass root for the Yankees; it's only noteworthy that more don't do so out of spite!

Let's go back to geography. Boston isn't necessarily the closest metropolis, nor is it the Big Apple of everyone's eye. Quite a few professors in the Five Colleges area of Northampton/Amherst maintain an apartment in New York City; only a few have one in Boston or Cambridge. If you live in the Berkshires, radio and network TV broadcasts usually come from Albany, New York.

Sports fandom also divides geographically. Like the famed Mason-Dixon Line to the south, demarcation lines are easily exaggerated. Still, Steve Rushin of *Sports Illustrated* places the fan line dividing New York and Boston rooters in the middle of Connecticut; that is, you find more Yankees (or Mets) fans to the south of that line and more Sox fans to the north, though allegedly both Hartford and New Haven contain more Yankees fans. Western Mass is located on the porous edge of this perceptual border.

Institutions such as UMass Amherst give further insight into divided loyalties. Of the roughly 23,500 undergraduate students on the Amherst campus, nearly a quarter hail from outside the Commonwealth. UMass also has more than 7,000 graduate students, just 40 percent of whom are Massachusetts residents. In each case, the Mid-Atlantic states, which include New York, make up about 20 percent of the student body.

The same split profile exists among the 1,700 plus students at the Massachusetts College of Liberal Arts in North Adams. It's even more profound elsewhere. Basketball was invented at Springfield College, and many of its 5,300 students major in physical education or sports studies; 72 percent of the student body hails from out of state. Colleges such as Amherst, Williams, Mount Holyoke, and Smith pride themselves on drawing students from across the nation and abroad. I've seen the applications for several of these schools, and rooting for the Red Sox is not an entrance requirement.

The Myth of Red Sox Nation

The term "Red Sox Nation" gets used as if it's a real thing. It's actually little more than a catchy throwaway line. *Boston Globe* writer Nathan Cobb coined the phrase in 1986, when it looked as if the Red Sox were about to break a 68-year World Series drought. Instead, an easily fielded groundball slipped under first baseman Bill Buckner's glove, the New York Mets won game six, and took the Series in game seven.

Prior to 1967—another almost-but-not-quite World Series frustration—not that many New Englanders would have thought of themselves as belonging to Red Sox Nation. Rooting for the Sox was an exercise in futility akin to hauling water with a teaspoon. In the pre-1967 days, scoring a ticket at Fenway Park could be done at the game-day ticket window. The Red Sox were perennial sad sacks who had only been to the World Series once (1946) since 1918. What some called the "Curse of the Bambino"[2] wasn't totally exorcised until 2004, when Boston won its first World Series in 86 years.

Red Sox Nation was and is a fiction that reflects the team's recent successes. As Rushin's data clearly show, there is no such thing as either a Red Sox or Yankees Nation; most fan loyalties are profoundly regional. Things do, however, get interesting along the borders between competing loyalties. The intersections of Western Mass with Northern Connecticut or Eastern New York are such places, but so too are the thin lines separating Dodgers fans from those of the Giants, or those where Astros and Rangers fans meet. The line dividing Cubs and Cardinal fans fuels passions every bit as intense as the Yankees/Red Sox split. I grew up in South-Central Pennsylvania, where fans were pretty equally divided among those rooting for the Philadelphia Phillies, Pittsburgh Pirates, and Baltimore Orioles. There were even diehard Washington Senators fans that *really* wallowed in futility, but I never met a Red Sox fan that far south.

Rabid (But Mostly Harmless) Fans

Put all these factors together, and the Yankees bat in Williamsburg makes sense. It also symbolizes the rabidity of sports fandom in Western Mass and stamps the region with part of its unique character.

Spend time in Western Mass and you'll learn that its residents have strong opinions about everything, including what they think of Boston, how much they like or loathe the Red Sox, and what snotty Boston writers can do with their perceptions of Western Mass. There's history, geography, and demographics associated with all of this that should be taken seriously, but not *too* seriously. Much of the outward rancor is simply passion and hot air that is the stuff of legendary pub debates and (mostly) good-natured arguments among sports fans and self-proclaimed political experts. I guess that makes debate the second most popular unofficial sport.

If longtime Red Sox and Yankees followers agree on anything, neither cares much for fair-weather fans who change loyalties when they move elsewhere, or jump onto or off the bandwagon depending upon how a team is doing in a given year. Fans are valued; fad-followers are scorned. Ask serious Red Sox devotees what they think of team mascot Wally the Green Monster or pink ball caps. Stand in the middle of the room when you pose the questions, lest you get burnt from blistering paint flying off the walls from the reply.

In similar fashion, folks like Russell Richardson are in for the long run. They are the kind of Yankees fan that can discourse on Don Larsen or Mickey Mantle as easily as a grizzled Sox follower can conjure up Ted Williams or Johnny Pesky.

If you can cool your own passions, take a quick look at the Williamsburg bat because it's a nice piece of folk art. It was fashioned from an aged 100-foot hickory tree that had to come down. The Yankees logo is on the barrel, and the bat's knob is adorned with a stitch-patterned baseball. The work represents 13 hours of carving by

Royalston's Sue O'Sullivan of Renaissance Girl Artwork. If you can't appreciate the irony of a woman with an Irish surname tackling a project that pays homage to a New York baseball team whose nickname is Dutch in origin, you need to work on your skills!

1 Full confession: I too am a Yankees fan. As noted, though, I was born in Pennsylvania, where few rooted for either the Yankees or Red Sox. I inherited my Yankees fandom from my Worcester-raised father, who idolized Joe DiMaggio. (The Weirs are Scottish, but my father's neighborhood was heavily Italian.) My boyhood idol was Mickey Mantle.

2 The "Curse of the Bambino" is the belief that the long misfortunes of the Red Sox resulted from their sale of Babe Ruth to the New York Yankees in 1919. It is a colorful piece of folklore embellished by sportswriters such as Leigh Montville, and passed into popular parlance by Dan Shaughnessy in a 1990 book. Many of the details cited by each are factually incorrect.

23
Wahconah Park: Pittsfield's Field of Dreams

In the previous chapter, we encountered a large baseball bat. Now let's talk *really* large. The first thing that greets a visitor to Pittsfield's Wahconah Park is a 27-foot-long baseball bat sitting in front of an odd rock-and-shrubbery grove. You don't want to touch the bat on a hot day; its rust-colored barrel is made of steel and heats quickly in the sun. The spiky shrubs behind the bat are supposed to suggest a catcher's mitt and the slab assemblage a ball. That doesn't quite work for me, but maybe your imagination is sharper than mine. The installation is the brainchild of landscape designer Jerid Hohn and has been around since 2006.[1]

Pittsfield and the National Pastime

A lot of people associate Cooperstown, New York, with early baseball. They shouldn't. First of all, the story of Abner Doubleday inventing baseball in 1839 is a tall tale that would make Pinocchio's nose snap off. Second, even if it were true, Doubleday would be a Johnny-come-late-

ly compared to what we know to be true about Pittsfield. A 1791 document discovered in the city contains the earliest known specific reference to "Baseball" and lists it separately from other ball-and-bat games often cited as possible parents: cricket, cat², wicket,

and fives. That document is actually a "ByeLaw [sic] for the Preservation of the Windows in the New Meeting House." It forbade all "Games with Balls" from being played within 80 yards of the building. The very existence of such an ordinance suggests that ball games were common, and that broken glass was a known hazard.

Whether Pittsfield is the original birthplace of baseball is debatable, but one thing is clear: the city has a deep and time-tested connection to watching America's pastime. The real attraction on Wahconah Street isn't the oversized steel baseball bat—though it's certainly an eye-catching addition—it's Wahconah Park itself, a place writer/editor Daniel Okrent called "baseball as it oughta be." He wrote:

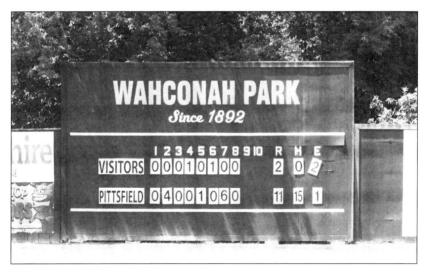

> Imagine this: you're in an old wooden ballpark where the action is so near … you can sometimes hear the batter talking to the umpire. If someone tries to start a wave, the fans in the next section generally have the taste to let it die. The players exert themselves ceaselessly, sprinting toward first on every routine pop-up, chasing every impossible foul fly. After the game, the players linger behind the dugout and greet kids … with autographs and pats on the head.

Okrent's words, written in 1990, capture the essence of the barn that is Wahconah Park. It is indeed an ancient facility. Think Fenway Park is the oldest baseball playing field in Massachusetts? Think again. There has been a baseball field on the Wahconah Park site since 1892, though the current grandstand is a relative infant, having opened only in 1919. It remains one of the last wooden grandstand parks in the United States.

Wooden stands are a holdover from professional baseball's 19th-century origins. Few remain for the simple reason that they had a distressing tendency to catch fire and burn to the ground. When Philadelphia's Shibe Park opened in 1909, its steel-and-concrete construction was hailed as a public safety breakthrough. Consider also that when Wahconah Park's new *wooden* grandstand opened, the concrete-and-steel Fenway Park was just seven years old and Chicago's Wrigley Field was celebrating its fifth birthday.

There simply aren't that many wooden throwbacks like Wahconah still around. Birmingham, Alabama's Rickwood Field, built in 1910, is said to be the oldest such facility in continuous *professional* use, though that claim is a bit of a stretch given that the Birmingham Black Barons moved out of the facility in 1987. Rickwood Field is now administered as a museum, and the Barons play just one game per year there. Insofar as heavy-duty use goes, Daytona Beach's Jackie Robinson Ballpark, which opened in 1914, could make a case for wearing the greybeard crown.

No matter. Just a few baseball parks of any sort predate the "new" Wahconah Park: Fenway, Wrigley, Rickwood, Jackie Robinson Ballpark, Burlington, Vermont's Centennial Field (1906), and Bisbee, Arizona's Warren Ballpark (1909), the last two of which are also concrete-and-steel structures like Fenway and Wrigley. Small wonder that Wahconah Park was placed on the National Register of Historic Places in Berkshire County in 2005.

Wahconah Park has hosted minor league baseball at every level except AAA, plus independent and amateur leagues. Since 1963, minor league baseball has used a classification system of: (top to low) AAA, AA, A (Advanced), A (Full-Season), A (Short Season[3]), and A (Rookie). Wahconah Park's glory days were its two stints in the AA Eastern League 1919–30 (then labeled A ball), and again from 1965 through 1988.

During the 1965–69 seasons, Wahconah hosted the Pittsfield Red Sox, and rabid Massachusetts fans got to see future Red Sox major leaguers such as Carlton Fisk, Sparky Lyle, Bill Lee, Billy Conigliaro, George Scott, and Reggie Smith. In all, more than 200 future major leaguers passed through Pittsfield on their way up. That list includes Joe Girardi, Mark Grace, Jamie Moyer, Rafael Palmeiro, and Hall of Fame member Greg Maddux.

Since 2002, Wahconah Park has played host to independent and collegiate leagues. Collegiate leagues are technically amateur baseball, as the players are unpaid, but they are akin in quality to minor league baseball's low-level A teams. The New England Collegiate Baseball League—in which Pittsfield had a franchise from 2005 through 2009—has produced dozens of major leaguers, and the older Cape Cod Baseball League even more. Since 2012, the Pittsfield Suns have been part of the Futures Collegiate Baseball League, which was formed in 2010.

The Suns is an appropriate name. Wahconah's dimensions are fairly commonplace—334 feet to the left-field line, 374 feet to center, and 333 feet to right—but it is one of the few parks oriented with home plate facing west, a remnant from a time when baseball was played during the daytime. Wahconah has had lights since 1946, but some day games are delayed because of sun glare. Netting in center field cuts the glare a bit, but depending on the calendar, some games simply stop until the angle of the rays permits batters to see the pitches again.

Wahconah Park is indeed a place where baseball turns back time. A pop foul behind home plate thunks off the roof, and the wooden grandstands invite languid viewing. There's also the corniness of lower-level baseball, including the gimmick of settling games tied after 10 innings with a home-run derby. But there are also the fresh, young faces of the players, many of them using wooden bats for the first time.[4] Metal is reserved for the sculpture garden in the parking lot.

[1] Hohn's sculpture originally stood in front of Pittsfield High School, but proved unpopular among students and was moved to Wahconah Park in 2008.

[2] Few people know the sport called cat, which is short for cat and dog, and is also called tip-cat, one-cat, pussy, and piggy. The basic idea is that a piece of wood called the "cat" is tossed into the air and a hitter with a tapered stick (the "dog") tries to hit in to prevent the cat from dropping into a hole or circle.

[3] In 2021, minor league baseball short season leagues were eliminated.

[4] Most high schools and colleges use metal bats. These save money, but are controversial as balls come off the bat at higher speeds, a potentially dangerous situation for pitchers standing just 60 feet six inches from the batter. Professional leagues use wooden bats, which is a greater transition than you might imagine for someone who has never used one.

24
Right Up Your Alley in Shelburne Falls

Shelburne Falls is a charming village on the Mohawk Trail just off Route 2. Most visitors rush to the Bridge of Flowers, a former trolley bridge across the Deerfield River that's now covered with colorful plantings that bloom from spring through autumn. Unhurried travelers then walk a few hundred yards to the foot of a power dam, where Ice Age glacial potholes reveal clues to the region's geological past. Those who linger shop in artisan galleries, grab a meal or a locally roasted coffee, and check out an open-air museum of old trolleys in Buckland on the other side of the river.

Roll with the Past

Few realize that a short stroll down a narrow walkway from Bridge Street reveals one of Shelburne Falls' most unique offerings: a bowling alley. If "so what?" was your first reaction, roll with me for a moment.

Contemplating how the "perfect ball" knocked down only four pins.

Humans have been tossing round objects down roads, across lawns, and through open spaces for much of recorded time; even the ancient Egyptians tried to knock down pins. Still, the unpretentious building with the wooden alleys in Shelburne Falls is, officially, the third-oldest bowling alley in the United States. Unofficially, it's the second oldest, as one pretender, Milwaukee's Holler House, opened in 1908, two years after the Shelburne Falls Bowling Alley (SFBA). Evidence suggests that only the Putnam Street lanes in Fitchburg, Massachusetts, which debuted in 1890, have been operating longer than the SFBA.

An enterprising man named C. W. Ward is responsible for the SFBA, which opened the first week of January in 1906. At the time, it was part of an amusement complex that also featured a garden, an arcade, a pavilion overlooking the river, and space for dances, concerts, and vaudeville events.

From the outset, the bowling alley held special "ladies' day" (and night) events, an idea still in its youth as far as sports were concerned. Historians generally credit major league baseball with popularizing ladies' day promotions, the idea being that the presence of women at sporting venues would bring middle-class respectability to the facility and weed out unsavory elements such as gamblers, drinkers, and rowdies. If that was Ward's idea, he picked the wrong sport. Bowling has historically attracted a working-class crowd less concerned with social niceties than with rolling the perfect ball and having a cold beer or two.

Check Your Seriousness at the Shoe Rack

Competition bowling takes place at the SFBA, but let's not confuse it with anything you might recall from last century's golden age of 10-pin bowling, or Professional Bowling Association heroes such as Earl Anthony, Dick Weber, and Don Carter. Carter was the first professional athlete to sign a million-dollar contract.[1]

Another thing that's special about bowling in Shelburne Falls is that it's a candlepin alley. Aside from a handful of professionals, most people who have tried it will tell you that candlepin kegling[2] encourages more snickers than seriousness. And you certainly won't find any Don Carter-like high rollers on the candlepin lanes.

Candlepin bowling is seldom experienced outside of New England and eastern Canada. Unlike its 10-pin cousin, luck often trumps skill in determining results. Even if you're a professional or league bowler, humility will win out in the end. As in 10-pin bowling, a perfect score is achieved by rolling 12 consecutive strikes, a feat no candlepin kegler ever has accomplished! The highest recorded score is 245, and that's only been done twice: by Ralph Semb of Erving in 1984, and by Chris Sargent of Haverhill in 2011. Professional candlepin bowlers generally average a much humbler 120–40.[3] My first trip to Shelburne Falls yielded a 107, total beginner's luck, as I've not gotten close to such a score since. Hackers like me can expect to roll in the 70s or 80s.

No wonder candlepin has rules that deviate from 10-pin bowling. The goal is the same: to knock down as many pins as possible. In candlepin, though, you get three balls to do so instead of two, and pins aren't cleared after each roll; dead wood stays in play. Strikes and spares are scored conventionally, but there's also a "10-box" if you clear the alley with your third ball.

Like most games, there is colorful lingo for specialists, but all you really need to enjoy the game is the ability to count and a sense of humor. An outing with friends soon brings gales of laughter when someone rolls a seemingly perfect ball that chops straight through the middle of the pack yet knocks down only two pins.

The pins are 15¾ inches high, cylindrically shaped, weigh 40 ounces each, and taper slightly at each end. This makes the pins more than a pound lighter than those in 10-pin bowling, and their shape makes them elusive prey. The 60 feet between the foul line and the pins is perfectly flat and the weapon in your hand is a 4.5-inch ball (without finger holes) that can weigh no more than the pins. The less said about how the pins are spaced, the better. Everything about candlepin bowling conspires against perfection.

Such devilish design invites speculation that Old Nick himself invented the game. The actual credit goes to Justin P. White, Jack Monsey, and Jack Sheafe of Worcester, though what exactly they were thinking back in 1890—some sources say 1885—is lost to history. White's name also surfaces in association with the development of duckpin bowling, but that's probably an apocryphal tale based on the fact that it, too, is an unforgiving game in which no one has yet rolled a perfect score.

Elusive mastery might explain why candlepins and duckpins have never shared the same bright spotlight as 10-pin bowling. The first TV broadcast occurred in 1958, and candlepin's popularity heyday was in the 1970s, but even then it was a poor cousin to the 10-pin stars associated with the Professional Bowlers Association. Interest has waned even for the once-mighty PBA, but candlepin has fallen into the proverbial gutter by comparison.

There has been no regular TV coverage of candlepin bowling since 2006, though the sport does have a YouTube channel. In 2017, Chris Sargent—whose three-game total of 530 is the highest ever recorded—complained that PBA bowlers can achieve stardom and earn millions in their careers, but candlepin professionals such as himself are unknowns who pay $100 entrance fees for a chance at winning $500.

Reports to the contrary, bowling is hardly a dead sport. Roughly 70 million people try their luck each year at one of the more than 3,500 bowling centers across the country. If we consider all sports with a competitive element, only weightlifting, running, swimming, basketball, cycling, and golf claim more participants than bowling.

New Englanders should appreciate their uniqueness—of all the bowling complexes, just 210 are devoted to candlepins or duckpins.4 Western Massachusetts is an epicenter, with candlepin alleys in Agawam, Chicopee, East Brookfield, Erving, Holyoke, North Adams, Palmer, Pittsfield, Southampton, Spencer, and Ware. But if you want to visit the Western Mass "birthplace," head to Shelburne Falls and wander through that narrow Bridge Street walkway. It's like a stroll back in time. Ladies are welcome any day. Prepare to be humbled.

1 Don Carter did so in 1964.

2 Keggling comes from the German word for bowling. Bowlers are often nicknamed keglers.

3 The highest score ever rolled by a female candlepin bowler is 207. Just three women have ever broken 200. Professionals generally average around 120.

4 This figure is accurate as of early 2019. Several older lanes closed in 2017, and a few others are reported to be near insolvency.

25
Revenge of the Broom Makers: Curling in Petersham

The town center of the western Worcester County settlement of Petersham affords a classic New England postcard view: a 19th-century library fashioned from round fieldstones, a greensward commons, a gazebo, town buildings of sturdy red brick and clapboards, a general store, steepled white churches, and a historic district lined with graceful houses. Petersham—as with Amherst, the "h" is always silent—is best known to history as the place where Shays' Rebellion ended in 1787, though today it's a quiet stopping place for those exploring the eastern side of the Quabbin Reservoir and Reservation.

Curling?

There's something about Petersham that marks it as different from other small hilltowns in the area. As you drive out of town on North Main Street/Route 32, the Country Club will be on your right. So is a nondescript one-story building with an attached barn, and a sign whose motif includes crossed brooms, a pair of thistles, and the information that you have stumbled upon the Petersham Curling Club.

Before the 2018 Winter Olympics, most Americans would have looked at those brooms, read the sign, and thought something on the order of, "Curling club? Is that some sort of weird hairdressing academy operated by a witches' coven?" Then, improbably, the United States won a gold medal in curling.

Nonetheless, you'd have to be quite an Olympics junkie to know that curling has been a competitive sport for a long time. It claims about 1.5 million devotees worldwide, but in the United States, a nation of over 325 million people, fewer than 20,000 folks have ever thrown a curling stone. Petersham has the only dedicated rink in Western Massachusetts where you can play or watch curling.[1] There is a smattering of "sheets," as curling surfaces are usually called, across the United States, but curling's most ardent fans are found in northern climes—New England, New York, and the Upper Midwest— because you need ice for curling.

The sport probably originated in medieval Scotland, which is why Petersham's sign sports thistles. The first known reference is from Perthshire, Scotland, in 1511, but that means it was likely played informally long before anyone thought to chronicle it. The gist of the game was then, as now, to slide a very heavy stone across an icy surface—frozen lochs, originally—and see how close one can get the stone to rest near a central target curlers call the "button."

Other places with lots of wintertime ice picked up the curling habit: Austria, Flanders, Sweden, South Island New Zealand, and Canada. Especially Canada; it's not unusual to drive through cities and small towns in Quebec and the Maritimes and spot a curling rink.

As with most sports, curlers have specialized gear—including shoes in which one sole is designed for sliding and the other for gripping—but an unofficial prerequisite is a skin thick enough to endure some good-natured ribbing. Much as in other quirky Scottish sports such as shinty[2], hammer hurling, or caber tossing, curling can seem a wee bit daft at first. Informal play requires hefting wicked heavy rocks, and usually takes place outdoors on frozen ponds in frigid weather.

The game's central feature invites amusement that's encapsulated by the crossed brooms on the Petersham sign. The sight of two uniformed players furiously sweeping the ice as a granite stone slowly inches down the sheet looks so odd to the uninitiated, that it has spawned jokes that curling was invented either by deranged housekeepers or by broom makers trying to boost sales. There are actually good reasons for the ice keeping that we'll get to in a moment.

Curling House Rules

Curling is a bit like a frigid version of bocce crossed with shuffleboard, though it's more complex. A curling sheet is 146–150 feet long and 14.5–16.5 feet wide, with backboards at each end. A vertical centerline bisects both the sheet and the targets at each end. Those targets ("houses") look something like an archery target, except they have just four scoring zones. The button lies at the center of each house, 16 feet from the backboard, and is surrounded by three concentric circles that are, from the button, four, eight, and 12 feet in diameter.

The center of the button is also bisected by the tee line from which "throwers" begin to glide their handle-assisted sliding stones down the ice, after having first pushed off from a "hack" located 12 feet behind the button. The hack serves roughly the same purpose as a pitcher's rubber in baseball; it gives the thrower leverage.

Teams consist of four players each: a lead, a second, a third ("vice"), and the "skip" (captain), who usually throws last. Each player slides two 36–44-pound granite stones toward the opposing button. When all 16 are thrown, this constitutes an "end." Big events generally have 10 ends, unless one side concedes. Each side has a time limit to complete their throws, and a match generally lasts about 2½ hours. (Informal games may have just eight ends.)

The team with the stone closest to the button wins the end unless none of the stones lies inside a target circle, in which case no points are awarded. The team that wins the end is awarded additional points for any other stones that lie closer to the button than those of their opponent.

About all that sweeping: few housekeepers ever swept a kitchen with such care! Like a hockey rink's Zamboni driver, sweepers clear the path of chips, rough ice, and debris that might impede the stone. They also heat the ice so that stones skim more easily. Skilled sweepers can influence the way the stone tracks, curls, and turns toward the target. Either the skip or the first kneels on the ice and barks instructions to the sweepers.

As in bocce, curling is a game of skill, tactics, and strategy. Stones are finessed down the ice, not flung haphazardly. There are all manner of strategies, such as throwing to "guard" a teammate's stone, or trying to "take out" one of the opponent's. No stone can cross the boundary lines at any point, and sweepers are expected to gallantly disqualify a throw if they accidentally "burn" a stone by touching it with their brooms.

Curling isn't as silly or easy as it looks. Still, it's decidedly a niche activity unlikely to dethrone any of America's major sports. As Olym-

pics viewers learned, it's a passion for its devotees, and since 1998, a sport that hands out Olympic medals.³

Why Petersham?

Petersham lies just nine miles from Athol, a town that straddles Franklin and Worcester counties. Until the 1980s, there was a factory in Athol operated by the Union Twist Drill Company, which fabricated metal cutting tools. In 1959, Stanley L. Holland was transferred to Athol from Rock Island, Quebec, to serve as president of Union Twist. Holland loved curling, as did several other Quebec transplants.

Holland and three other factory employees purchased land from the Petersham Country Club and broke ground on July 24, 1960. Naturally enough, they patterned their two-sheet rink on the one they frequented in Quebec. You get a sense of how much they adored curling when you contemplate the fact that they marshaled enough volunteers to build the rink for around $50,000. That's around $420,000 in today's money, which is an amazing value for a refrigerated facility. Still, that's more than loose change for a rink that only operates from October through early April, and is devoted entirely to curling. It is one of just four such facilities in all of Massachusetts.

The Petersham Curling Club still caters to true devotees. Regulars must pay club membership, and a board of governors oversees operations. The Petersham Club has several divisions, including men's, women's, mixed, juniors, various youth groups, and a "Signature" designation for the truly competitive who wish to participate in challenge matches against other clubs such as the Broomstones of Wayland, Massachusetts, or a club in Schenectady, New York, that's been around since 1907.

For all of that, curling is far more democratic than exclusive sports such as polo or yachting. You can also go to Petersham to watch, take part in just-for-fun events, or learn how to curl. I recommend the last of these. Remember how hard it is to shove a shuffleboard puck where you want it go? Try sliding a heavy stone a hundred feet down a frozen sheet, and you'll never again think the same way about ice, stones, or people with brooms.

1 A few other ice facilities occasionally have curling events, but they are ice skating/hockey arenas temporarily adapted for curling in much the same way that gyms are sometimes set up for roller derby.

2 Shinty is a ball-and-stick game closely related to Irish hurling. Both games bear similarities to field hockey, but are far more physical and allow things such as tackling and hitting airborne balls.

3 Curling was first made an Olympic sport in 1924, was dropped for the 1928 winter games, added as a demonstration sport in 1932, and remained so until 1998, when it again became an official Olympic sport. If you run across the term Eisschiessen, it's German for curling.

> WARREN GIBBS
> died by arsenic poison
> Mar. 23. 1860.
> Æ. 36 yrs. 5 mos.
> 23 dys.
>
> Think my friends when this you see
> How my wife hath dealt by me
> She in some oysters did prepare
> Some poison for my lot and share
> Then of the same I did partake
> And nature yielded to its fate
> Before she my wife became
> Mary Felton was her name.
> Erected by his Brother
> W.M. GIBBS.

Pelham gravestone. But is it authentic?

Section VI

(Not Your Ordinary) Museums

In this final section of the book, I'd like to spotlight intriguing museums. I can almost see you rolling your eyes. I know that lots of people associate museums with boring school field trips to hoity-toity places such as the Boston Museum of Fine Arts, or the antique-packed rooms of Historic Deerfield that seem to cater more to scholars and collectors than to the general public.

New Englanders often suffer from a type of museum fatigue that I call Colonial House Syndrome. I'm not sure anyone actually knows how many old-house museums there are in New England, but if you've spent time in one, you've seen paintings of people you've never heard of, trudged upstairs to see a cornhusk-filled mattress sitting on a rope foundation, and ended your tour in a dimly lit kitchen with an iron cauldron hanging in a fireplace and surrounded by mysterious implements.

I won't spotlight those kinds of museums, but I do want to speak in their defense. I love museums of all sorts. Most people have never been taught how to appreciate them. Please indulge me as I slip back into my educator role and offer a few tips for enjoying museums—of any sort.

1. Understand that you won't take in everything in your visit. At some point, you'll just glaze over and objects will pass you by like billboards on the interstate.

2. Do a bit of preparation, especially if it's a place to which you're unlikely to return. That's simple to do in the age of the Internet. Figure out what you really want to see.

3. See *first* the things that most interest you. Lots of people treat museums like math problems that have to be solved in order. They're more like collections of short stories; you can "read" them in any order you wish. Also like them, if you don't have time for or don't like certain chapters/sections, skip 'em. Always see what you came to see first, before you wear out.

4. Take breaks. Most museums allow you to leave and re-enter on the same day. See something, then have a cup of coffee at a café, or take a stroll. Repeat.

5. Know when you're "full." I adore the Boston MFA, but I never try to see it all. Many times either my wife or I will say, "My brain is full," our signal to collect our belongings and head out to do something else.

6. If you don't know what you're seeing, ask a docent or consider taking a tour. Museums have gotten hipper to the idea that they need to offer different kinds of tours for experts and for those who are not. I like Historic Deerfield too, but I know next to nothing about antiques, so a good tour guide is essential for me. A docent can explain lots of things to you, like the fact that the "gravestone" on p. 196 (from Pelham) is almost certainly a fake.

7. Don't be afraid to learn something. The old adage "Ignorance is bliss" is the biggest cowpat in all of New England! There's nothing you know that you once didn't, so allow yourself to be educated anew. I can't tell you the number of wonderful painters I've learned about by visiting the Clark and the MFA. They might have been famous once upon a time, but they meant nothing to me until I learned about them.

8. Do a recap. After my wife and I finish an exhibit, we retrace our steps. Each of us picks our favorite thing in each room or section and explains why it resonates. This has the added advantage of making us look more deeply at the exhibit.

9. Final game: Identify a takeaway point. What's the biggest, coolest, or most unusual thing you learned?

10. If you can, go back and repeat steps 1–9. The second biggest cowpat in New England is the statement: "Familiarity breeds contempt." No it doesn't. It's how we all learn. We start with what we know, then step into the unknown.

Now that I have this out of the way, I can also assure you that little of what you are about to read falls into the conventional idea of what a museum is. For me, a museum is simply a place where we can find displays, objects, and stories that instruct us. Or they're just fun. Take your pick, but let yourself be astonished.

26
Pelham: Small Tokens of Large Disputes

I've been harping on the idea that the past was often quite different from the way we imagine it. Not only are the concerns of yesterday not necessarily those of today, but also most of us sample the past's main courses without partaking of its side dishes.

Many Americans envision Colonial New England and the early American republic as a domain of pious English settlers and fiery patriotic revolutionaries. That's partly true, but if you really want to get some idea of the ebb and flow of daily life, get thee to a local historical museum. That's where you can learn things that humanize history, like workaday habits, petty squabbles, small details, and stories of malcontents that don't fit easily into the grand narratives found in textbooks. Sometimes, the smallest scraps help us understand things that mattered very much to people of their day. Such an item is a bite-sized lead token at the Pelham Historical Society.

Pelham communion token

Different Worlds

Pelham sits atop a ridge about seven miles from the center of Amherst. Today it is part of the Town of Amherst, but the greatest similarity between the two in the 18th century was that both were named for Englishmen. Amherst bears the surname of a controversial Colonial governor, and its inhabitants were mostly Puritans. Pelham's name honors an English statesman,[1] but most of the first settlers arriving in 1738 were Scots Irish Presbyterians. They incorporated Pelham in 1743.

As we shall see, that was one of the few early things done in Pelham with a minimum amount of controversy.

The aforementioned token can be a bit difficult to see when the light reflects off the glass case that encloses it, but it's stamped with the letter "P" for Pelham. It was given to church attendees deemed worthy of joining the Presbyterian Church and of receiving communion, a winnowing process dubbed "fencing the table." If you think this suggests social borders, you're right. Pelham residents were *very* particular about who could partake of and administer the Eucharist. Their reasons require a detour into European Reformation history.

The Reformation and Colonial America

Until 1517, the Roman Catholic Church monopolized orthodox Christianity in Western Europe. Martin Luther's challenge broke the Catholic monopoly and launched the Protestant Reformation. In its wake came social crises, religious wars, and faith-based persecutions that continued into the 18th century.

Unlike today, when individuals are free to choose what they believe, most Europeans adhered to a "faith follows the Crown" model in which the only accepted beliefs were those held by the sovereign; most others were illegal and heretical. The Reformation occurred simultaneously with the age of exploration and North American colonization. That wasn't a good thing; bloody European religious conflicts migrated across the Atlantic to the New World. New England was a major center of religious dispute.

My undergraduate medieval history professor would frown at this analogy, but if doctrine were ice cream, Roman Catholicism would be traditional vanilla in its uniformity and consistency. By contrast, there are more varieties of Protestant Christianity than flavors at a Herrell's scoop shop.

All Protestants rejected the religious authority of the Catholic pope. Nearly all believed in the Trinity, that faith alone is needed for salvation, and that the Bible is God's word. Beyond these things, however, there was more disagreement than accord.

The faith of 16th- and 17th-century English settlers in New England was supposed to follow the Crown. That would have meant accepting King Henry VIII's 1534 Act of Supremacy, which made the English monarch head of the Church of England (Anglican). Instead, New England was filled with more malcontents than the license-renewal line at the Department of Motor Vehicles.

The reason for all the squabbling was simple enough: Anglican theology was "soft" in an age in which people paid a lot of attention to such matters. Henry VIII was no great thinker; he simply wanted to rid himself of a wife and Pope Clement VII wouldn't sanction an annulment. Aside from the Protestant basics mentioned above, Henry's critics complained that Anglicanism was basically Catholicism without the pope.

The Pilgrims who came to Plymouth in 1620 were Separatists who quit Anglicanism in favor of a more austere form of Protestantism. The Puritans who came to Massachusetts Bay 10 years later never officially left the Anglican church, but their efforts to "purify" it gave them their name, and made Puritans quarrelsome and borderline heretical. But at least in the eye of the Church of England, Puritans had the right kind of church governance—the kind that put congregations in charge of most decision-making.

That was not the case for the Scots Irish Presbyterians who settled Pelham, but brought unsanctioned theology with them. In the 17th century, English monarchs tried to pacify Ireland by transplanting Protestant Lowland Scots into Ireland hoping they would intermarry with locals and breed Catholicism out of the Irish.

Instead, many of the Scots gravitated toward the stern Presbyterianism of John Knox (1513–72), a follower of John Calvin (1509–1604), who preached doctrines that included predestination, limited free will, rejection of pomp, and rigid ritual. Today we might use the phrase "epic fail" to describe the English hope that Anglicanism would prevail in Ireland.[2] Anglicanism got more organized and refined its rituals and doctrines in the *Book of Common Prayer* (1549), and did so even more emphatically in the 1646 *Westminster Confession of Faith*. Scottish Calvinists—most of whom would be dubbed Presbyterians—had no love for Anglicanism. Presbyterian Calvinists developed differing practices in various editions of *The Book of Common Order*. The only commonality between Scots Presbyterians in Ireland and English Anglicans is that the Irish disliked both of them! Ultimately, those more properly known as "Scots in Ireland" fled to non-Irish shores.

Pelham's Argumentative Presbyterians

Pelham began to take shape in 1718, when the Reverend William Boyd met with Governor Shute to discuss Scots-Irish immigration. On February 2, 1739,[3] land was purchased from Colonel John Stoddard of Northampton, construction of a Presbyterian meetinghouse commenced, and Pelham was populated. The Rev. Robert Abercrombie led the first congregation, first as a "supplayer," a substitute, and then as its official minister during 1744–45. He was dismissed for being too lenient in forgiving sinners.[4]

Pelham Scots Irish proved every bit as disputatious as those in Europe. There is no patriarch within Presbyterianism, but governance and decision-making are supposed to flow downward from general assemblies to synods, presbyteries, and elders. In theory, Presbyterianism reversed the Puritan (Congregational) model of granting power to local congregations. In practice, American Presbyterianism looked much like the Puritan "New England Way" in which higher bodies advised but could not supersede local decision-makers. Presbyterian ministers—also called teaching elders, bishops, or ministers of word and sacrament—were simply the first among equals of "ruling elders." In small places such as Pelham, the elders included most male property-owners though not all were viewed as equal. Pews were rented, with preferential seating given to those who paid the highest taxes. Local elites also influenced church governance, as there weren't enough Presbyterians in New England to develop higher bodies that could overrule elders.

So much bickering marked Pelham's early religious history that one wonders how locals found time to clear land and tend to their farms. After Abercrombie's dismissal, it took nearly nine years to find a permanent pastor. The Rev. Richard Crouch Graham (1739–71) served 1763–71, often complaining of the inadequacy of his £60 salary. His successor, the Rev. Andrew Bay, pastored for less than two years, and his replacement, the Rev. Nathaniel Merrill, stuck it out from 1774 to 1780, when he, too, was dismissed.

More turmoil ensued, not the least of which was the intensification of the American Revolution. After Merrill, it took four years to find another minister. Stephen Burroughs (1765–1840), depending upon whose version one believes, was either badly treated or was—in the words of Charles Parmenter's 1898 town history—an "unregenerate imposter," con man, and plagiarist named Davis. The latter seems closest to the truth. His exit in 1784 gave way to Shays' Rebellion in 1786–87 of which Pelham was in the center of the crisis. Then came the "stormy" pastorate of Elijah Brainard (1799–1805), who seems to have pleased no one.

Pelham congregations—there were two for a time—and ministers battled constantly. Town members railed against uninspiring (or unorthodox) preaching styles, dictatorial behaviors, and lax application of Westminster Confession discipline. They also accused several ministers of financial malfeasance, fought each other over the propriety of infant baptism,[5] and questioned the faith of several ministers. Of the Rev. Matthias Cazier— who served just one year, 1793—members expressed the view, "We are total strangers to the gentleman's character and know not whether it is religious or moral."

For their part, an endless parade of ministers complained of low pay, inadequate supplies of firewood, and substandard lodging; several brought lawsuits against the town. Unrelenting dispute exhausted Presbyterian fervor. The Rev. Winthrop Bailey (1784–1835) served Pelham during the years 1821–25, and was among those who transitioned Presbyterians to Calvinist Congregationalism, thus ending nine decades of tumult. Not coincidentally, the shift to Congregationalism officially invested the local body of believers with the governance power they had asserted from the beginning. It could also be said that Pelham Scots Irish ultimately fenced themselves from the table.

Whew, that's a lot of history! I warned you that small objects sometimes tell complex stories. Pelham's religious drama offers a different view of New England piety. Historians will rightly tell you that most of what you were taught about Colonial history has been severely airbrushed. Pelham will make you believe it.

To add a small footnote to our story, the Pelham Historical Society contains another artifact that suggests that the change of church did little to purify moral character. A gravestone with whimsical engraving recounts the alleged 1860 demise of Warren Gibbs. He supposedly met his maker courtesy of oysters poisoned by his wife. (See picture in Section VI introduction.) Given shaky supporting documentation for this alleged murder, the marker is probably a fake, perhaps the invention of an overzealous mid-20th-century individual wishing to enhance New England's colorful gravestone lore. But given Pelham's stormy social relations, we can all imagine every word carved upon the stone, even if it never happened!

1 Lord Jeffery Amherst (1717–97) is controversial because he wrote a letter during Pontiac's War (1763) in which he suggested introducing smallpox into Indian populations via traded blankets. It is not known if his suggestion was actually carried out, but it would not have been an original idea for white men of his era. His words, of course, play badly today. Amherst College removed the Lord Jeffs as the name of its sports teams, and some have advocated changing the very name of the town.

2 Protestantism did prevail in counties that now make up Northern Ireland, which is why they were partitioned from the Republic of Ireland in 1922 and made part of Great Britain. This has been a source of contention ever since, but that is a different discussion.

3 This date shows up as 1738 in many sources. In 1752, the Julian calendar from Roman times gave way to the Gregorian calendar. In September 1752, 11 days were dropped to readjust calendars. Remarkably, there were Calendar Day riots in various places, but slowly the changes took hold. This has been a bit of a headache for historians. Dates, including George Washington's birthday, are often listed first by Gregorian dates and then in a bracketed Old Style date.

4 Early Presbyterians were even more concerned about sin than Puritans, and they earned a reputation for severity.

5 Although most Protestants allow infant baptism, those affected by Anabaptist Reformation ideas assert that only adults who have had a conversion experience should be baptized. Many Puritans, Separatists, and Presbyterians practiced only adult baptism, so even discussing infant baptism led to bitter disputes.

27
Gigantic Obsession: Indian Orchard's Titanic *Museum*

The *RMS Titanic* sank on April 15, 1912, with a loss of 1,517 lives. Its wreckage rests in 1,200 feet of Atlantic Ocean trench roughly a thousand miles northeast of Boston, and it's another 98 miles from Boston's Revere Beach to Springfield. So why is there a museum devoted to the *Titanic* in Springfield's northeastern neighborhood of Indian Orchard, where the only sizable body of water is the Chicopee River? That stream once powered mills, but none of them produced items remotely maritime.

From Obsession to Museum

As is often the case with specialty museums, the one in Indian Orchard began with an obsession, that of Edward Kamuda (1939–2014), who first opened his collection to the public in 1963. Blame his *Titanic* obsession on the movies.

The world's largest collection of *Titanic* memorabilia rests in Belfast, Ireland, and another trove resides in the Maritime Museum of the Atlantic in Halifax, Nova Scotia. Both make logical sense; the *Titanic* stopped at Ireland before setting its course with destiny, and many of the recovered bodies were brought to Halifax, where some were buried. But how do we explain the fact that there are also *Titanic* museums in Branson, Missouri; Pigeon Fork, Tennessee; and Las Vegas, Nevada?

There's no denying the drama surrounding the supposedly unsinkable *Titanic*, but it took popular culture to make it into a quintessential tale of tragedy and hubris. If measured by loss of life, the 1945

Model in the Titanic *Museum*

sinking of the *MV Wilhelm Gustloff* is the worst maritime tragedy of all time. It went down with at least 9,400 lives lost. Nor is the *Titanic* the greatest non-military shipping disaster, a dubious distinction earned by the Filipino ferry *Dona Paz* in 1987, when 4,386 people drowned. The *Titanic* ranks just seventh on lists of tragic civilian maritime disasters. But the only other ship in the top 10 to star in a movie was the *RMS Lusitania*, which was torpedoed by the Germans in 1915 with a loss of 1,198 lives. By then, several movies had already immortalized the *Titanic*.

Film scholars have dubbed the 1910s as the golden era of silent movies. This means motion pictures were still a novelty for most viewers in 1912, and the idea of a "feature" film was in its infancy.[1] The *Titanic* tragedy proved irresistible and an American film, *Saved from the Titanic*, appeared just 29 days after the ship sank. On its heels came efforts from German and French studios: *In Nacht und Eis* and *La hantise*. Before a year had passed, there was also a thinly disguised Danish *Titanic* film, more than a hundred songs, and dozens of *Titanic* poems, including one by Thomas Hardy.

The *Titanic* has seldom been absent from popular culture in some form or other, expressions that included stage shows and dance extravaganzas. "My Sweetheart Went Down with the Ship" (1912) is generally regarded as the first popular musical effort, and the *Titanic* quickly became a staple for blues, folk, and country musicians. Movies, though, have kept afloat memories of the *Titanic* more than any other medium. By some estimates, more than one-half billion people have seen James Cameron's 1997 film *Titanic*, and at least six major features predated it between 1913 and 1996. Several were blockbusters, including *Titanic* (1953), *A Night to Remember* (1958), and *The Unsinkable Molly Brown* (1964). To date, there have also been two IMax films, at least three animated films, and three post-1997 features about the tragedy. The box office magic of *Titanic* films has had a spillover effect. There have been untold numbers of television shows and episodes using the *Titanic* as a theme. Performers as diverse as Lead Belly, Woody Guthrie, Sissy Spacek, Paul Newman, Kylie Minogue, Bob Dylan, and U2 have weighed in with *Titanic* offerings. And, yes, there are video games.

Popular culture's dominance in telling the *Titanic's* story is part of what inspired the project in Indian Orchard. Edward S. Kamuda, his wife Karen, and three others opened the museum in 1963. Kamuda claimed that his initial passion was fired by viewing the 1953 film *Titanic*, directed by Jean Negulesco, which he first saw in the now-defunct Grand Theater, across the street from the current museum. As he got older, though, he began to worry that the memories of aging survivors would be lost. Good academic studies were rare prior to Walter Lord's 1955 book *A Night to Remember*, which is better remembered as a 1958 film adaptation.

Even today, academic output on the disaster is the thinnest part of the *Titanic* oeuvre. Such concerns led Kamuda to spearhead the founding of the *Titanic* Historical Society (THS), which is devoted to studying the disaster, especially the biographies of the ship's passengers and crew. The THS newsletter quickly became a clearinghouse for both scholarly and general-interest news.

An Idiosyncratic Collection

It is important to remember that Kamuda and his wife Karen began both the museum and the THS 22 years before oceanographer Robert Ballard, a THS member, located the *Titanic's* resting place in 1985. The Kamudas did not feature salvaged items, a pursuit Edward found ghoulish. Only a few *Titanic* items displayed were flotsam, among them a small carpet fragment, a deckchair, a rivet punching, and a lifeboat flag. All of the passenger artifacts came from survivors, including the lifejacket worn by Madeleine Astor (1893–1940), the new bride of tycoon John Jacob Astor IV; he went down with the ship. One of the larger collections comes from second-class passenger Selena Rogers Cook (1890–1964), who donated the clothing, handbag contents, veil, and assorted other articles she managed to take with her to the lifeboat, including an extracted tooth!

Veil worn by Selena R. Cook

Cook's tooth is among the things that make the Indian Orchard museum idiosyncratic. Oddities begin with the building itself. The front half of its 208 Main Street location is Henry's Jewelry Store, an establishment that still feels like a slice of 1950s Americana.

In the midst of its baubles sits a nine-foot scaled model of the *Titanic,* the only object on view without paying admission to the museum proper. Also on display the day I visited were the political views of Kamuda's widow in the form of three photographs marking perceived historical "disasters:" the *Titanic,* the *Hindenburg,* and Barack Obama!

Persevere, even if your political views veer more leftward. It's safe to say that you won't find too many museums like this one anymore. It invites adjectives such as throwback, antiquarian, shopworn, chaotic, and eclectic. The overall experience is like opening dusty trunks in search of treasure. The interior reflects its founders' fascination with things *from* and *about* the *Titanic.* Letters, recollections, table settings, and survivors' objects stand cheek by jowl with sheet music, movie posters, facsimiles, and kitsch. In an age in which museums are going high-concept, high-tech, and high-cost admission prices, a modest entry fee gives you access to two rooms and some 600 artifacts in which scholarly pursuits and popular culture metaphorically smash into an iceberg and allow their respective cargoes to mingle indiscriminately.

Pop Culture's Lessons

The *Titanic* Museum is a testament to how history can be teased from popular culture, even when the latter seeks only to entertain. Kamuda begrudgingly understood this. He, like those most familiar with the real-life events, was initially critical of the James Cameron movie, especially of invented characters such as Jack (Leonardo DiCaprio) and Rose (Kate Winslet). Yet he too was eventually charmed, spent time on the set, and welcomed Cameron as a THS member.

Kamuda and fellow THS member Paul Phaneuf gave a further nod to popular culture in 2012, when they dedicated a monument to *Titanic* victims in Springfield's Oak Grove Cemetery. The front of the 10,000-pound, four-by-nine-foot monument donated by the St. Pierre-Phaneuf Funeral Home depicts an etching on granite of the ship. The back contains these final lines: May the memory of the *Titanic* be preserved forever. "Nearer, my God, to thee."

The last line references the song that legend holds was played by the ship's orchestra as the ship broke apart and plunged to its watery grave. That legend, however, is consistent only in movies; eyewitness accounts disagree over what tune was being played. No matter. History meets legend, and maybe Western Massachusetts isn't so far from the coast when one considers that among the 1,517 victims were two Springfield locals: 47-year-old Jane Carr, a third-class passenger; and 29-year-old Milton Long, the son of a judge and former city mayor who was among the first-class passengers who gallantly went down with the ship.

[1] *The Story of the Kelly* is usually regarded as the first feature film. It was made in Australia, and released in 1906.

28
Dalton: Give a Damn about Greenback Dollars

Whether you know it or not, each time you reach into your wallet, you touch a piece of Dalton, Massachusetts. All bills in circulation are engraved on paper made in that small Berkshire County town (population 6,624) east of Pittsfield. Dalton is home to the Crane Paper Company, which has been producing United States currency paper since 1879—even longer if we stretch what we mean by "United States currency."

All Paper is Not Created Equal

As you might expect, money is printed upon a very special kind of paper. There are parts of the process that cannot be revealed lest the nation's financial security be compromised, but there's quite a lot you can learn by visiting the Crane Museum of Papermaking and Center for the Paper Arts located just off West Housatonic Street.

This small museum tells a unique tale, starting with the fact that no one else is allowed to make currency paper. The museum is housed in the Old Stone Mill Rag Room, built in 1844, and its name tells you something that's special about the dollars in your pocket. Crane paper is made of three-quarters cotton and one-quarter linen, not wood pulp. Moreover, the cotton comes from rags, so you're a double recycler every time you send a buck into circulation.

The museum, which first opened in 1930, is a glorious throwback. There's not a lot of glitz inside, just a video, scale models, wallboard displays, old tools, paper samples, knowledgeable docents, and hands-on exhibits. My favorite display is one in which you can use a magni-

Entrance to the Crane Museum's rag room

fying glass and a black light to see some of the unclassified security measures used to thwart counterfeiters. There are also fun things for kids to do such as making a piece of paper, creating a watermark, and dabbling with ink designs.

The museum also tells the story of the Crane family, whose workers created both currency stock and high-quality writing paper. Stephen Crane (1734–1777?) set up shop near Boston in 1770, when paper of all kinds was hard to come by. He may have died during the Revolutionary War, but before doing so sold cartridge papers for munitions, as well as higher-grade stock that engraver Paul Revere used to print currency for the Massachusetts government.

Stephen's son Zenas (1777–1845) bought land in Dalton in 1801, and formed Crane and Company in partnership with two others. One of his sons, Zenas Marshal Crane (1815–77), oversaw construction of the rag room that now houses the Crane Museum.

A Wrinkled Path to Paper Money

From 1801 on, Crane and Company produced a variety of papers, including those used for local, state, bank, and U.S. currencies. That plural speaks volumes. In 1962, folksinger Hoyt Axton wrote, "I don't give a damn about a greenback dollar." Seldom have such ahistorical words been written. You're in the same boat if you take paper money for granted, as if the buck jammed into your jeans pocket is the most natural thing in the world. Paper money is one of the mostly hotly contested issues in American history. Until 1971, just about everyone gave a damn about greenback dollars, and a lot of people were against them!

Vintage photo of the rag room

Furious debates have raged over what money is, who could make it, how its value would be determined, and whether paper could be used for exchange. Printed bills are fiat money, meaning they have no intrinsic worth. Even today, bills aren't worth the paper on which they are printed. All that makes them valuable is the government's promise they can be used to purchase a set value's worth of goods and services.

That's not always been true, which is one reason it took a long time before many people had greenbacks in their jeans. Those bills printed on Stephen Crane's paper during the Revolutionary War weren't worth much. Wars are expensive, so the Founders did what many people do in a crisis: they borrowed money. Remember, the United States broke with England, and the revolution meant that London lines of credit were severed. The revolutionary government printed money called "Continentals," and hoped that bankers, merchants, soldiers, shopkeepers, and others would accept them. Mind you, the Continental Congress didn't actually *have* the equivalent value of the greenbacks it printed; it traded in the hope the Colonists would first win independence, and second, that prosperity would make that paper valuable.

They were half right. The war was won, but much of the new nation was awash in debt. For years, greenbacks could not be redeemed at anything close to face value; hence the phrase "not worth a Continental damn" entered popular parlance. Most of those with Continentals sold them for next to nothing. Later, a handful of speculators cashed in, but high taxes and a lack of money with which to pay them were primary causes of Shays' Rebellion (1786–87), which began in Western Massachusetts.

Article I of the U.S. Constitution (1789) contains six mentions of money, none of which involves printing it. When the U.S. Mint opened in 1792, it issued coins. Credit—and paper money was a form of it—was a tougher sell. When the First Bank of the United States (B.U.S.) was proposed in 1790, it generated so much opposition that even George Washington was skeptical.

It took six years to capitalize the first B.U.S. The bank's charter expired in 1811, with a single individual, Stephen Girard, buying most of its stock. The Second B.U.S. was chartered for 20 years in 1818, but did not long survive President Andrew Jackson's assault on it in 1833, and sputtered to dissolution in 1841.

By the 1830s, money generally meant copper, silver, or gold coins. Money supplies were limited, to the delight of some and the detriment of others. The rest of the 19th century saw heated debate over "hard" versus "soft" money. The limited circulation of hard money linked to precious metals was favored by lenders, who could charge higher interest rates. Those favoring soft money (greenbacks or cheap silver)—such as farmers or small shopkeepers—argued for greater circulation and controlled levels of inflation that would cause prices to rise and make loans easier to pay. Banks also printed their own bills after 1836, but these were rudimentary lines of credit allegedly backed by government bonds; technically, only the federal government could issue money.

From the start, the nation's monetary system was a mess. Paper money was issued again during the Civil War. In its midst, the National Banking Acts of 1863 and 1864 established a single national currency in the North, and the bills of the Confederacy lost all value when the war ended. Sounds good, right? It wasn't.

By the time Winthrop Crane (1853–1920) secured a contract to deliver paper to the Bureau of Engraving and Printing in 1879, money supplies had tightened so much that the year before, Congress passed the Bland-Allison Act seeking to stimulate circulation by requiring the Treasury Department to buy more silver. But wait; it gets worse! Congress had gone to a gold standard six years earlier, and silver was anathema to self-proclaimed "gold bugs." Quite a few banks refused to accept "silver certificates" that could be redeemed for silver coins, even though they were allegedly required to do so. About the only ones who gave a damn about greenback dollars were farmers and labor activists. Farmers hoped that greenbacks would touch off controlled inflation that would make farm goods more valuable and loans easier to repay. Labor leaders seeking to broaden support tended to side with farmers, a strategy with which some urban workers agreed and others bitterly opposed.

The post-Civil-War period was marked by controversial experiments over backing U.S. money with silver, gold, or both (bimetallism). Each was tried in various forms, though a certain yellow substance remained the gold standard. (From 1877 to 1933, paper money could be exchanged for gold.) Speculation, watered stocks, worthless bank notes, and bank failures were commonplace. From 1865 to 1900, nine recessions occurred. In total, nearly 19 of those 35 years involved economic hardship. Things didn't really get on the right track until the

1913 Federal Reserve Act brought all commercial banks under its wing and even then, the Great Depression (1929–41) loomed.

The 1933 Banking Act—which included the FDIC and a ban on private ownership of gold—eventually stabilized the money supply, but silver certificates could still be exchanged bills for hard currency as late as 1964, and it wasn't until 1968 that all U.S. paper money became Federal Reserve notes. Citizens can no longer convert them into precious metals, but the value of reserve notes cannot be devalued.

Crane Paper has weathered all of these battles. So when you reach for a dollar, think of Dalton. If you're near Pittsfield, drop into the museum and take the kids. While you're thinking about how complex money has been and can be, the kids can have some fun— at your expense.

Ten Loose-Change Facts

1. There is no dollar sign on U.S. currency other than the $1 coin.

2. Spanish money bore the name "dollar" before the United States was created. The dollar sign derives either from the way the words "Spanish peso" were rendered (with an intersecting upper case S and lower case p), or from the two vertical lines that represent the Pillars of Hercules that adorned Spanish silver. No one is absolutely sure.

3. The dollar sign was used informally before 1875, when it became standard.

4. The phrase "In God We Trust" was not on U.S. paper currency until 1957. It was added during the Cold War as part of a propaganda strategy that juxtaposed the purported piety and goodness of the democratic United States against the "godless authoritarianism" of the Soviet Union.

5. The average lifespan for a dollar bill is about 18–21 months. Wear and tear decreases as the face value of the bill increases, but part of

Crane's business plan rests on the fact that the supply of Federal Reserve notes must be replenished often.

6. Bills also get replaced when designs change, which they do periodically. (Before 1929, designs weren't standardized.) Design changes in 1996 and 2003 were made to enhance security against counterfeiters. Changes ordered in 2016 will increase the presence of women and people of color on bills.

7. There have been periodic discussions about opening currency paper production to competitive bid, but these have been derailed citing security risks and invitations to counterfeiting.

8. In 2015, the stationery product line of Crane was separated from the currency company. The former is now an international business.

9. There has not been a Crane family member on the management team since 2013.

10. The Old Stone Rag Room is on the National Register of Historic Places.

29
Cummington:
The Story Behind The Cummington Story

Museums and towns are filled with things ordinary and extraordinary. The trick lies in knowing which is which. Often, the most revealing stories are embedded in overlooked objects and the unexamined past.

Small Town, Big Story

At a glance, Cummington looks like numerous other Western Massachusetts hilltowns. And its museum, partly housed in the 19th-century Kingman Tavern, appears similar to other local history museums. The tongue-twisting Cummington Kingman Tavern Museum holds photos, antiques, family mementos, and period furniture arranged to

Cummington Kingman Tavern Museum

evoke bygone domestic life. Outwardly, its major distinguishing feature is that it's more extensive than most local history museums. It's a complex that includes a room decked out as a general store; a two-story barn stuffed with implements, tools, and machines; an 1840s cider mill; and a parsonage. But the Kingman Tavern also houses a changing array of small objects and paintings rendered by artists with surnames you might not normally associate with a small village nestled in a trough formed by the Westfield and Swift Rivers. These items tell a remarkable story.

Cummington lies in the Berkshire foothills, 21 miles southeast of Pittsfield. It's a village of fewer than 900 people that, like other hilltowns, has been steadily shrinking in population. Most travelers ignore it altogether, which is easy to do as Route 9 bypasses the village center and the area's big attraction is the homestead of poet/journalist William Cullen Bryant (1794–1878), which lies about two miles to the northwest.

Let me tempt you into wandering into the village if you're cruising through in the summertime by telling you that Cummington is the only Massachusetts town that was ever the subject of a U.S. Information Agency propaganda film. *The Cummington Story* is a romanticized tale of how reluctant residents came to accept outsiders. Some of the displays in the Kingman Tavern illumine the legacy of a for-real 1940s village drama.

The adjective "sleepy" is often applied to villages, but it's seldom accurate. There's always plenty of drama anywhere human beings reside. Too often, descriptors such as sleepy are just self-congratulatory labels applied by smug urban dwellers and suburbanites.

Cummington is an old village named for Colonel John Cumings (with just one "m" and sometimes spelled without an "s"), who bought land there in 1762. He fought in the Revolutionary War, as did several other local men. The village incorporated in 1779, and was a self-contained farming community for a while, though not one untouched by the Industrial Revolution. By the 1830s, small concerns—tanneries, cutlery shops, forges, metal shops, and grist and lumber mills—lined the riverbanks.

Agriculture and Western Mass hilltowns have long been a challenging match, and Cummington slowly evolved into an intriguing but sometimes tension-fraught mix of Yankee traditionalists and newcomers. There was, for instance, strong abolitionist sentiment in the village that was often fanned by visiting agitators. There was equally vociferous opposition; seven men were booted from the local Congregationalist church for their devotion to the antislavery cause.

The future of Cummington depended upon reconciling old and new ways. Farming declined to the point where, in 1869, a local cattle show was held to encourage agriculture. It didn't revitalize farming, but the parade of bovines dovetailed nicely with the first Cummington Fair held the previous year. These days the fair is regarded as a quintessential "old-time" fair and is one of the oldest in the Commonwealth.

Nostalgia, though, is by nature backward looking. Cummington's most revered local, William Cullen Bryant, embodied the transition between old and new. He was born in the village, but the family homestead was sold in 1835. Bryant bought it back 30 years later, by which time he had won acclaim elsewhere. As he rebuilt his home, Cummington began to look different from the village of his childhood. In 1881—just three years after Bryant's death—Cummington hosted a suffrage convention that attracted speakers such as Lucy Stone and Julia Ward Howe.[1]

Tilling the Soil for *The Cummington Story*

The circumstances behind *The Cummington Story* emerged from those who marched to different drummers, especially in the 20th century. The film's theme of learning to accept outsiders, including Jews, isn't quite as dramatic when placed in context. Nonconformity and heterogeneity were suspect in the 19th century, but by the 1910s, at least some Cummington residents had grown accustomed to different ways of doing things.

For instance, not all villagers rallied to World War I, as they had to previous wars. Stories circulate of young men hiding from recruiters, and of an unnamed resister who lived in a cave along the Westfield River. Though he did not arrive in Cummington until 1921, the Rev. Carl Michael Sangree Sr. (1894–1977) was also a conscientious objector during the war, and it speaks volumes that he pastored the very Congregationalist church that once expelled abolitionists.

More changes were on the wing. In 1923, Katherine Frazier founded the Cummington School of the Arts, a playhouse inspired in part by the famed Provincetown Players. It quickly evolved into a broader arts and educational mission that offered six-week summer programs for gifted children, writers, actors, playwrights, musicians, and artists. Before it closed in 1993, its alums included talents such as photographer Diane Arbus, artists Helen Frankenthaler and Willem de Kooning, writer Archibald Macleish, and poet Marianne Moore. In 1939, the school also inspired Henry Duncan to found Cummington Press, nationally renowned for its high-quality handset letterpress books.

Cummington's creative reputation was such that the Greenwood Music Camp relocated there. It was started by Dorothy ("Bunny") Fay and Rumsey McGregor in 1933. They first set up programs in Isle La Motte, Vermont, and then Harvard, Massachusetts. In 1940, the camp shifted to Cummington, which Fay knew from teaching music at summer programs held at Smith College. It remains a haven for children studying classical and chamber music.

The final piece of *The Cummington Story* is that the village was also home to Meadowbrook Lodge, informally known from 1910 through 1940 as the "Jewish summer camp." Numerous Jewish children from New York City and elsewhere frolicked on the 630-acre campus. It was never as large or as well appointed as Jewish resorts in the Catskills several hours west, but Judaism was not entirely mysterious to Cummington's Yankee Protestants as the storms of World War II gathered.

Cummington and World War II

By 1940, Hitler's armies had swept across most of Europe. The Rev. Sangree attended the General Council of Congregational Churches in Cambridge, Massachusetts, and asked what a pacifist minister could do to alleviate the suffering. He was told, "Take care of the refugees."

Sangree sought $10,000 to develop a refugee program, but the money never came. Although he and the Rev. Roland Johnson of Ashfield raised a small amount of money, Sangree struck a bold blow; he gave up his own 17-room home for the cause. From May 1940 through September 1944, Sangree's Main Street home operated as the Cummington Refugee Hostel.

An estimated 50 individuals—mostly Jews and blended Jewish/Christian families— spent varying amounts of time in the village. Many were highly educated and/or possessed skills that fit well at the local School for the Arts and the Cummington Press. Some studied with Philip Hicken (1910–1985), a well-known artist who lived in Cummington in the 1940s and also painted murals for the New Deal's Works Progress Administration.

This house was a refugee hostel during WWII.

The first refugee was Johannes H. Gaides, a German political refugee and agricultural economist, who had escaped from two concentration camps. He went on to study at Harvard. Others included Dr. Kurt Jellinek and his wife, who left Nazi-held Austria; Paul Frank, a lawyer from Vienna; George Beer, a German radical; Czech language teacher and translator Paul Amann[2] (1884–1950); and Viennese insurance salesman Werner Koenigsberger and his wife, who assumed the roles of Joseph and Anna in the Cummington propaganda film.[3]

The best-known refugees were those who distinguished themselves in the arts: painter Paul Wieghardt and his sculptor wife Nelly Barr, whose work was displayed the Berkshire Museum; painter and graphic artist Gustav Wolf (1887–1947); folk art wood carver Ana Niesel; and German Jewish poet Joel Picard. Other refugees generally found work in various local enterprises.

Promoting the American Way of Life

When World War II ended, the U.S. Information Agency empowered its Motion Picture Bureau to produce a series of films promoting the virtues of the American way of life. *The Cummington Story* (1945) was its New England entry, a spur-of-the-moment choice, as scouts had previously considered a Maine location.

The film is unabashedly propagandistic and, from a contemporary perspective, a saccharine mash-up of Norman-Rockwell-like sentimentality, charm, nostalgia, and naïveté. Sangree narrated the movie, which is a fictionalized account of the Refugee Hostel and the village's struggle to overcome cultural barriers. Several of the refugees assumed character roles, and locals appeared as extras.

Cummington emerged as a postcard "white village" (see chapter 15) in which fearful villagers and displaced refugees eventually bond through work, music, love of the land, religious faith, participation in the local economy, and the Cummington Fair. Breakthrough moments include Joseph's acceptance into the Old Stove League, a group of men who gathered for checkers and chat at the general store.

The film fades out with Sangree sermonizing that the "strangeness of people breaks down when they live, work, and meet together as neighbors." Cut to the bittersweet ending as Joseph delivers a farewell speech at the local church, before he and his family board a bus that is the first leg of their journey back to their homeland. Sangree intones that Cummington had been "reluctant to greet strangers," but was now "reluctant to say goodbye to friends."[4]

Much of the script seems dated today, and those who know local geography will snicker at aerial shots of fields and features along the Connecticut River, not the streams that course through Cummington. The film treats conflict as mere suspicion and ignores xenophobic responses in the wake of Pearl Harbor, including villagers' calls for Sangree's ouster. There is, however, a musical bonus: Aaron Copland (1900–1990), one of the nation's greatest composers of elegiac theme music, penned the score.

A Poignant Legacy

Sangree left the pulpit in 1946, but continued to summer in Cummington. The then-widowed minister married Florence Lyon—a former Northfield School admission director—and the two promoted international understanding. Among other things, they built connections between the Northfield and Mount Hermon schools and Le Collège-Lycée Cévenol International (1938–2014) in France, a training school for peace activists located in a village that sheltered Jews during World War II.

The Sangrees were not the only ones in Western Mass to build bridges across cultures. Sections II and III of the Selective Training and Service Act of 1940 provided draft deferments for those working in agriculture, but seasonal laborers, part-time workers, and numerous others were subject to conscription. The war thus caused manpower shortages among Western Mass farmers.

By October 1944, some 700 German prisoners of war held at Chicopee's Westover Air Force Base worked on various farms. Many were part of a special (and semi-secret) project that included English-language classes and cultural training in the hope that indoctrinated

POWs would help improve future U.S./German relations. American International College in Springfield also had a program that operated into the 1950s that trained more than 100 European artisans from 11 nations to work in local industries.

Cummington's Refugee Hostel remains an inspiring and enlightened effort that unfolded against a backdrop of global bloodshed and tyranny. The 1945 film cast Cummington as a typical New England village but, as we've seen, it has long been a place where contrarians and creative talents have lived and made their voices heard. Pulitzer Prize-winning poet Richard Wilbur (1921–2017) lived there, and MSNBC anchor Rachel Maddow calls it home. Also tucked away in folded hills and back roads you'll find scores of potters, ceramic artists, woodworkers, painters, graphic designers, and niche farmers. When The Creamery, a beloved local general store and hangout, was threatened with closure in 2009, locals resurrected it as a community-owned cooperative. The Rev. Sangree certainly would have applauded that spirit.

1 Lucy Stone was involved in most of the key events of the early suffrage movement, including organizing the first national conference. She was also the first Massachusetts woman to obtain a college degree (Oberlin, 1847). Julia Ward Howe was also an important activist, though she is best remembered for penning the lyrics to "The Battle Hymn of the Republic."

2 Paul Amann exemplified the difficulty refugees faced. He, his wife, and children were originally placed with a Quaker family in Philadelphia, but post-Pearl-Harbor suspicion forced him to go to Northampton and then to Cummington, but alone. Sangree sought to secure work for Amann as a language teacher, mostly unsuccessfully. Amann and his family left Massachusetts for New York state in 1946, where he finally got work at various upstate colleges.

3 The film depicts "Joseph" and "Anna" as returning home after the war. In truth, the Koenigsbergers stayed in Cummington. As the film shows, both were fine musicians with a devotion to classical music.

4 The film can be viewed on YouTube: http://www.youtube.com/watch?v=t08g07 IBa4A.

30
Gardner and Greenfield: When Factories Founder

New Englanders sometimes use the expression "people from away" to reference tourists. When people from away venture outside of Boston, they comment on three things: New England's "pretty" villages, its scenic splendor, and its massive redbrick factories.

Follow the Red Brick Road

This chapter is about red brick. Outsiders generally think of red brick as a housing material, but if you live here, you mostly associate it with jobs that no longer exist. Much of Springfield Technical Community College (STCC), for example, is housed in red brick hulks that had been part of the United States Armory system from Colonial times through 1968; the Massachusetts Museum of Contemporary Art (Mass MoCA) in North Adams repurposed the buildings of the former Sprague Electric Company. Both are wonderful institutions, but neither comes close to replacing the same number of workers who once collected paychecks at those sites.

 Western Mass has a lot of red brick, and most of it has yet to find a second act comparable to STCC or Mass MoCA. What's the best way to remember bygone lifestyles? The giant chair of Gardner is a whimsical memorial. Greenfield's Museum of Our Industrial Heritage takes a more serious approach.

A Big Chair for a Big Loss

As we have seen, big things fascinate Americans. If you set your GPS for 130 Elm Street in Gardner, you'll find yourself outside an elementary school whose front lawn sports a 20'7"-high ladder-back chair. If you want one like it for your den, reinforce the floor; it weighs over 3,000 pounds.

Gardner's giant chair is impressive, silly, and fun. It's also sad, as it's the last link to a once-thriving enterprise that earned the town nicknames such as "Chair City" and the "Furniture Capital of New England."

Gardner bicentennial chair

Gardner incorporated in 1785, and 20 years later, James Comee began using a foot-powered lathe to produce wooden and flag-bottom chairs, the latter term meaning it had a seat constructed of rushes (twisted, wet cattail leaves). Soon thereafter, one of Comee's apprentices, Elijah Putnam, started making cane-bottomed chairs.

By 1878, there were a dozen chair shops in Gardner. One was Heywood Brothers —established in 1835—which became one of the most revered chair manufacturers in the country. It merged with the Wakefield Company in 1897 and continued to make high-quality furniture in Gardner until 1979.1 Other local firms included Conant-Bell Furniture, C. H. Hartshorn, S. Bent and Brothers, Gem Industries, and Nichols and Stone.

In 1900, there were at least 20 furniture factories in Gardner, with P. Derby and Company reputed to be the second-biggest chair manufacturer in the United States. Each year, Gardner workers made more than four million chairs and untold numbers of baby carriages, household furnishings, cabinets, cribs, sewing tables, and other useful items.

As anyone smaller or bigger than the norm knows, chairs may be common, but finding a comfortable one for your particular *tucas* is a difficult and selective process. In that spirit, Gardner chair makers produced their goods in various styles, sizes, and materials, though they tended to favor natural-material seats: rush, cane (split and woven), wicker (split willow or palm), and rattan.[2] Gardner's reputation within the furniture business was such that building giant chairs became a marker of one-upmanship and rivalry sometimes jocularly labeled the "Chair Wars."

Before it closed in 2002, Gardner Heritage State Park displayed a 12-foot-high chair built in 1905, that was once billed as the "world's tallest chair." In 1927, upstarts in Thomasville, North Carolina, built one 13½-feet tall. The very next year, Gardner manufacturers responded with a 15-foot Mission-style chair. And to rub mud in Thomasville's eyes, Gardner tore down its big chair in 1935, and replaced it with a 16-foot Colonial Hitchcock.

The Depression and World War II temporarily halted the chair competition but in 1948, Thomasville chair makers unveiled an 18-foot Duncan Phyfe and set it on a 12-foot pedestal. At that point, the floodgates opened and reason rushed out. Among the new contenders for the world's tallest chair: Bennington, Vermont (19'); Washington, D.C. (19'6"); Morristown, Tennessee (20'); and Gardner's own Bicentennial chair, which now sits on Elm Street. Then came Binghamton, New York (24'9"), and two in Wingdale, New York, a 25-footer and a 30-footer that toppled during a 1996 storm. Alabama, Texas, South Dakota, Colorado, Missouri, and Indiana also did their best to get a rung up on the competition.

Don't look for Gardner to launch a new Chair Wars attack; no chair factories remain. It would be a tall order in any event. Overseas manufacturers got into the act, and the current record is a 65-foot ladder-back in the middle of a Manzano, Italy, traffic circle.

I first spent time in Gardner in the mid-1980s when the Commonwealth launched a program called "Shifting Gears: The Changing Nature of Work in Massachusetts, 1920–1980." It set scholars loose across the state to look at the Bay State's industrial heritage and to study the impact of deindustrialization. The thinking was that perhaps Massachusetts had something to teach the nation. After all, the American Industrial Revolution was born in the Blackstone River corridor that runs from Worcester to Pawtucket, Rhode Island.

Forget those "pretty" New England villages; Massachusetts was Ground Zero of the mass-production factory system. It was first to industrialize, but also the first region to experience empty red brick factories. The decline began to be noticeable after World War I, when Bay State corporations—especially in shoes, textiles, and woolens—pulled up stakes and fled to the low-wage South. The Great Depression accelerated the exodus; aging infrastructure exacted a toll after the Second World War, and then came foreign competition, automation, the 1970s energy crisis, deregulation, and changes in tax policy that rewarded outsourcing.

By the 1980s, Gardner still called itself "Chair City," but it was one of the cities slated to receive a Heritage State Park, museums with staffs tasked with documenting disappearing modes of work and studying what came next. When the Heywood-Wakefield plant closed in 1979, its Central and Elm Street plant in West Gardner was soon placed on the National Register of Historical Places (1983), and it became part of a local historical district in 1985, the year Gardner's Heritage Center opened.

These things were more akin to tombstones than to tourist attractions. History couldn't save Gardner; the Heritage Center closed in 2002. Six years later, famed New York furniture maker L. and L. G. Stickley bought out Nichols and Stone, and Gardner lost its remaining large-scale chair manufacturer.

Gardner's fate was similar to many of its Route 2 neighbors. Fifteen miles east of Gardner, Leominster was once known as "Comb City," then "Plastics City." No more. Ten miles north of Gardner, Winchendon displays a 12-foot wooden rocking horse from its days as the "Toy City." To the west, Athol's machine-tool industry has shrunk in size and output, and New Home sewing machines pulled the plug in the town of Orange. Further west still, North Adams no longer manufactures shoes, textiles, or electrical capacitors.

What used to be called "smokestack industries" took big hits elsewhere too. It's been decades since Holyoke was called "Paper City" or Westfield "Whip City" for actually making those products. Decaying red brick in the Connecticut River Valley and the Berkshires once fronted manufacturing associated with a who's who of American industrial might. Among the firms now gone or fading:

- Adams: Berkshire Fine Spinning
- Chicopee: Ames Manufacturing, Duryea, Spalding, Stevens/Savage, Victor Bicycle, Uniroyal
- Florence: Corticelli Silk, Pro-Brush Company, Nonotuck Silk
- Holyoke: American Pad and Paper, Boston Associates (textiles)
- Millers Falls: Millers Falls Company (tools)
- Pittsfield: General Electric
- Springfield: American Bosch, Good Housekeeping, Indian Motorcycle, Jones and Lamson, Milton Bradley, Rolls Royce, U.S. Armory
- Turners Falls: John Russell Cutlery
- Westfield: Columbia Bicycle, Stanhome (cleaning products)

Greenfield and the Runaway Machine Tool Trade

Many Western Mass towns and cities once had thriving machine-tool shops, which is where Greenfield enters our drama. Its Museum of Our Industrial Heritage (MOIH) on Mead Street occupies a remnant of the once mighty Greenfield Tap & Die Company (GTD), which was once the nation's largest such company.

The museum tells the story of local industry, collects the stories of former workers, and seeks to be part of Greenfield's revitalization. These are serious tasks; hence the museum lacks the waggish humor of the Gardner chair. It does, however, help us understand the meaning of crumbling red brick.

It's this basic: until recently, there were no machines without machinists. They were the ones who built the tools that cut metal and made it possible to fashion it into parts from which machines were built. If it drilled, screwed, bore, cut, sharpened, sheared, ground, planed, shaped, or joined, machinists were the reason. They also made parts interchangeable. Some jobs could be learned quickly, but machinist was not among them; machinists were highly skilled and well compensated.

GTD's story begins with an English immigrant named John Grant, who made his way to Greenfield in 1872. He came up with a two-piece system—taps and dies—that cut and threaded connectible metal pieces. A simple example is a nut and bolt, once Greenfield's stock in trade (along with screws). Imagine the intricacies of a large machine and the many pieces that must be cut, shaped, and joined.

Making taps and dies is precision work with tolerances so small that it took computer programmers years to develop software that could best the exactitude of top machinists.

GTD officially formed in 1912 as a holding company that consolidated several smaller firms. By 1920, the GTD complex along the Green River mushroomed to 145,000 square feet and produced more than two dozen distinct cutting and threading sets. By decade's end, GTD had annual sales of $3.5 million and roughly a third of its sales were overseas. Although GTD suffered during the 1930s Great Depression, its specialized production meant it was not hit as badly as other industries. GTD boomed during World War II, when it operated around the clock and employed several thousand workers with half again that number enrolled in training programs. GTD workers enjoyed high wages and generous benefits that ranged from insurance plans to company-sponsored recreation leagues, picnics, scholarships, and outings.

Alas, like many other Massachusetts firms, decline accelerated in the late 1950s. Mergers in 1958 and 1962 led to contraction, though GTD—as part of TRW[3]—still pumped around $10 million annually into Greenfield's economy into the 1970s.

The 1970s recession hurt GTD badly and, in 1986, it was sold to investor Samuel Fox, who promised to modernize production and raise wages. Instead, he slashed wages by $4 per hour and sold GTD to Kennametal in 1992. By 1996, just 400 workers remained in Greenfield. Kennametal slashed jobs further, and as of 2019, employs a workforce of around 250, the number fluctuating according to company needs. In all, the number of GTD workers has fallen by some 90 percent since its post-World-War-II high-water mark. Competition is only partly to blame; hundreds lost their jobs due to automation, outsourcing, and disinterested profit-takers.

There are a handful of small machine shops left in Western Mass, but if you see taps and dies anywhere these days it's likely to be part of an innovative scrap metal sculpture by renowned area artist James

Kitchen, or perhaps made into Jewish ritual objects by Archie Nahman, a former machinist, self-taught metals artist, and former MOIH board member.

Job loss isn't a pleasant story, but it's also part of what Western Mass is about. What is to be done with all that red brick? Maybe, as in North Adams or Springfield, we retrofit some of it as a museum or an educational facility. Conceivably, some could become housing, office space, or a specialty manufactory. Perhaps some waste materials from the industrial past find their way into creative hands such as those of Kitchen or Nahman. But the challenge for towns like Gardner or Greenfield is replacing high-paying jobs and lost tax revenue. One measure suggests the scale of the problem. When Greenfield assessed the value of the remaining GTD buildings and 10 acres of land in 2000, it was just $99,300.[4] The next time someone "from away" asks about the red brick, tell them the truth: it's debris from a tragedy.

[1] Fans of the PBS broadcast *Antiques Roadshow* will know that Heywood-Wakefield furniture is greatly valued by collectors.

[2] Many items claiming to be rattan are simulated. Pure rattan comes from tropical palms, preferably from Borneo, and is rather expensive.

[3] TRW was the handle for the Thompson Ramo Woodbridge Corporation, an Ohio-based firm with ties to the automotive and aerospace industries.

[4] Much of the site was demolished in 2002. The remaining buildings need extensive renovation, and the site is part of a pollution-cleanup initiative.

31
You Can Get Anything You Want (Including Alice's Church): The Guthrie Center of Great Barrington

"Alice's Restaurant" ranks high on the list of iconic stories from the 1960s. What Baby Boomer could not spontaneously bust out the tag line: "You can get anything you want, at Alice's Restaurant"? In 18 minutes and 34 seconds, composer and song hero (anti-hero?) Arlo Guthrie laid out a masterpiece that is equal parts talking blues[1], ragtime melody, comedy, farce, and morality play. For those too young to remember, "Alice's Restaurant" is a hilarious partly fictionalized version of an actual, though improbable, event.

The Guthrie Center

As anyone who has heard the song or seen the spin-off movie knows, Alice Brock's actual restaurant is just a catchy song hook; culinary skills don't have much of a role to play in the comic drama. Arlo Guthrie never went into food services nor, to the best of my knowledge, did he acquire all of his life desires at Alice's Restaurant. He did and does, however, pursue quite a few of them in the church where much of the Alice's Restaurant drama unfolded. Guthrie now owns that building, which operates as the Guthrie Center. You can visit it at 2 Van Deusenville Road, in the Berkshires village of Housatonic, part of the town of Great Barrington.

Fiction is Stranger than Truth

Perhaps it seems odd to include the Guthrie Center in a section about museums. After all, museums collect the past, and Guthrie remains an active and beloved performer who still lives part of the year in Western Mass.

Let's expand what we mean by the word museum. A good one opens doors to what historians call the usable past, pieces of the past that also inform the present. Since remnants of 1960s idealism live on at the Guthrie Center, it's appropriate to take a stroll back in time to place it in context. Though it pains me to say it, some of the events commemorated in the old church are at least vintage, if not antique.[2] As of 2020, the events described in Arlo's tale reached their 55th anniversary.

Arlo Guthrie was born July 10, 1947, one of the four children of folk music legend Woody Guthrie and his second wife, Marjorie Mazia Guthrie. Arlo spent much of his childhood in Brooklyn, but finished grades nine through 12 at Stockbridge (MA) School, a private progressive boarding campus. Ray and Alice Brock worked at the school, Ray as a shop teacher and Alice as school librarian. They purchased the church as their home in 1964, and Arlo was among a group of high school students who visited them there.

Guthrie graduated in the spring of 1965, and enrolled in Rocky Mountain College in Billings, Montana, in the fall, with a vague idea of pursuing a forestry degree. The trouble began when he and a friend, Rick Robbins, decided to spend Thanksgiving break back East with Alice and Ray, Alice having recently purchased a space in Stockbridge where she would run a restaurant.

Guthrie took many liberties in his tale; it was, after all, a slice of musical shtick, not a documentary.[3] There never was an Alice's Restaurant; the Stockbridge eatery was called The Back Room and accounts differ as to whether it had opened in November 1965.[4] But the gist of Guthrie's story is true. The Brocks really did live in a church that was old even in the 1960s.

A foundation stone bears the year 1866, but that's a re-founding date. It began life as St. James Chapel in 1829, and enlarged to something close to its current configuration in 1866, when it became Trinity Church. It operated as an Episcopal Church until 1964, when it was deconsecrated and sold to the Brocks, who decided to live there. More accurately, they lived in the choir loft, as the main floor was an ongoing construction site. The new owners were among the legions to discover that the *idea* of renovating an old building is more romantic than actually *doing* so.

As Guthrie related in "Alice's Restaurant," there was plenty of room for "a Thanksgiving dinner that couldn't be beat" on the main floor "where the pews used to be." Guthrie told *Rolling Stone* reporter Patrick Doyle in 2014, "To have what happened to me actually happen and not be a work of fiction … remains amazing." After their repast, Guthrie and others bundled up the dinner waste and quite a lot of construction debris, and drove a VW microbus to the Stockbridge landfill. To their chagrin, it was closed, so they dumped the trash onto another pile of garbage they spied near the Indian Hill School. As it transpired, though, they disgorged their contents onto private property, which led to their arrest by "Officer Obie," Stockbridge Police

Chief William J. Obanhein. Arlo and his compatriots spent the night in jail before making bail the next morning.

Guthrie greatly embellished his arrest. Photographs of the "crime scene" were, indeed, taken but Guthrie was not handcuffed, nor did Obanhein remove the jail cell's toilet seat or bathroom tissue as overzealous precautions against suicide. The defendants appeared before Special Justice James E. Hannon, who really was blind. They were fined $25 and were ordered to haul the trash back up a hill soaked by a recent rainstorm, and then take it to the legal landfill.

Guthrie spent the remainder of the break hanging out with the Brocks, laughing over the events, and improvising verses for the first half of a song that evolved collectively and spontaneously. The great "massacre," as Guthrie described it—borrowing an Ozarks colloquialism for an improbable situation—led to another fateful choice: Arlo left college.

If Guthrie had stayed in school, we probably would have never heard of the incident. Suffice it to say, Arlo Guthrie was not destined for a forestry career. In 1966, leaving school—and with it his 2-S student draft deferment—made the soon-to-be-19-year-old Guthrie subject to military conscription. He received his draft notice and reported to the induction center in New York City, his legal residence. Although the irreverent tale he told of his experience there was consonant with youthful skepticism toward militarism and the Vietnam War, Guthrie invented most of what transpired at the center. He was, however, told that he was unfit for the Army, and was never called to serve.

You Can Make It Anything You Want

Creative people such as Guthrie take the strings of a tale and weave them into ropes. The first public version of "Alice's Restaurant" aired as a 1966 live performance on WBAI Radio in New York, where counterculture disk jockey Bob Fass hosted a show titled "Radio Unnameable." The song caused an immediate stir and Guthrie recorded it as one entire side of an album, which was released in 1967, the same year Guthrie performed the piece at the Newport Folk Festival.

Call it a song that captured the zeitgeist or a work of genius, but "Alice's Restaurant" took on a life of its own. Director Arthur Penn turned it into a full-length motion picture, with Guthrie, Obanhein, and Hannon portraying themselves. The movie hit the theaters on August 19, 1969, just days after Guthrie performed at Woodstock. For a time, the demand for the story was so great that Guthrie refused to perform it, lest he fall prey to what he called "Ricky Nelson syndrome," having one's art held hostage to audience expectations. These days, he dusts it off for significant anniversaries and has even recorded a longer version with added comic interludes, wry comments, and greater sensitivity to a few remarks that would today ruffle feathers.

Guthrie eventually made his home in the Berkshires and, in 1991, purchased Trinity Church. After the Brocks sold the building in 1971, it had several owners prior to Guthrie. He renovated it, built a small addition, and made it the center of enterprises such as Rising Son Records, the Guthrie Foundation, a music and spoken-word series, and social outreach. On Sundays, ecumenical religious services unfold under the rubric of "Bring Your Own God." In 2017–18, the church underwent renovations to replace the ceiling, restore the stained glass window, and increase its energy efficiency.

In the best spirit of 1960s idealism, all faiths and points of view are honored. The Guthrie Center's outlook is embodied in words from Ma Jaya Sati Bhagaviti (born Joyce Green), a Jewish/Hindu spiritual leader:

One God — Many Forms
One River—Many Streams
One People—Many Faces
One Mother—Many Children

Most visitors to the Guthrie Center come to attend concerts in the inviting former sanctuary, where tables accommodate attendees and diners who sample café items from the kitchen just off the lobby. Alice has nothing to do with the fare on offer, but one can visit the loft and imagine the Brocks' time there.

The lobby best fits traditional ideas of a museum. It is home to wonderful archival photos and posters for those seeking a time-warp experience. There is also a small shop where one can purchase CDs and other Guthrie-related merchandise.

The spirit of the Sixties is most evident, though, in things concert-goers *don't* see: the work of the Guthrie Foundation. The old church now has vitality as a community center where all manner of activities take place that bring '60s idealism into the 21st century: free community lunches, tutoring, yoga classes, and (of course!) a Thanksgiving feast. It is also the pivot around which charitable events spin, particularly those related to raising awareness of and money for research into Huntington's chorea, the disease that killed Woody Guthrie. In a wonderfully ironic twist, the major calendar event in the latter effort is an annual "Garbage Trail Walk to Massacre Huntington Disease."

Alice's Restaurant Side Dishes

Here's some trivia for "Alice's Restaurant" fans:

- A story circulates that the 18:34 length of the original "Alice's Restaurant" was wry commentary on the length of the erased gap in the Nixon Watergate tapes. This is apocryphal, as the actual length of Guthrie's stage patter varied each time he performed it. The album version clocks in at 18:16.
- Guthrie claims that the style of the song/story has four major inspirational threads. They are: 1. Storytelling inspired by comedians Lord

Buckley and Bill Cosby. 2. Guitar-picking borrowed from Mississippi John Hurt, Elizabeth Cotton, and Doc Watson. 3. The talking blues learned from his father. 4. The political worldview of Pete Seeger.

- Alice's Restaurant" also has four parts: the concept of massacre, the tale of the incidents, the response to the incidents, and a broader moral.
- Although often called an "antiwar song," Guthrie insists it's more an "anti-stupidity" composition.
- Officer Obanhein claimed that if there had only been a few bags of garbage, he would have altered history by picking them up himself!
- Alice Brock's Stockbridge eatery occupied the bottom of a building that was once artist Norman Rockwell's studio. Bill Obanhein was one of Rockwell's occasional models.
- Obanhein admitted he had little sympathy for longhaired youths at the time, but he came to see them as "good kids." He agreed to be in the movie version of "Alice's Restaurant" because he thought it best to make a fool of himself rather than let an actor do it. He and Guthrie became friends on the set and remained so. Obanhein died in 1994, five weeks before his 70th birthday.
- Alice Brock moved to Provincetown in 1979, where she works as an artist and operates a gallery.
- The shortened single version of "Alice's Restaurant" never cracked the Billboard Top 100, though the album rose as high as #17.
- Guthrie long ago removed a word from the performance that would today be viewed as anti-gay.
- Despite tales to the contrary, Guthrie made it clear that Alice Brock was not promiscuous and never cheated on Ray. The two remain friends.
- Guthrie thinks the enduring success of "Alice's Restaurant" has much to do with its takedown of "idiocy" and the fact that it's a classic little-guy-versus-the-system tale.
- The Stockbridge School operated from 1948 to 1976. It closed for financial reasons, as did a subsequent private school. The campus now houses a nursing facility. Chevy Chase is also a Stockbridge School alum; film director Christopher Guest attended but did not matriculate.

1   The talking blues should not be confused with the style of music that evolved from African American spirituals and slave songs. The talking blues is a form of folk music—usually influenced by country and old-time music—with a free-flowing melody that accompanies a spoken-word performance. The latter, though, is usually very rhythmic and is not quite speech and not quite singing. Nor is the instrumentation like classic 12-bar blues; the talking blues usually depend upon a repeated chord progression. Arlo Guthrie is known for his tall tales and funny stories. He borrowed the talking blues from his father, Woody Guthrie, and from Pete Seeger, known raconteurs.

2   The definition of an antique is a matter of dispute among collectors and assessors, and I'm content to leave them to it. For the record, though, it used to be that an object had to be 100 years old or more to be an antique, though some experts now use 50 years as their guideline. Complicating matters, a home or building only has to be 50 to be an "historic" structure, though it must meet other criteria of social and historic importance, not merely be old. Items, objects, and homes take just 20 years to become vintage, but when they turn into antiques is disputable. Historians are all over the map on how far in the past an event must have occurred to be considered "history." Some say the past is as recent as yesterday, or that some of the participants must be deceased. Still others apply arbitrary timeframes such as 20 years or a generation. Now do you understand why I'm content to let others argue over this stuff?

3   You can find a version of "Alice's Restaurant" with lyrics at http://www.youtube.com/watch?v=m57gzA2JCcM. Arthur Penn's film can be viewed on YouTube at http://www.youtube.com/watch?v=FDI-mtoR6SI.

4   Guthrie recalls that Alice had opened her café, but Brock claims she opened it shortly *after* Thanksgiving. It was short-lived; she closed it in the spring of 1966 and moved to Boston. The Brocks divorced in 1968 and sold the church in 1971. Alice Brock later had a take-out in Housatonic, then a bigger restaurant in Lenox that was foreclosed in 1979.

32
The Skinner Museum in South Hadley: The Attic of Western Mass

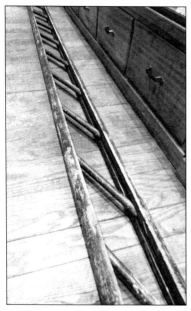

A folding wooden ladder

I've saved the quirkiest museum for last! A lot of "updated" museums are too slick for their own good. Splashy websites trumpet upcoming events, audio tours are readied, and curators busy themselves with displaying works that make a statement. Often you can borrow an iPad as you make your way through featured shows or amuse yourself at kiosks that display everything from rotating holograms of objects to short videos explaining what your eyes see. That is, when they're not boring you to kingdom come with information you'll never need to know.

You can count on the fact that a well-stocked gift shop will offer memories of your visit in every form imaginable—from books, postcards, and posters to T-shirts, coffee mugs, scarves, and plush toys. There are even well-crafted reproductions from the exhibition for those willing to shell out serious money.

Gloriously Old-Fashioned

You won't find *any* of that at the Skinner Museum in South Hadley, a place so gloriously behind the times that it nearly doubles back on itself to become cutting edge! The experience of visiting is like prowling in the treasures-and-trash attic of a slightly batty great aunt who never tossed anything. The 7,000-object collection appears eclectic, random, and chaotic. Why, for example, is there a wooden monkey hanging on a wall festooned with tribal spears? Or case after case of seashells and rocks?

There's more organization than you think, but you will find new and unusual things each time you visit. One of my favorites lies along the floor of the right-hand side of the main hall. It looks like a debarked wooden log that I first imagined was a wooden water pipe from days past. A friendly docent showed me that it's cleverer than that; she pushed up from the bottom, which revealed it to be one side of a folding wooden ladder, complete with collapsible rungs. (See previous page.) Another push and voila: an easy-to-store ladder. Ladders are mere tools, of course, but I experienced the thrill of viewing something I had never before seen.

The Skinner Museum is such a throwback that some worry that it needs to get with the times. I hope that doesn't happen. The Skinner does something that few museums do anymore: take us back in time the moment we enter the doors. After all, how often are you greeted by two suits of armor flanking a carved tribal figure and standing amidst a jumble of pewter, musical instruments, old bicycles, and mounted animal heads?

The museum doors, incidentally, are attached to what used to be a Congregational church in the Swift River Valley town of Prescott, one of the four towns abandoned when the Quabbin Reservoir was built. In 1929, silk mill operator Joseph Allen Skinner (1862–1946) paid to have the church dismantled, removed to South Hadley, and rebuilt, a painstaking process completed in 1932. Skinner opened the church doors in 1932 and continually added objects to his museum until his death, at which point it was deeded to Mount Holyoke College, whose art museum now administers it.

The wonders inside the Skinner are quite different from the formal paintings and sculptures on display in the campus art museum. You go to the Skinner to see third-century Roman oil lamps share space with glass pigs, cigar crimpers, birds' eggs, Colonial tableware, masks from Oceania, a hippopotamus skull, snuff bottles, and a parlor dome filled with stuffed birds. I've not even scratched the surface; there are more than 7,000 objects at the Skinner but it feels like more. Wise visitors drink it in through small sips rather than large gulps.

Skinner's approach was once innovative. Most sources credit painter Charles Willson [sic] Peale (1741–1827) with opening the first American museum worthy of being called such, though Peale called

his a "cabinet of curiosities." Peale unveiled his displays in Philadelphia in 1786, just three years after the Treaty of Paris officially recognized the independence of the United States. He showcased his own canvasses, but also architectural finds, a woolly mammoth skeleton, taxidermy, and fossils. Upon Peale's death, P. T. Barnum (1810–91) bought much of the collection.

Barnum is best remembered for trafficking in hoaxes and freak shows, but there was also an educational component to his hucksterism. For instance, he operated a Chinese museum in Boston from 1840 to 1847 that spotlighted items secured by maritime traders. Crowds lined up outside his New York City museum to see outsized paintings of the Grand Canyon, a place few Easterners would have seen in person at a time when most rail lines ended in Chicago. Among Caucasians, only a handful of westward-bound settlers and surveyors had gone deep into Southwestern canyon lands.

In fact, until the 20th century, sailors, soldiers, explorers, arriving immigrants, and the well-heeled were among the few who actually saw much of the world beyond where they lived. Cabinets of curiosities were a way for the American masses to learn about the broader world, including their own nation.

One of the original distinctions between museums and historical societies was that museums collected broadly and historical societies mostly locally. You've probably also noticed that some places in Massachusetts—Boston, Pittsfield, and Westfield among them—have museums and libraries designated as *athenaeums*. That ancient Greek term was deliberately chosen to indicate a "scientific" approach to art, literature, and material objects that were allegedly untainted by Barnum-like hokum. In essence, many quality museums were cabinets of curiosities. Their intent was to be educational, hence *not* like your great aunt's attic.

The Family Behind the Skinner Museum

William Skinner (1824–1902) was born in London, England, and immigrated to Northampton in 1843, where he worked briefly at a dye works before entering into a silk mill partnership. In 1853, Skinner struck out on his own. He built a factory along the Mill River between Haydenville and Williamsburg, which he expanded four years later. Skinner called it the Unquomonk Silk Company—an Algonquin word meaning "at the end place"—and the small hamlet where most of Skinner's workers lived was dubbed "Skinnerville."

William Skinner married, built a handsome house near his factory, and sired five children. Two of his sons—William Cobbett (1857–1947) and Joseph Allen (1862–1946)—later entered the silk trade. Joseph Skinner recalled a childhood of collecting arrowheads, bird eggs, and rock specimens in the fields and along the Mill River. Don't look for the Unquomonk Mill or Skinnerville. Today, the Mill River is a humble, shallow stream that looks incapable of inflicting damage worse than a damp basement. Still, it drops 700 feet in its 13½-mile run to the Connecticut River, which made it useful in the age of water-powered industry. It earned its name; by 1870 at least 70 manufactories lined its banks and the Mill River was dammed in numerous places.

On May 16, 1874, shoddy construction and a wet spring collapsed a dam upstream near Williamsburg, a disaster that killed 139 people and swept away most of Skinnerville. Joseph Skinner was one week from his 12th birthday when the river knocked his home from its foundation.

William Skinner was back in business in six months, but this time in Holyoke, where the local power company offered him generous terms to locate along a power canal watered by dams across the Connecticut River. William even moved his damaged Skinnerville home to Holyoke, where it was rebuilt on Cabot Street and renamed "Wistariahurst" [sic].[1] Skinner prospered and his business changed its name to Skinner and Sons Manufacturing in 1876, when William C. Skinner began working in a company office in New York. Joseph A. Skinner also joined the firm upon his graduation from Yale in 1886. By then, Joseph was already an ardent collector. He forged intellectual relationships with Mount Holyoke College President Mary E. Woolley, and with South Hadley neighbor and town historian Sophie Eastman. Skinner was an early devotee of the Colonial Revival Movement (1880–1940) and was well known in antiquarian circles throughout the East.

He also earned a reputation for being civic-minded, and was deeply involved in building The Orchards, a world-class golf club; for helping Mount Holyoke rebuild after a devastating 1896 fire; and for purchasing the very mountain for which the college is named. Skinner bought that land—including Summit House—in 1916. In adjacent South Hadley, Skinner's homestead became a repository for buildings saved from the wrecking ball. His home, Mount Holyoke College, and the carriage house at Wistariahurst housed numerous objects that later found their way into the Skinner Museum.

Not Quite Chaos!

One person's chaos is another's filing system. The Skinner Museum's helter-skelter appearance is somewhat deceptive. Skinner's collections reveal several themes.

One is linked to the Colonial Revival Movement's focus on preserving fading ways of life. In some ways, the Skinner Museum is a more offbeat version of Old Greenfield Village in Michigan or Historic Deerfield in the Connecticut River Valley, both of which are rough contemporaries. The basement of the Skinner is the clearest example of this; it's a relatively tidy collection of tools, farm implements, kitchenware, and other everyday items. There is an implied antimodern disdain throughout the museum, one that favors tradition over change.

The glaring exceptions to this are mechanical innovations. Skinner was, after all, a manufacturer and a graduate of Yale's Sheffield Scientific School. Like many men of his age, he equated science with industrial progress. Not surprisingly, he saved things related to the silk industry, from worm to garment, as it were. Other items also pay homage to industrial progress, though these are usually smaller items like the aforementioned cigar crimper. Still others relate to the need for businesspeople to flog their wares; think of cigar store Indians as an analog for Skinner Company advertisements.

The Mill River flood left an impression on young Joseph Skinner. As University of Massachusetts researcher Cheryl Harned observes, Skinner developed a fascination with and collection of things related to the Mill River disaster: photos, clippings, items salvaged from 1874, and so on.[2]

One might also imagine there's a lot of the 12-year-old boy in the museum: all those eggs, shells, fossils, bicycles, ship models, and animal heads. Ditto objects that suggest a boy's romantic daydreams: fierce tribesmen, Native Americans in buffalo robes, and knights in shining armor.

Across the river at Wistariahurst, the Skinners opened the carriage house to the public in 1927 as the Holyoke Museum. Its taxidermy displays were an instant hit with children, especially one fashioned by Burlington Schurr, who curated all house exhibits from 1927 until his death in 1951. Schurr was an amateur naturalist who liked to stuff things. His whimsical *piece de résistance* is "Frog Circus," taxidermy frogs, reared on back legs and holding flutes, woodwinds, drums, and brass as if they were the circus band.

When Wistariahurst was deeded to the city of Holyoke in 1959, serious-minded curators—desirous of displaying late-Gilded-Age splendor, not amusements for the hoi polloi—locked the frogs away. Bad move! Popular demand forced staff to bring it into the house where, today, most visitors find it a lot more interesting than silk-brocaded elegance.

I tell that tale to sing the praises of capturing the inner child, something the Skinner Museum does a lot better than most "updated" museums. When the docent opened the folding ladder, mine was the glee of a 12-year-old.

1 Wistariahurst acquired additions in 1913 and 1927.
2 As of this writing, Ms. Harned was still writing a Ph.D. dissertation based on the Skinner family.

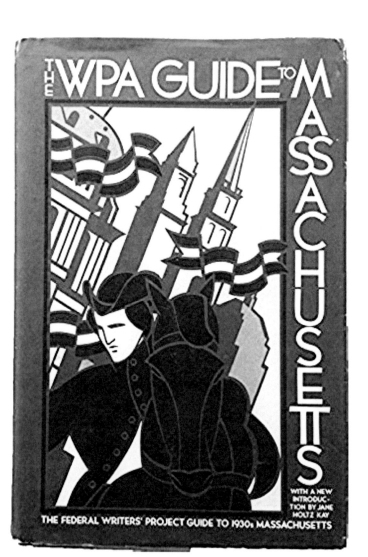

Bibliographic Essay

This book is one of the few scholarly works I've written that doesn't rest mostly upon primary sources. Much of what I found comes from my travels to the places mentioned, chatting with locals, visiting libraries, and surfing the Internet. Consider this bibliography as a start for those who want to read more.

Basic Stuff

One of best ways to see how things have changed is to consult *The WPA Guide to Massachusetts*, published in 1937, as part of the New Deal Federal Writers' Project. Various writers recorded what they saw without judgment. The *Guide* is a chronicle more than a narrative, one that opted for breadth not depth.

Few have captured the sublime within the ridiculous as well as John Margolies, a photographer/social commentator who frequently pointed his lens at roadside oddities. His *Signs of Our Times* (1993) looked at commercial signs designed to lure drivers off the highway through their gargantuan size, whimsical design, humorous catch phrases, or some combination of these. He repeated this approach with bizarre, human-made come-on sculptures in *Fun Along the Road: American Tourist Attractions* (1998). Alas, there wasn't much Western Mass material in his books.

Karal Ann Marling's *The Colossus of Roads: Myth and Symbol along American Highways* (1984) remains a delight. She concentrated on iconic content—everything from Mount Rushmore and images of Abraham Lincoln to figures like Paul Bunyan and Smokey the Bear—plus offbeat advertising and tourist constructions. Most of her material was collected in the Midwest.

Gwyn Headley's *Architectural Follies in America* (1996) surveys fanciful visions, broken dreams, and vivid imaginations as expressed in built structures. Massachusetts has nine references, only two of which come from Western Mass, and one of those never actually existed!

Massachusetts gets a better workout in Jeff Belanger's *Weird Massachusetts: Your Travel Guide to Massachusetts' Local Legends and Best Kept Secrets* (2008). It's no longer in print, but I like its punchy style. A lot of his material, though, is more analogous to TV shows like *Ghost Hunters,* that is, rumors, fanciful imagination, legends, and paranormal tales. There's not much serious history in the text, but it's a fun "leaf-through," even if it is Boston-centric.

Arcadia Publishing's *Images of America* series is invaluable. With more than 7,000 titles in print, one is seldom far from a town covered by one of their books. They are nostalgic and rich in images. Other than the photo captions, though, there's not much to educate readers who don't already know these towns.

Section I: Western Mass BC

I spent time chatting with people at Smith College and surfing the Internet for this section, but a few basic guides include Richard Little, *Dinosaurs, Dunes, and Drifting Continents: The Geology of the Connecticut River Valley,* 2003; Nicholas McDonald, *Windows into the Jurassic World,* 2010; James O'Connell, *Inside Guide to Springfield and the Pioneer Valley,* 1986; and Donald B. Weishampel and Luther Young, *Dinosaurs of the East Coast,* 1986. Weishampel's projects are good sources for many things related to dinosaurs. The Massachusetts Geological Survey also provides a wealth of information: http://mgs.geo.umass.edu/resources/education. It's easy to find information about Nash Dino Land. Mark Roessler's piece in the April 13, 2010 *Valley Advocate* was very useful, but Carlton Nash has been the subject of dozens of features. Just Google his name and you'll find plenty. I am also indebted to his son Kornell for some of the material in my chapter.

Three less conventional places to gather information include immersion at the Beneski Natural History Museum at Amherst College, informative display panels at the Smith College Botanic Garden and Greenhouse, and taking good notes when you visit the dinosaur tracks at Smith's Ferry in Holyoke.

Burnt Hill is harder to research, as most of the exotic interpretations of the site fall into the category of speculation. A starting point—though the work has been soundly criticized by academics—is Barry Fell, *America B.C.: Ancient Settlers in the New World*, 1976. It's always good to sample the outliers! A more thorough, though many would say still overly speculative, report is that of Daniel V. Boudillion and Edward R. Cornish, "Burnt Hill: A Stone Circle in Western Massachusetts," *New England Antiquities Research Association Field Report*, October 1, 2009. The late Judith S. Young of the University of Massachusetts Amherst astronomy department wrote many scholarly as well as mystical papers on standing stones. Finally, for reasons mysterious even to myself, I too am fascinated by standing stones and clues from the human past. I wrote a piece for *Celtic Heritage* (Winter 2008), "Where Heritage Begins: Skara Brae and Celtic Origins," and a local investigation for *Hampshire Life: The Gazette's Weekly Magazine for the Pioneer Valley*, "Stone Circles: Shedding Light on an Ancient Mystery," September 19, 2008.

Section II: Hard to Overlook

Works on Native Americans in Massachusetts and New England are voluminous, so I will simply mention a few: Lisa Brooks, *Our Beloved Kin: A New History of King Philip's War*, 2018; Alfred Cave, *The Pequot War*, 1996; John Demos, *The Unredeemed Captive: A Family Story from Early America*, 1994; Jill Lepore, *The Name of War: King Philip's War and the Origins of American Identity*, 1999; and Neal Salisbury, *Manitou and Providence: Indians, Europeans, and the Making of New England 1500–1693*, 1982. Salisbury is widely regarded as the dean of New England Native American studies, and anything he wrote illumines. If you still haven't gotten enough, the series titled "Native Americans of the Northeast," Brian Halley series editor, has—at last count—21 active titles. There is no shortage of information on the Mohawk Trail, most of it easily accessible on the Internet.

The Whately Town Library has a vertical file on its milk bottle, and its staff is very helpful. See also Enna M. Cline, *Whately 1771–1971: A New England Portrait,* 1972; Burt Feintuch and David Watters, editors, *The Encyclopedia of New England,* 2005; and Masslive.com, "Whately's Iconic Giant Milk Bottle Gets a Makeover," July 19, 2013. I also raided the Smith College art library for works on folk art and found works from Frederick Fried, Jean Lipman, Herbert Hemphill, Jr., and Gerard Watkins to be very helpful.

As for the Northampton monument, I queried just about everyone who would listen on the subject. If you want more information, consult the Northampton Historical Society website links for "The Daley and Halligan Bicentennial Commemoration," http://www.historic-northampton.org/daleyandhalligan/daleyandhalligan.html. For everything else, read my much longer piece on the monument, "Romancing the Stone: Invented Irish and Native American Memories in Northampton," *Historical Journal of Massachusetts* 46:2 (Summer 2018). A special thank you to Elise Bernier Feeley of the Hampshire Room for Local History and Genealogy at the Forbes Library in Northampton.

Gary Leveille has written the definitive work on the newsboy monument: *The Mystery and the History of the Great Barrington Newsboy Statue,* 2016. I also perused the web extensively for sites dealing with Lewis Hine newsboy and child labor images. Joe Manning's work on the "Lewis Hine Project" has been heroic and Herculean in identifying the children in Hine's photographs: https://morningsonmaplestreet.com/lewis-hine-project-index-of-stories/lewis-hine-project/. David Nasaw, *Children of the City: At Work and at Play,* 1985, is very useful, as was *The Historic New York Times* for tracking down information on Colonel William Brown.

Marshall Field has several biographers, including Axel Madson, whose *The Marshall Fields*, 2002, is a fine family history. A good place for short, professional biographies is *American National Biography*, 1999. Timothy Sullivan's entry on Field is outstanding. James Gilbert, *Perfect Cities: Chicago's Utopias of 1893*, 1993 is excellent for placing Field in the urban environment. The Field Memorial Library has published a short pamphlet that details its architectural features.

The "Three Men Down" monument is another one about which I pestered local people for information. It has a Facebook page with links: https://facebook.com/pg/MarianneLabargeWard6/photos/?tab=album&album_id=587176428016235. The online *Daily Hampshire Gazette* index of articles from the 1990s on was useful, as was a card catalogue file of older articles maintained by the Forbes Library in Northampton. I stumbled upon a piece from the *Fitchburg Sentinel*, July 10, 1947, that gave me details of that year's crash atop Mt. Tom. There are numerous good books on the Berlin Airlift. I like the readability of Barry Turner's, *The Berlin Airlift: The Relief Operation that Defined the Cold War*, 2017. Another fine work is Daniel Harrington, *Berlin on the Brink: The Blockade, the Airlift, and the Early Cold War*, 2012. Though it doesn't deal with the airlift, my favorite look at the Cold War is Paul Boyer, *By the Bomb's Early Light: American Thought and Culture at the Dawn of the Atomic Age*, 1985.

Surprisingly little that's verifiable has been written about whether Melville imagined Mount Greylock as a white whale, though an on-site winter visit makes it plausible. Nathaniel Hawthorne remains the main source for the association, and not even staff at Arrowhead could verify that Melville thought so. The *Boston Globe* reported it as a fact in a September 24, 2017, New England Travel piece on the Berkshires. Because I'm not a literature scholar, I consulted quite a few Melville biographies including: Andrew Delbanco, *Melville: His World and*

Work, 2005; Gavin Jones, *Failure and the American Writer: A Literary History*, 2014; Edward H. Miller, *Melville: A Biography*, 1975; James E. Miller, Jr., *A Reader's Guide to Herman Melville*, 1978; and Faith Pullin, editor, *New Perspectives on Melville*, 1978.

The best way to discover a bird's-eye of Western Mass is to follow my example by getting into your car and finding a few!

Section III: Famous Long Ago

The first thing anyone should read about Edward Bellamy is his *Looking Backward* (1888). It is simply the most famous work on utopian thought that the United States has yet produced. I recommend giving it context by looking at works on American utopian experiments such as: Charles Nordhoff, *The Communistic Societies of the United States*, 1966; Timothy Miller, *The 60s Communes: Hippies and Beyond*, 1999; Donald E. Pitzer, ed. *America's Communal Utopias*, 1997; and Foster Stockwell, *Encyclopedia of American Communes 1663–1963*, 1998.

Dwight L. Moody is a fascinating character. To appreciate his educational vision, start with the official record: Sally Atwood Hamilton, editor, *Lift Thine Eyes: The Landscape, the Buildings, the Heritage of Northfield Mount Hermon School*, 2010. Magazines such as *Christianity Today* and *Christian History* periodically revisit Moody's theological thought. Moody's biographers include: Lyle W. Dorsett, *A Passion for Souls: The Life of D. L. Moody*, 1997; Bruce J. Evensen, *God's Man for the Gilded Age: D. L. Moody and the Rise of Modern Mass Evangelism*, 2003; and James F. Findlay Jr. *Dwight L. Moody, American Evangelist, 1837–1899*, 1969.

Erastus Salisbury Field is slippery as a biographical subject. The best work is Mary Black, *Erastus Salisbury Field*, 1984, which was produced as part of an art exhibition catalog. Thomas Maytham's "Two Faces of New England Portrait Painting" for the *Bulletin of the Museum of Fine Arts* 61:323 (1963) is useful, as is the uncredited "The Historical Monument of the American Republic: Cotton Mather Meets the Millennium, http://xroads.virginia.edu/~cap/field/hmar.html. Anyone gazing upon Field's masterpiece should seek a copy of his *Descriptive Catalogue of the Historical Monument of the American Republic*, 1876.

I've been interested in anti-Chinese discrimination for quite some time, and published "Blind in One Eye Only: Western and Eastern Knights of Labor View the Chinese Question," *Labor History* 41: 4 (2000). Excellent books on the subject include: Iris Chang, *The Chinese in America*, 2003; Doris Chu, *Chinese in Massachusetts: Their Experiences and Contributions*, 1987; Andrew Gyory, *Closing the Gate: Race, Politics, and the Chinese Exclusion Act*, 1998; Frederick Rudolph, "Chinamen in Yankeedom: Anti-Unionism in Massachusetts in 1870," *American Historical Review*, 53: 1 (October 1947); and Alexander Saxton, *The Indispensible Enemy: Labor and the Anti-Chinese Movement in California*, 1971. Lue Gim Gong's amazing adventure has been told in Virginia Aronson, *Gift of the Unicorn: The Story of Lue Gim Gong, Florida's Citrus Wizard*, 2002.

Among my sources for thinking about the Hadley Green were: Dona Brown, *Inventing New England*, 1995; Ellen Elizabeth Callahan, *Hadley: A Study of the Political Development of a Typical New England Town from the Official Record (1659–1930)*, 1930; Joe Conforti, *Imagining New England*, 2001; Clifton Johnson, ed. *Old Hadley Quarter Centennial Celebration 1909*, 1909; Sylvester Judd, *History of Hadley*, 1905; Alice Morehouse Walker, *Historic Hadley: The Story of the Making of a Famous Massachusetts Town*, 1906. Southern Vermont College and the Laumeister Art Center run a very informative Covered Bridge Museum, https://artcenter.svc.edu/covered-bridge.

See also John Burk, *Images of America: Massachusetts Covered Bridges*, 2010; Benjamin and June Evans, *New England's Covered Bridges: A Complete Guide*, 2004; and Patricia Harris and David Lyon, "Spanning Generations," *Boston Sunday Globe*, August 20, 2017.

Section IV: Follies, Choices, and Causes

My major source for Santarella was *The Kitson Papers 1887–1934,* held by the New York Historical Society. I also consulted numerous websites about Santarella and Kitson. Useful publications included: *Benezit Dictionary of Artists,* 2006; Don Davis, "The Story of Tyringham Galleries," *American Artist,* February 1955; Eloise Myers, *A Hinterland Settlement: Tyringham, Massachusetts and Bordering Lands,* 1944; and Brian Mastroianni, "Santarella: Fairy Tale or Wayside Chapel?—Minute Man Sculptor Henry Hudson Kitson's House in Tyringham," *Berkshire Eagle,* July 18, 2013. I also pulled various articles from the archives of *Berkshire Life,* the *Springfield Sunday Republican,* and the *Worcester Sunday Telegram.* See also Christine C. Neal, "Sculptor Theodora Alice Ruggles Kitson: 'A Woman Genius,'" *Historical Journal of Massachusetts,* 44:1 (Winter 2016).

Brian McCue graciously gave me a personal tour of Montague Castle and fielded my many questions. Much has been written about the Brotherhood of the Spirit, and the University of Massachusetts Amherst Special Collections holds papers from the Brotherhood. The best way to find more information is to watch *Free Spirits: The Birth, Life, and Loss of a New-Age Dream,* a 2006 Acorn Productions film directed by Bruce Geisler.

Although I consulted newspaper articles in the *Daily Hampshire Gazette* and perused the Three Sisters Sanctuary's official website: https://threesisterssanctuary.com/, my main source for this chapter has been repeated visits to the site and discussions with Richard M. Richardson, creator of the sanctuary. There are also numerous YouTube videos about the gardens, including a 30-minute documentary titled, *Three Sisters Sanctuary Documentary,* http://www.youtube.com/watch?v=Wmo-NRfAkYQ.

To learn about the earnestness of anti-alcohol crusaders, see Jack S. Blocker, *Alcohol, Reform and Society: The Liquor Issue in Social*

Context, 1979; Ruth Bordin, *Women and Temperance: The Quest for Power and Liberty*, 1981; Eric Burns, *The Spirits of America*, 2004; Paul Cimbola and Randall Miller, editors, *Against the Tide: Women Reformers in American Society*, 1997; K. Austen Kerr, *Organized for Prohibition: A New History of the Anti-Saloon League*, 1985; Mark Linder and James Kirby Martin, *Drinking in America: A History*, 1982; Daniel Okrent, *Last Call: The Rise and Fall of Prohibition*, 2010. See also "Mohican History: The Story of the Konkapot Family," http://www.konkapot.com/history-of-the-stockbridge-munsee-band-of-the-mohicans/. Information on Amelia Jeanette Kilbon was obtained from the Sophia Smith Collection of Smith College. Information on local temperance fountains can be found in Randy Gordon, Jason Scavotto, and Leah Berkenwald, *Monumental History of the Pioneer Valley*, 2007.

Orange is discussed in Allen Young, *North Quabbin Revisited*, 2002. See also John Carr. "Massachusetts Route 2 History," http://www.mit.edu/~jfc/Route%202.html. I spent a considerable amount of time in the Smith College art library looking at biographical dictionaries that mentioned sculptor Joseph Pollia. I also searched images online to get a sense of his work. Peace organizations proliferate in Western Massachusetts. They also often change offices and names. Good websites for tracking them include: https://www.theresistancecenter.org/organizations and https://www.afsc.org/category/location/florence-ma. The New England Peace Pagoda has a Website: https://newenglandpeacepagoda.org/.

Section V: Sports

The *New York Times* has produced a really good map of baseball rivalries based on Steve Rushin's work. See Tom Gratikanon, Josh Katz, David Leonhardt and Kevin Quealy, "Up Close on Baseball's Borders," April 24, 2014, https://nytimes.com/interactive/2014/04/23/upshot/24-upshot-baseball.html. Nathan Cobb confessed to coining the term "Red Sox Nation" in a September 26, 2005, *Boston Globe* article titled "Sox Fan's Words Led to a Birth of a Nation," http://archive.boston.com/sports/baseball/redsox/articles/2005/09/26/sox_fans_wor ds_led_to_the_birth_of_a_nation/. For an amusing (if not always accurate) piece, see Dan Shaughnessy, *The Curse of the Bambino*, 2004.

Daniel Okrent's elegiac "Just a Little Bit of Heaven: Pittsfield's Wahconah Park is Baseball as it Oughta Be" appeared in *Sports Illustrated* on July 23, 1990. *Wikipedia* has an excellent page on Wahconah Park: https://en.wikipedia.org/wiki/Wahconah_Park. Adam Sege wrote a piece on Wahconah Park when the Suns established a Collegiate Futures team there in 2012. See "In Pittsfield, Baseball Tradition Takes Fans Way Back," https://bostonglobe.com/metro/2012/07/06/pittsfield-baseball-tradition-shines-brightly-wahconah-park/zKGzH4eXNx73VHjvm49QbO/story.html. Good luck trying to determine which baseball park is actually America's oldest! This question is endlessly parsed. Rickwood's claim, for instance, rests on being the oldest used professionally, as many parks predate it. It also rests on being in "continuous" use, a claim I question.

The International Candlepin Bowling Association hosts a website: https://candlepin.org/. Mainly, though, one has to surf the Internet to find out much about the sport and its history. As professional competition, candlepin bowling has fallen from public view to the point where a recent champion, Chris Sargent, poured out his frustrations to *Boston Globe* correspondent Billy Baker: "No One Can Hold a Candelpin to Him," *Boston Globe*, May 5, 2017. Perhaps its future lies with recreational fun-seekers such as myself. Some of the Shelburne Falls alley's history can be found at http://www.shelburnefallsbowling.com/our-history/.

Curling also has a governing body, the World Curling Federation (http://www.worldcurling.org/). You can find out about curling stones at https://folklife.si.edu/resources/festival2003/scot_curling2.htm. A March 1944 magazine article titled "Game of the Magic

Broom" remains a classic consulted by most looking into the sport. It is now online at: http://books.google.com/books?id=ht8DAAAA MBAJ&pg=PA78&dq=popular+mechani c+antitank+1941&hl=en& ei=jeiaTKeaN82jnQeWl4SADw&sa=X&oi=book_result&ct=re sult &resnum=3&ved=0CDsQ6AEwAg#v=onepage&q&f=true. Pieces of curling's intricacies and history can be gleaned from the USA Curling website, https://.teamusa.org/USA-Curling. See also Scott Cacciola, "What is Curling? Power Plays, Scoring, Rocks, and Hammers," *New York Times*, February 8, 2018. Information on curling in Petersham can be found on the Petersham Curling Club website, https://.petersham-curling.org/.

Section VI: Museums

The go-to source for pre-20th-century Pelham is Charles Parmenter, *History of Pelham, Massachusetts: From 1738 to 1898*, 1898. Parmenter often included large excerpts from primary-source documents in his narrative. Two classic works on American religion are Sydney Ahlstrom, *A Religious History of the American People*, Two Volumes, 1975; and Martin Marty, *Pilgrims in Their Own Land: 500 Years of Religion in America*, 1984.

There are scores of books on the *RMS Titanic*, but to understand what inspired the museum in Indian Orchard, Walter Lord, *A Night to Remember*, 1955, is a must. It's also worth viewing the 1958 film directed by Roy Ward Baker that was adapted from Lord's book. It's not the first film made about the *Titanic*, but it did much to fixate the disaster in popular culture. Another good place to start is Eugene Rasor, *The* Titanic*: Historiography and Annotated Bibliography*, 2001. The Titanic Historical Society (THS) has a website, https://titanichistoricalsociety.org/. Selected issues of *The Titanic Communicator*, the official THS journal, are available through Amazon.com. Beyond these sources, there are specialty works devoted to virtually every aspect of the *Titanic*.

For those looking to connect the *Titanic* to other maritime disasters, *Wikipedia* provides a strong list from which to begin your study: https://en.wikipedia.org/wiki/List_of_maritime_disasters.

I learned a lot simply by touring the Crane Paper Museum in Dalton. Those seeking a readable account on the development of capitalism should consult Joyce Appleby, *The Relentless Revolution: A History of Capitalism*, 2010. H. W. Brands is also a lively writer; see his *Greenback Planet: How the Dollar Conquered the World and Threatened Civilization as We Know It*, 2011. For more on the greenback controversy, a very thorough work is Gretchen Ritter, *Goldbugs and Greenbacks: The Antimonopoly Tradition and the Politics of Finance in America*, 1997. I touched upon money-supply issues from organized labor's perspective in Robert E. Weir, *Knights Unhorsed: Internal Conflict in a Gilded Age Social Movement*, 2000. Some information on the Crane family and the rag-paper process can be found at: https://en.wikipedia.org/wiki/Crane_and_Company_Old_Stone_Mill_Rag_Room.

One of the best ways to appreciate the history of Cummington is to start with the 1945 film *The Cummington Story* and work backward. It is available for free viewing on YouTube: http://www.youtube.com/watch?v=to8gQ7IBa4A&t=8s. For context, see Richie Davis, "The Cummington Story (2005)," *The Recorder* (Greenfield), August 19, 2016. I made extensive use of Forbes Library's vertical files when researching Cummington institutions and artists, especially articles found in the *Daily Hampshire Gazette* and the *Springfield Republican*. For more on POWs during World War II, see John Bonafilia, "Hospitality Is the Best Form of Propaganda: German Prisoners of War in Western Massachusetts, 1944–1946," *Historical Journal of Massachusetts* 44:1 (Winter 2016). Papers from the Cummington School of the Arts are housed in Special Collections at the University of Massachusetts Amherst. The Cummington Historical Society holds many documents, especially a rich collection of those linked to the antislavery movement: https://cummingtonhistoricalcommission.weebly.com/.

A good general history of labor in Massachusetts is Tom Juravich, William E. Hartford, and James R. Green, *Commonwealth of Toil: Chapters in the History of Massachusetts Workers and Their Unions*, 1996. An excellent look at the impact of deindustrialization in Western Massachusetts is Robert Forrant, "The Rise and Demise of the Connecticut River Valley's Industrial Economy," *Historical Journal of Massachusetts*, 46:1 (Winter 2018). The Partner Library at the University of Massachusetts Lowell holds some of the material collected from the "Shifting Gears" project. See https://libguides.uml.edu/c.php?g=492497&p=4030943.

Some of Gardner's history can be gleaned from Esther G. Moore, *History of Gardner, Massachusetts, 1785–1967*, 1967. The South Gardner Historical Society collectively produced *Gardner, Massachusetts (Images of America Series)*, 2011. For Greenfield Tap and Die, see Rebecca Ducharme, "Greenfield Tap and Die: Economic and Historical Analysis," *Historical Journal of Massachusetts* 34:2 (Summer 2006) and Tom Goldscheider, "At Sword's Point," *Historical Journal of Massachusetts* 46:2 (Summer 2018). The website for the Museum of Our Industrial Heritage is http://industrialhistory.org/.

Those unfamiliar with Arlo Guthrie's recording of *Alice's Restaurant* (1967), or have not yet seen the film of the same name directed by Arthur Penn (1969), should correct those errors immediately! The tale is the stuff of Massachusetts legend. Guthrie has given many interviews concerning his escapades and the church, among them an interview with Patrick Doyle in *Rolling Stone*, November 26, 2014; and with Doug Most in the *Boston Globe*, August 26, 2015. A recent *Globe* article, Thomas Farragher, "Striking a Chord: Immortalized in 'Alice's Restaurant,' a 1960s Landmark Has a Revival," May 5, 2018, recounts renovations at the Guthrie Center. The Guthrie Center also has a brochure available at various locations in the Commonwealth. Full disclosure: I am a contributor to the Guthrie Center and a sometime attendee of concerts at the site. University of Massachusetts Amherst doctoral student Cheryl Harned is writing her dissertation on the Skinner family and the Skinner Museum. I'd like to thank her for sharing her prospectus. See also Kate N. Thibodeau, *Holyoke: The Skinner Family and Wistariahurst Museum*, 2005. The best account of the 1874 Mill River flood is Elizabeth M. Sharpe, *In the Shadow of the Dam: The Aftermath of the Mill River Flood of 1874*, 2004. For the Skinner Museum website see: https://artmuseum.mtholyoke.edu/collection/joseph-allen-skinner-museum. For those looking to chew on some heavy-duty theoretical material about what and how museums collect, Tony Bennett, *The Birth of the Museum: History, Theory, Politics*, 1995, is a good starting point.

Back cover images, clockwise from top left: Historical Monument *by Erastus Salisbury Field (Springfield), newsboy statue (Great Barrington), Waconoh Park (Pittsfield), Skinner Museum Collections, (South Hadley)*